PMP® EXAM PREP

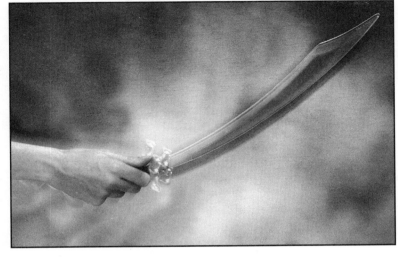

Review Material,
Explanations,
Insider Tips,
Exercises,
Games and
Practice Exams…

…To Pass PMI®'s PMP® and CAPM® Exams

Rita Mulcahy, PMP

RMC Publications, Inc.

To Tim, who always encourages me to make a great thing better.

To the hundreds of people who sent me comments on the book. Thank you for making the effort.

To my team and my editor; when someone is running like a tornado, it is great to have an anchor!

Third Printing

ISBN   0-9711647-3-8

RMC Publications

PHONE: 952.846.4484
FAX: 952.846.4844
EMAIL: info@rmcproject.com
WEB: www.rmcproject.com

RMC Project Management is a Project Management Institute (PMI) Registered Education Provider. (R.E.P.) RMC Project Management is committed to enhancing the ongoing professional development of PMI Members, PMI-certified Project Management Professionals (PMP), and other project management stakeholders through appropriate project management learning activities and products. As a PMI R.E.P., RMC Project Management, has agreed to abide by PMI-established operational and educational criteria, and is subject to random audits for quality assurances purposes.

Table of Contents

Introduction to the Fourth Edition of PMP® Exam Prep

It is my intention to update this book frequently to make certain it contains the latest materials available and my most recent knowledge about the exam.

The main approach to the *PMP® Exam Prep* book has not been changed, nor have the major exercises. We have added 151 more questions, included explanations and added exercises and additional information on the topics on which people are currently scoring poorly so that you do not face their problems. In total, we have added over 100 pages of additional information. There are over 300 changes in this edition!!

I have enjoyed my sleepless nights coming up with devilish ways for you to get ready for the exam faster and easier. I hope you enjoy this edition and that you will contact me with your comments. They keep me going!

This Edition Will Go Out of Date!

RMC products are frequently updated to give you the latest information available. Please check www.rmcproject.com to see our latest edition.

Rave Reviews from Around the World!

"I have seen all the PMP® prep material out there and even attended other classes. Your material is unbelievably far and away the best!"

"I would like to thank you for writing your book - without it I would never have passed the PMP®! Your advice on how to approach the exam, the topics that you covered and the level of questions were spot on. I am based in Cayman so I was studying for the exam purely by myself. Your book helped provide a structured way to approach the exam and covered and provided advice on many topics not in the PMBOK® Guide. The examples that require working through difficult topics such as PERT, earned value and working out critical paths enabled me to get full marks in the exam. I think the personal touch that you brought to the book also helped to make things easy to remember. I am recommending your book to a number of people I have met."

"I just wrote the PMP® exam and passed with a good margin. I wanted to drop this note to let you know how valuable I found your PMP® Exam Prep book in preparing for the exam. This is without a doubt the most valuable resource I used during my study. Of the two other guides I used, the practice exam you developed most closely emulated those on the actual exam. I found your tips and games very useful in remembering concepts and formulae on the exam. This is a very easy to use book that focuses on the areas critical for study. It simplifies preparation by boiling down the myriad of books suggested as resources to help prepare for the exam. Thanks for putting this excellent resource together."

© 2002 - 1998 Rita Mulcahy, PMP
PHONE: (952) 846-4484 - EMAIL: info@rmcproject.com - WEB: www.rmcproject.com

About the Author

Rita Mulcahy, PMP, is an internationally recognized expert in project management and a sought-after project management speaker, trainer and author. She has four project management books to her credit, has taught over 10,500 project managers from around the world and helped over 18,000 people prepare for the PMP® exam.

Rita's speaking engagements draw record crowds. People have stated: "Rita makes you think! The most informative presentation I have ever seen." In fact, Rita has spoken at PMI®'s annual project management symposium to standing room only crowds and been asked to present encore presentations at the symposium for an unheard of four years!

She has over 15 years and US $2.5 billion of hands-on project experience on hundreds of IS, IT, new product, high-tech, service, engineering, construction and manufacturing projects. She has served as an acting PMI® Chapter President and Vice President for more than seven years and has taught project management courses for four major universities.

Rita is the founder of **RMC Project Management,** an international project management speaking, training and consulting firm, and a Global Registered Education Provider with PMI®. RMC specializes in interpreting the *PMBOK® Guide* for real-world use; helping companies use the latest project management tools and techniques to complete projects faster, with less expense, better results and fewer resources. RMC provides training in project management, advanced project management and PMP® and CAPM® training. Since its founding in 1991, RMC has provided many quality products to prepare you for those exams. Classes offered include:

- PMP® Certification Training
- Project Management Tricks of the Trade®
- Tricks of the Trade® for Risk Management
- Tricks of the Trade® for Determining Customer Requirements
- What Makes A Project Manager Successful?
- Why Do Projects Fail and How To Prevent It
- Tricks for Avoiding Common Project Problems
- Avoiding Common Stumbling Blocks in Risk
- Project Management for Teams, Senior Management, Sales and Functional Managers
- All PMI® *PMBOK® Guide* Subjects

How to Use This Book

This book is the only accelerated learning guide for passing the Project Management Institute's Project Management Professional (PMP®) and Certified Associate in Project Management (CAPM®) Exams. In order to get the most out of this book, and save time studying, you should look for and use all the following features and benefits:

- Identifies the hardest topics and what to expect on the exam
- Review of the topics not in the *PMBOK® Guide*
- Closely indexed to the *PMBOK® Guide*
- Insider tips about the exam that are not readily available elsewhere
- PMI®-isms
- TRICKS for studying and taking the exam
- Determine what you know and do not know
- Determine what to study and focus on
- Gain familiarity with the types of exam questions
- Increases your probability of passing the exam

Over ten years of experience helping project managers prepare to take the Project Management Institute's PMP® Exam, plus US $2.5 billion dollars of real-world project experience, and feedback from around the world have gone into this book. Although you will certainly learn a lot about project management, this book is <u>not</u> designed to teach you all you need to know about how to manage a project, or the art and science of project management. You must have project management training before you take the exam.

This book is intended to work hand-in-hand with PMI®'s *A Guide to the Project Management Body of Knowledge* and our other materials. For the sake of brevity, we will refer to the *Guide to the Project Management Body of Knowledge* as the *PMBOK® Guide* in this book. All page references in this document refer to the *PMBOK® Guide* unless otherwise stated!

Each chapter is organized the same: an introductory paragraph, a list of hot topics, review materials and a practice exam.

Introduction to Each Chapter – The introductory paragraph provides an overview of the chapter.

Hot Topics – The hot topics give you an understanding of what topics are important and my impression as to their order of importance.

Review Materials – The review materials are current and contain the latest updates on the exam. Both the PMP® and CAPM® exams are covered in this book. Both exams cover the same material, just from different experience levels. Any time the word "exam" is used it should be taken to mean either exam.

Lists and summaries instead of long-winded paragraphs are used whenever appropriate. Feedback from students indicates that the review material covers all the major items on the exam.

Practice Exams – The practice exams are placed at the end of each chapter so you can review the material, test yourself and move to the next chapter. If you are taking the CAPM® exam, refer only to the questions marked for that exam; the other questions are designed for the PMP® exam. Those taking the PMP® exam should utilize all questions in the book. On the next page is a score sheet to use as you go through the practice exams. Make a copy of it for each of the sets of sample questions in the book.

NOTE: The questions in this book are tests on the chapter content. Because the questions are in book format, they cannot simulate the complete range and depth of the PMP® Exam questions. You can find such a simulation in the *PM FASTrack®*, PMP® exam simulation software program.

Question Number	3rd Time	2nd Time	1st Time
1			
2			
3			
4			
5			
6			
7			
8			
9			
10			
11			
12			
13			
14			
15			
16			
17			
18			
19			
20			
21			
22			
23			
24			
25			
26			

Question Number	3rd Time	2nd Time	1st Time
27			
28			
29			
30			
31			
32			
33			
34			
35			
36			
37			
38			
39			
40			
41			
42			
43			
44			
Total Score	3rd Time	2nd Time	1st Time

What will you do different next time?

Other Materials to Use

(Our products are used in more than 43 countries.)

If you have had training in project management, you should not need any materials other than this book, the *PM FASTrack®*, the *Hot Topics* flashcards, and the 2000 *PMBOK® Guide* to pass the PMP® Exam. If you have difficulty understanding material in this book, you many need more project management training, not another book. If, however, you need help in only a few areas, the most useful books are listed in the bibliography at the end of this book. Only products purchased directly through RMC are supported by RMC. Go to www.rmcproject.com to order materials. Pass the exam **GUARANTEED** with our 2 day **PMP® Exam Prep Class!**

RMC PMP® Exam Prep System

Our materials are designed to work together! The book *PMP® Exam Prep* covers the <u>knowledge needed</u> to pass the exam. *PM FASTrack®* helps you <u>test and apply your knowledge</u>. *Hot Topics* helps you <u>improve recall</u>.

PM FASTrack® - PMP® Exam Simulation Software

Online Version or CD-ROM

Over 1,300 questions in 4 testing modes!

PM FASTrack® is an exam simulation program, modeled after the actual PMP® Exam. It is **UNIQUE** because it:
- Contains over 1300 questions, answers and explanations
- Created with the help of hundreds of experienced project managers from around the world
- Created based on a psychometric review and sorts questions **SIMILAR TO THE ACTUAL EXAM**
- Helps you practice the actual test-taking environment (a key aspect to passing the exam)
- Charts your progress with printable charts and graphs
- Helps you sort questions by knowledge area, process group or any key word you enter
- Helps you discover what you know and do not know

Hot Topics - Flashcards for Passing the PMP® Exam (Book or CD)

Shorten your exam study time and increase your understanding with 656 pages of Hot Topics Flashcards or about 90 minutes of audio Hot Topics. As part of RMC's PMP® Exam Prep System, this portable book/audio CD helps test knowledge recall, a must for both the PMP® and CAPM® exams.

The Exam

Keep in mind two things. First, THIS IS NOT A TEST OF THE INFORMATION IN THE *PMBOK® Guide*! Second, you cannot rely on real-world experience. It is training in project management using these terms that is critical! This does not mean that you need weeks of training or a masters certificate in project management to take the exam.

WARNING: The exam changes frequently! You must visit www.pmi.org for full details. Any differences between what is listed here and what is listed on PMI®'s website should be resolved in favor of PMI®'s website.

A summary of the exams

CAPM

Category	General Education	PM Education	PM Experience	Experience within last	Number of questions	Time to take the exam	Sign Code of Conduct
One	Bachelors degree	23 contact hours	1,500 hours	3 years	150	3 hours	Yes
Two	High School graduate	23 contact hours	2,500 hours				

PMP

Category	General Education	PM Education	PM Experience	Experience within last	Number of questions	Time to take the exam	Sign Code of Conduct
One	Bachelors degree	35 contact hours	4,500 hours	3 years minimum	200	4 hours	Yes
Two	High School graduate	35 contact hours	7,500 hours	5 years minimum			

Applying To Take the Exams
PMI®'s turnaround time to review applications is currently only a few days for electronic submissions. If they accept your application, you will receive a letter authorizing you call the testing center to make an appointment to take the exam. PMI® is quickly moving to offer computerized testing around the world in many languages.

Watch out! **Once you receive your authorization letter, you must take the exam within six months!** In some instances, testing centers do not have openings for several weeks from when you call. The CAPM® exam may not be offered as frequently as the PMP® exam.

PMI® often makes changes to the way the exam is administered. Therefore, read the authorization letter carefully to uncover any differences from what is described here.

What are the Exams Like?

The PMP® exam includes 200 multiple-choice questions with four answers per question. The exam must be finished in four hours. The CAPM® exam includes 150 questions and must be completed in three hours. (HINT: If your study material has five choices per question, don't use it! It is either related to the old exam and therefore at least four years out-of-date, or it has not been created using the same modern test creation standards as the exam.)

The CAPM® exam is knowledge-based, whereas the PMP® exam is knowledge, application and analysis-based, and includes more situational questions. The questions for both exams are randomly generated from a database containing hundreds of questions. The questions may jump from topic to topic and cover multiple topics in a question. You get one point for each correct answer. There is no penalty for wrong answers.

For many people the toughest knowledge areas on the exam are integration, procurement and time. The toughest process groups are controlling and closing. Make sure you study these carefully.

WARNING: The PMP® exam is not like any exam you have taken before. The passing score may be 137 out of 200 in 2002 for the PMP® (about 68%) but because the exam is written psychometrically, there are questions on the exam that even experts find difficult! Do not get frustrated!

Taking the Exam

You must bring your authorization letter from PMI® to the test site as well as two forms of ID with exactly the same name you entered on the exam application.

Once you arrive at the test site you will be given scrap paper, pencils (and possibly even earplugs) and have the chance to do a 15-minute computer tutorial (if your exam is given on computer, to become familiar with the computer and its commands).

When you take the exam, you will see one question on the screen at a time. You can answer a question and/or mark it to return to it later. You will be able to move back and forth throughout the exam.

When you finish the exam, you will have multiple chances to indicate if you are done. The exam will not be scored until you are ready or your time is up. If you pass the exam, the computer will print out a certificate and a report, and you will officially be certified. If you do not pass the exam, PMI® will be notified and will send you information on retaking the exam. You will have to pay an additional fee to retake the exam.

Why Take the Exam?

Let me quote from one of my students. *"The exam has changed my life. (Could I be more dramatic?) The process of studying for the exam, taking your class and passing the exam has changed how others look at my abilities."* By passing the exam, you can say that you have passed an international exam designed to prove your knowledge of project management. That is impressive. There are other benefits. Should I put this in writing? PMI®'s salary survey has found that PMP®s are paid at least 10% more than non-PMP®s in the United States (and even more in some other countries), and I have had many students who have received a US $15,000 bonus AND a 15% raise when they passed the exam. Others have said they got a job over 200 others because they were a PMP®. Such benefits reflect well on the future of the CAPM® as well. These are good reasons to finally get around to taking the exam.

Are You Ready To Take the Exam?

From my experience, 90% of those who fail the exam do so because they have not had project management training that uses PMI® terminology. Take this seriously! Real-life experience or just reading the *PMBOK® Guide* is not enough to pass this exam! This is so important that, beginning in 2002, project management training has become required before one can take the PMP® exam.

If you have not had formal training in project management, or are unfamiliar with the step-by-step process of project management, I suggest RMC Project Management's "Tricks of the Trade® for Project Management" course in addition to our "PMP® Exam Prep" course.

To help you determine how much you really understand about project management before you study for the exam, I have included the following short list as a test.

How Do You Know If You Need To Improve Your Knowledge?

PART 1:   If you experience many of the following problems on projects:
- Cost or schedule overruns
- Unrealistic schedules
- Changing scope of work or schedules
- Poor communications and increased conflict
- Running out of time near the end of the project
- Unsatisfactory quality
- Low morale
- People on the team are unsure of what needs to be done
- Excessive rework and overtime
- Too many project meetings

PART 2:   If you do not understand, or do not use, two or more of the following:
- A step-by-step process for managing projects and why each step is necessary
- The project manager, senior manager, sponsor and team roles
- Project charter
- What is a work breakdown structure, how to create it, and that it is not a list in a Gantt chart
- How to manually create a network diagram
- Critical path - how to find it and what benefits it provides the project manager
- PERT and estimating with PERT
- Monte Carlo simulation
- Earned value
- Schedule compression, crashing and fast tracking
- Dealing with unrealistic schedules
- Project plan development – creating a realistic and approved project plan
- Project plan execution – managing the project to the project plan by looking for exceptions to the plan and taking corrective action
- Risk management process and that risk management is not just using a checklist
- Expected value
- Calculating budget reserves and their relationship to risk management
- Controlling the project to the project plan

How to Study for the Exam

You can write and rewrite things you need to know, read and reread many books or use other methods to study for the exam. After working with thousands of people, I have perfected what my students say is the most efficient and shortest process for studying for the exam! Please consider this method before you determine how you will study. If you have the *PM FASTrack®* (PMP® exam simulation software), use it instead of the practice exams in this book. If you have the *Hot Topics* flashcards (described earlier), use them after you read each chapter in this book and keep reviewing them until you take the exam. They are great to keep yourself in test-taking mode. Both products come with further instructions on how to make the best use of them.

The Magic Three

Studies have shown that if you visit a topic three times, you will remember it. Therefore, you should read this book and use our products three times before you take the exam.

Be in Test-Taking Mode

Get used to jumping from one topic to another and practice taking an exam for hours. Do not underestimate the physical aspects of taking an exam that lasts four hours.

An Efficient Step-By-Step Process

1. Before you review the materials, take the practice tests in one sitting – as you would during the actual exam. If you have *PM FASTrack®* software, use it instead of the questions in this book.

2. Do not analyze your right and wrong answers at this point; just note the chapters where you have the most and least difficulty. This will help you determine an overall study plan. It will also help you determine if you really do understand project management and how much studying you will need.

3. Read the material in this book for the first time, focusing on the chapters where you had the most errors. At the same time, skim through the same chapter in the *PMBOK® Guide* to get an understanding of the flow of the processes. As you finish each chapter, use the *Hot Topics* flashcards to improve recall and test your understanding for that chapter.

4. If it is at all possible, form a study group. This will actually make your study time more effective and shorter! You will be able to ask someone questions and the studying (and celebrating afterward) will be more fun. A study group should consist of only three or four people.

    Meet with a study group and pick someone to lead the discussion of each chapter (preferably someone who is **not** comfortable with the chapter). Each time you meet, go over questions about topics you do not understand and review the hot topics on the exam using the *Hot Topics* flashcards, if you have them. Most groups meet for one hour per chapter.

    NOTE: This book is written for individual use. Because it includes exercises and activities, each member of the study group will need their own copy.

5. Either independently or with your study group, do further research on questions you do not understand or answered incorrectly. This does not mean read many books! Simply refer back to this book, the *PMBOK® Guide*, your project management class materials, or to the books recommended in the bibliography at the end of this book.

6. Take and retake the practice tests until you score over 90%.

7. Use the *Hot Topics* flashcards, if you have them, to retain the material you have studied until you take the exam.

How are the Questions Written

Feedback from thousands of my students has provided the following insights:

- Knowledge is tested on the CAPM® exam. Questions tend to be straightforward as illustrated in the first set of questions at the end of each chapter of this book.

- The PMP® exam tests knowledge, application and analysis. This makes the PMP® exam more than a test of memory. You must know how to apply the information in this book and be able to analyze situations involving this information. Do not expect the exam to have all straightforward, definition-type questions.

- It is important to realize that the PMP® exam deals with real-world use of project management. It contains about 125 "what should you do in this situation?" questions (situational questions). These questions are extremely difficult if you have not used project management tools in the real world or do not realize that your project management efforts include common errors. You have to have been there.

- Both exams emphasize the process of project management (project management life cycle or process groups). The following breaks out the number of questions for the PMP® and CAPM® exams. NOTE: This list changes from year to year. See www.pmi.org for the latest list.

	PMP® Exam		CAPM® Exam	
PM Process	**Number of Questions**	**Percent of Questions**	**Number of Questions**	**Percent of Questions**
Project Initiating	17	8.5	14	9.3
Project Planning	47	23.5	33	22
Project Executing	47	23.5	40	26.7
Project Controlling	46	23.0	32	21.3
Project Closing	14	7.0	14	9.3
Professional Responsibility	29	14.5	17	11.3
Total	200		150	

- There are a few instances where the same set of data is used for additional questions later in both exams. This is particularly true of network diagram questions.

- Only a few questions on either exam expect you to MEMORIZE the step-by-step *PMBOK® Guide* processes. Only ten to twelve questions expect you to MEMORIZE the inputs or outputs from the *PMBOK® Guide*. These are discussed in later chapters.

- There may be only eight to ten formula-related calculations on either exam.

- There should only be ten to twelve earned value questions on either exam. Not all of these require calculations using the formulas.

- Most acronyms (e.g., WBS for work breakdown structure) should be spelled out.

- The correct answers should not include direct quotations from the *PMBOK® Guide*.

- Most students feel uncertain of only 40 of the 200 questions on the PMP® exam.

- Many students have needed only 2½ hours to finish the PMP® exam and then taken the rest of the time to review their answers.

Types of Exam Questions

Many people ask me what the questions on the exam are like. The questions are mostly situational, many are ambiguous and some even seem like they have two right answers. Be prepared for these types of questions so you will not waste time or be caught off guard when you are taking the exam.

1. **Situational questions only on the PMP® exam** – These questions require you to have "been there."

   You receive notification that a major item you are purchasing for a project will be delayed. What is the BEST thing to do?
   - A. Ignore it, it will go away
   - B. Notify your boss
   - C. Let the customer know about it and talk over options
   - D. Meet with the team and identify alternatives

   The answer is D.

2. **Two right answers** – Questions that appear to have two right answers are a major complaint from many test takers. You should be prepared for this and realize that only those with inadequate project management training before taking the exam think they have a lot of questions with two right answers.

   Let's look again at the question above. Couldn't we really do all of them? The "right" answer is certainly D, but isn't it also correct to tell the customer? Yes, but that is not the first thing. Essentially this question is really saying, "What is the BEST thing to do *next*?"

3. **Extraneous information** – It is very important to realize that not all information included in a question will be used to answer the question. Here, the numbers are extraneous:

   Experience shows that each time you double the production of doors, unit costs decrease by 10%. Based on this, the company determines that production of 3,000 doors should cost US $21,000. This case illustrates:
   - A. Learning cycle
   - B. Law of diminishing returns
   - C. 80/20 rule
   - D. Parametric cost estimating

   The answer is D.

4. **Out of the blue questions** – No matter how well you study, there will ALWAYS be those questions where you have no idea what the question is asking. Here is an example:

   The concept of "optimal quality level is reached at the point where the incremental revenue from product improvement equals the incremental cost to secure it" comes from:
   - A. Quality control analysis
   - B. Marginal analysis
   - C. Standard quality analysis
   - D. Conformance analysis

   The answer is B.

5. **Words you have never heard before** – Sometimes words that you have never heard before are used as possible choices. How many of you understand that a "perk" is an abbreviation for "perquisite?" Non-English speakers – practice dealing with this before you take the exam.

Parking spaces, corner offices and access to the executive dining room are examples of:
  A. Perquisites
  B. Overhead
  C. Herzberg's "motivators"
  D. Entitlements

The answer is A.

6. **Where understanding is important** – In order to answer many of the questions on the exam, you must understand all the topics. Memorization is not enough!

The process of decomposing deliverables into smaller, more manageable components is complete when:
  A. Project justification has been established
  B. Change requests have occurred
  C. Cost and duration estimates can be developed for each work element at this detail
  D. Each work element is found in the WBS dictionary

The answer is C.

7. **New approach to known topic** – There will be many instances where you understand the topic but have never thought about it in the way the question describes.

In a matrix organization, information dissemination is MOST likely to be effective when:
  A. Information flows both horizontally and vertically
  B. The communications flows are kept simple
  C. There is an inherent logic in the type of matrix chosen
  D. Project managers and functional managers socialize

The answer is A.

Keys to Answering PMI®'s Questions

1) Understand the material cold. Do not assume this exam tests memorization; it tests knowledge and application! You must understand the items in this book, how they are used in the real world and how they work in combination with each other.

2) Have real-world experience using all the major project management techniques.

3) Read the *PMBOK® Guide*.

4) Understand the areas PMI® emphasizes (PMI®-isms, explained later in this book).

5) Be familiar with the types of questions.

6) Be familiar with and practice interpreting ambiguous and wordy questions.

7) Practice being able to pick an answer from what appears to be two or three right answers.

8) Get used to the idea that there will be questions you cannot answer.

Tricks for Taking the Exam

1. A major TRICK is to answer the question from PMI®'s perspective, not the perspective you have acquired from your life experience. If this approach does not give you an answer, rely on your training and lastly, your life experience.

2. Another major TRICK is to first read the actual question in the words provided (often the last sentence), then read the rest of the question. Note the topics discussed in the question and the descriptors (e.g., "except," "includes," "not an example of"). This should help you understand what the question is asking. Determine what your answer should be and then look at the answers shown.

3. One of the main reasons people answer incorrectly is because they do not read all four choices. Do not make the same mistake! Practice reading the questions and all four choices when you take the practice exams. A good TRICK is to practice reading the choices backwards (choice D first, then C, etc.) Practice in this area will help you locate the BEST answer.

4. Practice being able to quickly eliminate answers that are highly implausible. Many questions have only two plausible options and two obviously incorrect answers.

5. There will be more than one "correct" answer to each question but only one "BEST" answer. Practice looking for the BEST answer.

6. Be alert to the fact that information in one question is sometimes given away in another question. Write down things that you do not understand as you take the exam and use any extra time at the end of the exam to go back to these questions.

7. Attempts have been made to keep all choices the same length. Therefore, do not follow the old rule that the longest answer is the right one.

8. A concerted effort has been made to use "distracters" - choices that distract you from the correct answer. These are plausible choices that less knowledgeable people will pick. Distracters make it appear as though some questions have two right answers. To many people, it seems as though there are only shades of differences between the choices. Look for this type of question as you take practice exams.

9. Look for words like "first," "last," "next," "best," "never," "always," "except," "not," "most likely," "less likely," "primary," "initial," "most," etc. Make certain you clearly read the question, and take note of these words, or you will answer the question incorrectly! There are many questions that require you to really understand the process of project management and its real-world application.

10. Watch out for choices that are true statements but not the answer to the question.

11. Watch out for choices that contain common project management errors. They are intentionally there to determine if you really know project management. Therefore, you may not know that you answered a question incorrectly! Look for errors in your knowledge and practice as you go through this book.

12. Options that represent broad, sweeping generalizations tend to be incorrect, so be alert for "always," "never," "must," "completely" and so forth. Alternatively, choices that represent carefully qualified statements tend to be correct, so be alert for words such as "often," "sometimes," "perhaps," "may," and "generally."

13. When a question asks you to fill in a blank space, the correct answer may not be grammatically correct when inserted in the sentence.

14. As soon as you are given paper at the exam, write down all the formulas and major processes.

15. Visit the exam site before the test to determine how long it will take to get there and to see what the testing room looks like. This is particularly helpful if you are a nervous test taker.

16. Do not expect the exam site to be quiet. Be prepared for some noise. Many testing sites will have earplugs or headphones available.

17. Look for the "rah, rah" answer (e.g., "the project manager is so important," "the WBS is so useful").

18. Take the night off before the exam to do something relaxing and get a little extra sleep. DO NOT STUDY! You will need time to process all you have learned so you can remember it when you take the exam.

19. Make sure you are comfortable during the exam. Wear layered clothing and bring a sweater to sit on in case the chairs are uncomfortable.

20. Bring snacks! Bring lunch! You will not be able to bring snacks into the exam room, but having them stored close by may stop hunger pains.

21. Use deep breathing techniques to help relax. This is particularly helpful if you are very nervous before or during the exam and when you notice yourself reading the same questions two or three times.

22. Use all the exam time. Do not leave early unless you have reviewed each question twice.

23. Prepare a test-taking technique and stick to it. This may mean, "I will take a ten minute break after every fifty questions because I get tired quickly," or "I will answer all the questions as quickly as possible and then take a break and review my answers."

24. It is okay to change your answers as long as you have a good reason.

25. Create a test-taking plan before you take the exam. Mark a question for review if you do not answer it. This will allow you to find it faster later.

26. If you are unsure of the answer to a question, but have narrowed down the answers, mark down on your scrap paper the question number and the possible best answers. It will save you time when you return to the question.

27. Let me repeat myself to save you anguish. WARNING: This exam is not like one you have taken before. The passing score is 137 out of 200 in 2002 (about 68%) but because the exam is written psychometrically, there are questions on the exam that even experts find difficult to answer correctly! You cannot score 90% correct as you did on college exams. This exam is different. Any passing score is great.

28. Do not get frustrated while you take the exam! If you understand that there will be questions you cannot answer, they will not bother you and you will thus score higher. Just say to yourself, "This must be one of those questions that experts find difficult that Rita warned me about!" Then get on and pass the exam!

Inputs and Outputs

You can't help noticing that the *PMBOK® Guide* is full of inputs and outputs in each of the knowledge areas. What is an input? Something you need before you can begin a process. Doesn't it make sense to have everything you need before you begin? Wouldn't having those inputs make work faster, better, more complete?

What about outputs? An output is what you have when you are done with a process. Wouldn't it be useful to know what you are trying to achieve when you are doing something?

Inputs and outputs are logical and are reasonable questions on the exam. Many people think passing the exam means memorizing these. It does not. The exam is testing real-world application, not memorization. You need to know inputs and outputs, but if you know project management, these are logical and should not require memorization.

Do not expect all the inputs tested on the exam to be clearly listed in the *PMBOK® Guide*. For example, you know that you need a team (or at least the initial team) to create a work breakdown structure, yet team is not specifically listed as an input to scope definition (where a WBS is created). You should rely on this book to understand inputs and outputs but also be able to see the logic behind the inputs and outputs in the *PMBOK® Guide*.

Exercise: The following are the most important project management processes to know the inputs and outputs. Make sure you add in this exercise real-world inputs and outputs that are not in the *PMBOK® Guide*. When you are finished, check your answers with the *PMBOK® Guide* and the rest of this book.

Project Management Process	Key Inputs	Key Outputs
Activity Definition		
Activity Sequencing		

Project Management Process	Key Inputs	Key Outputs
Administrative Closure		
Initiation		
Procurement Planning		
Project Plan Development		
Project Plan Execution		

Project Management Process	Key Inputs	Key Outputs
Resource Planning		
Schedule Development		
Scope Planning		
Scope Definition		
Scope Verification		

Project Management Process	Key Inputs	Key Outputs
Solicitation		
Solicitation Planning		
Source Selection		

Interpreting the *PMBOK® GUIDE*

Many people have difficulty making sense of the terms in the *PMBOK® Guide*, yet it is important to know these terms and what they mean in order to gain new ideas toward improving our project management practices and to pass the exam.

Exercise: Here is a TRICK to getting more familiar with the *PMBOK® Guide*. You should try this exercise AFTER you have read the rest of this book. For each of the project management processes listed, fill in the rest of the columns.

Project Management Process	Knowledge Area	Process Group	What Does It Mean?	What Knowledge Area Process Comes Before?	What Knowledge Area Process Comes After?
Activity Definition					
Activity Sequencing					
Admin. Closure					
Initiation					
Procurement Planning					
Project Plan Development					
Project Plan Execution					
Resource Planning					

Project Management Process	Knowledge Area	Process Group	What Does It Mean?	What Knowledge Area Process Comes Before?	What Knowledge Area Process Comes After?
Schedule Development					
Scope Definition					
Scope Planning					
Scope Verification					
Solicitation					
Solicitation Planning					
Source Selection					

Answer: As you read the answers to this exercise, notice the words, "Whatever needs to be done." They repeat often and are meant to hint at all the soft, interpersonal activity needed, as well as the project management and technical activity needed. Using the phrase "whatever needs to be done" is a TRICK to understanding the full range of activity to which each topic relates.

Project Management Process	Knowledge Area	Process Group	What Does It Mean?	What Knowledge Area Process Comes Before?	What Knowledge Area Process Comes After?
Activity Definition	Time	Planning	Whatever needs to be done to create an activity list from the work breakdown structure	None	Activity Sequencing
Activity Sequencing	Time	Planning	Creating a network diagram	Activity Definition	Activity Estimating
Admin. Closure	Communi-cation	Closing	Whatever needs to be done to close out the project	Performance Reporting	None
Initiation	Scope	Initiating	Whatever needs to be done to create a project charter	None	Scope Planning
Procurement Planning	Procure-ment	Planning	Whatever needs to be done to create the scope of work and the procurement management plan	None	Solicitation Planning
Project Plan Development	Integration	Planning	Whatever needs to be done to create a project plan that is bought-into, approved, realistic and formal	None	Project Plan Execution
Project Plan Execution	Integration	Executing	Producing work according to the project plan and identifying changes	Project Plan Develop-ment	Integrated Change Control
Resource Planning	Cost	Planning	Whatever needs to be done to determine resource requirements for the project	None	Cost Estimating
Schedule Development	Time	Planning	Whatever needs to be done to create a bought-into, approved, realistic and formal schedule and schedule management plan	Activity Estimating	Schedule Control
Scope Definition	Scope	Planning	Whatever needs to be done after the scope statement and scope management plan in order to create the work breakdown structure	Scope Planning	Scope Verification

Project Management Process	Knowledge Area	Process Group	What Does It Mean?	What Knowledge Area Process Comes Before?	What Knowledge Area Process Comes After?
Scope Planning	Scope	Planning	Whatever needs to be done after the project charter to create a scope statement and scope management plan	Initiation	Scope Definition
Scope Verification	Scope	Control-ling	Inspecting project work and meeting with the customer to gain formal acceptance at the end of each project phase	Scope Definition	Scope Change Control
Solicitation	Procurement	Executing	Whatever occurs after the procurement documents are ready and before the proposals are received	Solicitation Planning	Source Selection
Solicitation Planning	Procurement	Planning	Whatever needs to be done after the statement of work is ready to create a procurement document	Procurement Planning	Solicitation
Source Selection	Procurement	Executing	Whatever needs to be done after the proposal is received to obtain a signed contract	Solicitation	Contract Administra-tion

Recurring Themes - PMI®-isms

There are two important reasons for this section of the book. First, an objective of any certification exam is to continuously expand the base of industry knowledge. If there are areas where certain fundamentals are lacking, and this is certainly true in project management, the certification exam will most likely emphasize them. PMI® does the same thing.

The second reason for this section of the book is that I have heard hundreds of comments from students about concepts on the exam that surprise them. Sometimes students are surprised because they may be using incorrect project management principles, or their culture supports project managers with a different approach to project management than the approach represented on the exam. PMI® assumes that you are doing proper project management, which may be different from the way your company is actually doing it. As a result, there are some potential problem areas or gaps in your knowledge that you should review before you even start studying for the exam. I call these PMI®-isms.

PMI®-isms are not stressed and sometimes not even mentioned in the *PMBOK® Guide*! An understanding of them has come from over 10 years experience helping people pass the exam. Understanding PMI®-isms will help you pick the right answer from what seems like more than one correct answer. It will help you answer many more questions correctly than is possible by relying only on life experience. Look for more on these topics in the body of this book.

- There is a basic assumption that you have records (historical information) for all past projects that include what the tasks were, how much each task cost, and what risks were uncovered. You are probably laughing right now because you do not have such information. You may even be saying, "That is a good idea!" For the exam, assume that you have them for all projects and that you create them for existing projects. Historical records are an input to almost every step of the project management process.

- You must understand the process of project management; e.g., what to do first, second, etc., and why! See the Life Cycle Game.

- For most of the main bolded topics covered in this book, you must understand what they are and why you should care about them; e.g., why they can help the project and project manager.

- You should understand what role a project manager plays, what work he must do and what work involves other stakeholders. Many people fail the exam simply because a project manager in their company has very little power and they do not realize what powers a project manager really should have or what they should be doing. Others fail the exam because they think the project manager is supposed to plan the project on his or her own and TELL everyone what to do. In either case they are incorrect.

- Everything should be coordinated with stakeholders on a project. Stakeholder skills, communications needs and EXPECTATIONS must be considered throughout the management of the project. You might not have formally taken this approach on your projects.

- All roles and responsibilities must be CLEARLY assigned to specific individuals on the project. Since the lack of clear assignment is the number one complaint of team members in my studies, you could probably use some additional understanding of what PMI® suggests in this area.

- You should realize a project plan is not Gant chart nor is a WBS created in a Gantt chart.

- Work breakdown structures (WBS) are the foundation of all project planning and should be used on every project.

- A work breakdown structure is not a list.

- Project managers are "wonderful," "great," and must be very skilled (a "rah! rah! for project management" topic).

- PMI® does not approve of gold plating (adding extra functionality).

- The definition of kickoff meeting used on the exam may be different than a "kickoff meeting" you might hold.

- The project manager must be proactive. Although PMI® does not use this word, correct answers indicate that the project manager must find problems early, look for changes, prevent problems, etc.

- Planning is very important and all projects must be planned.

- Make sure you know what it takes to create a real project plan - project plan development.

- Project managers must have a plan (a management plan) for how they are going to manage everything on the project. This may be a formal document for larger projects or a less formal plan for smaller projects. It becomes part of the project plan. See this phrase throughout the book, e.g., scope management plan, staffing management plan.

- Most project managers have never developed a project plan that meets the *PMBOK® Guide*'s definition of a project plan. In time, as more project managers are properly trained and allowed to use project management in the workplace, this will change.

- Project managers MUST control the project to the project plan – project plan execution and integrated change control.

- For most people, what is described in the *PMBOK® Guide* is a much more extensive process than what they have done in the real world!

- Watch out for the word "audit" as in "Procurement Audit" and "Quality Audit!" It may mean something different than you think.

- If you do not manage cost on your projects, you should be more careful studying cost.

- Notice how many times corrective action is mentioned in the *PMBOK® Guide*. Know what it is and when it is needed.

- Make sure you check your knowledge of what activities are included in controlling and closing.

- There is a basic assumption on the exam that you have company project management policies (don't laugh, we will get there) and that you will adapt them for use on your project. These may include project management methodologies and quality procedures.

- The project manager has some human resource responsibilities of which you might not be aware.

Project Management Framework
(*PMBOK® GUIDE* Chapters 1-3)

This chapter covers the foundation for project management and conveys important concepts. Most of the questions are easy, but watch out for questions about weak or strong matrices (explained below). Make sure you MEMORIZE concepts, definitions and approaches. Make certain you read these chapters in the *PMBOK® Guide* at least once. TRICK: It would be helpful to use an electronic copy of the *PMBOK® Guide* to search for these words: sponsor, stakeholder, project management and senior management. It will help you to better understand these roles.

Hot Topics

- Project management life cycle
- Stakeholder
- Stakeholder management
- Forms of organization
  - Matrix
    - Strong
    - Weak
    - Balanced
  - Functional
  - Projectized
  - Project expeditor
  - Project coordinator
- Tight matrix
- Triple constraint
- Definition of a project
- Definition of a program
- Project office
- Social-economic-environmental sustainability
- Project life cycle

DEFINITION OF A PROJECT (page 4; all page number references are to the *PMBOK® Guide*): You must understand the definition of a project.

- Temporary endeavor with a beginning and an end
- Creates a unique product, service or result
- Done for a purpose
- Has interrelated activities
- Is progressively elaborated – distinguishing characteristics of each unique project will be progressively detailed as the project is better understood

DEFINITION OF A PROGRAM (page 10): "A program is a group of projects managed in a coordinated way."

STAKEHOLDER, STAKEHOLDER MANAGEMENT (page 16): You should think of stakeholders as more than the project manager, sponsor and team. A stakeholder is someone whose interests may be positively or negatively impacted by the project. They may also include those who may exert influence over the project but would not otherwise be considered stakeholders. See also the section titled "Roles and Responsibilities" in the Human Resources chapter. PMI® defines stakeholders as:

- Project Manager – The individual responsible for managing the project
- Customer – The individual or organization that will use the product of the project
- Performing organization, government agencies
- Sponsor – The individual/group who provides the financial resources for the project
- Team – Those who will be completing work tasks on the project
- Internal/external – Stakeholders can come from inside or outside the organization
- End users – The individuals or organizations that will use the product of the project when it is completed
- Society, citizens – Often members of society can be stakeholders – e.g., instances when a new road is being build through a community or a new emergency phone number (such as a 911 number) is being set up
- Others – Owners, funders, sellers

What is stakeholder management? "The project management team must identify the stakeholders, determine their requirements, and then manage and influence those requirements to ensure a successful project." Stakeholder management is made up of the following steps:

- Identifying stakeholders
- Assessing their knowledge and skills
- Analyzing the project to make sure their needs will be met
- Getting and keeping them involved in the project through assigning them work, using them as experts, reporting to them, involving them in changes and the creation of lessons learned
- Getting their sign-off and formal acceptance during closure

The key to customer satisfaction is careful and accurate needs analysis; therefore, stakeholder management is a proactive task. The project manager should not just receive a scope of work and then strive to complete it, but rather determine all the stakeholders and incorporate their requirements into the project in order for the project to be a success.

What if there is a difference between the requirements of the stakeholders? PMI® suggests that such differences should generally be resolved in favor of the customer - the individual or organization that will use the product. Please see more about this topic in the Professional Responsibility chapter.

Stakeholder expectations are more ambiguous than requirements and may be intentionally or unintentionally hidden. Expectations should be identified and managed throughout the life of the project to the same extent as stakeholders' requirements. Stakeholder expectations has been removed from the definition of stakeholder management in the 2000 edition of the *PMBOK® Guide*, but it remains in the description of stakeholders.

SOCIAL-ECONOMIC-ENVIRONMENTAL SUSTAINABILITY (page 27): There is a trend in the PMP® exam and the *PMBOK® Guide* of more project responsibility and accountability toward the environment and the people and economy within which projects take place. The effect of this accountability can remain long after the project is completed. For example, consider all the homes that are not worth renovating even 20 years after they are built, let alone 100 years later. Another example; a project manager taking into account the number of trucks that would have to go through the community, and the negative impact that would have on the community, if a new facility is built in a particular city.

TRIPLE CONSTRAINT (page 29): The triple constraint (the concept started with three items) are cost, time, scope of work (requirements or scope statement), quality and customer satisfaction (or stakeholder satisfaction). These are so intertwined that a change in one will most often cause a change in at least one of the others. The triple constraint is part of the constraints mentioned continuously in the *PMBOK® Guide*. See also the Professional Responsibility chapter.

Management sets the priority of each of the components and they are used throughout the project by the project manager to properly plan the project, evaluate the impact of changes and prove successful project completion.

Cost / Time
Quality
Scope
Customer Satisfaction

LIFE CYCLE (pages 11-15, pages 29-38): There are two different life cycles referenced in the exam: project life cycle and project management life cycle. You must be very familiar with the project management life cycle as there are 40 to 60 questions on this topic!

PROJECT LIFE CYCLE (pages 11-15): This life cycle describes what you need to do to *do the work* on the project. Many companies (especially those in software development) mistakenly consider this type of life cycle to be the same as project management. Questions about this life cycle are not often part of the exam and are more correctly part of exams for technical disciplines such as engineering, information systems, telecommunications, construction, etc.

Construction – feasibility, planning, design, production, turnover and startup.

Information systems – requirements analysis, high-level design, detailed design, coding, testing, installation, conversion and operation.

PROJECT MANAGEMENT LIFE CYCLE (process groups, pages 32-37): This life cycle describes what you need to do to *manage* the project. It follows PMI®'s process groups:
- Initiating
- Planning
- Executing
- Controlling
- Closing

For small projects these process groups represent the whole of a project life cycle. For large projects, the project management life cycle may be repeated for each phase of the project life cycle (see *PMBOK® Guide* page 31 figure 3-3). The process groups do not necessarily follow one after the other, but frequently overlap during the life of the project (see *PMBOK® Guide* page 31 figure 3-2).

To test your knowledge of the project management process, the next exercise was created. When reviewing the chart, please note, a few of the core and facilitating processes noted in the *PMBOK® Guide* are not listed because projects do not always address these topics during the part of the project management life cycle listed in the *PMBOK® Guide*.

You should MEMORIZE and understand the overall project management process (a PMI®-ism), what each term means, the phase of the project management life cycle when each should be done and the specific order of the planning and closing phases. Be prepared for questions that describe situations and ask you to pick the next thing to be done or to describe what step, process or phase of the project management life cycle one is in. Read pages 29-38 in the *PMBOK® Guide*, but make certain you MEMORIZE the following chart. When you are ready, play the Life Cycle Game on the subsequent pages.

Initiating	Planning	Executing	Controlling	Closing
Select project	Create scope statement	Execute the project plan	Integrated change control	Procurement audits
	Determine project team			
Collect historical information	Create WBS	Manage project progress	Project performance measuring	Product verification
	Finalize the team			
Determine project objectives	Create WBS dictionary	Complete work packages	Performance reporting	Financial closure
	Create network diagram			
Determine high-level deliverables, estimates	Estimate time and cost	Distribute information	Scope change control	Lessons learned
	Determine critical path	Quality assurance		Update records
Determine high-level constraints and assumptions	Create risk management plan	Team development	Quality control	End of project performance reporting
	Develop schedule			
	Develop budget	Hold progress meetings	Risk monitoring and control	Formal acceptance
Determine business need	Determine communication requirements	Identify changes	Schedule control	Project archives
Develop product description	Determine quality standards	Use work authorization system	Cost control	Release resources
Define responsibilities of the project manager	Risk identification, qualification, quantification and response planning	Manage by exception to the project plan	Scope verification	
	Iterations – go back		Ensure compliance with plans	**Overall**
				Influencing the organization
Determine high-level resource requirements	Create other management plans – scope, schedule, cost, quality, staffing, communications, procurement		Project plan updates	Leading
				Solving problems
Finalize the project charter	Create project control system		Corrective action	Negotiating
	Final project plan development			Communicating
	Gain formal project plan approval			Holding meetings
	Hold kickoff meeting			Stakeholder management

NOTE: Team building (included as part of team development), risk planning and identification are focused on where they are placed in the previous chart. These activities start where they are listed and do not end until project closure. You can identify risks and build a team throughout the life of the project.

Also note that planning is iterative. For example, a project manager may lead the creation of the WBS, but need to change it during planning to add work related to risk responses.

Life Cycle Game

The following pages contain the phases and activities of the project management life cycle (a shorter version of the list on the previous page). Cut them out and practice putting them into the correct phase on your own or in a group. When you think they are all in the correct phase, put planning and closing in order. Lastly, check your answers using the chart on the previous page.

I have said that you must understand project management to pass the test. If you do not understand many of the items or you do not agree with the order in planning, you are lacking a basic understanding of project management. In this case, you might want to consider additional project management training before taking the exam.

SELECT PROJECT	DETERMINE PROJECT OBJECTIVES	FINAL PROJECT PLAN DEVELOPMENT
DETERMINE HIGH-LEVEL DELIVERABLES, ESTIMATES	DETERMINE HIGH-LEVEL CONSTRAINTS AND ASSUMPTIONS	HOLD KICKOFF MEETING
DETERMINE BUSINESS NEED	DEVELOP PRODUCT DESCRIPTION	DETERMINE PROJECT TEAM

Chapter 2
Project Management Framework

Intentionally
left
blank

PHONE: (952) 846-4484 - EMAIL: info@rmcproject.com - WEB: www.rmcproject.com

DEFINE RESPONSIBILITIES OF THE PROJECT MANAGER	DETERMINE HIGH-LEVEL RESOURCE REQUIREMENTS	GAIN FORMAL PROJECT PLAN APPROVAL
FINALIZE THE PROJECT CHARTER	INITIATING	CREATE SCOPE STATEMENT
RISK IDENTIFICATION, QUALIFICATION, QUANTIFICATION AND RESPONSE PLANNING	CREATE PROJECT CONTROL SYSTEM	CREATE WBS
CREATE OTHER MANAGEMENT PLANS	DETERMINE COMMUNICATION REQUIREMENTS	FORMAL ACCEPTANCE
FINALIZE THE TEAM	CREATE WBS DICTIONARY	DISTRIBUTE INFORMATION

Chapter 2
Project Management Framework

Intentionally
left
blank

CREATE NETWORK DIAGRAM	ESTIMATE TIME AND COST	TEAM DEVELOPMENT
DETERMINE CRITICAL PATH	DEVELOP SCHEDULE	DEVELOP BUDGET
CORRECTIVE ACTION	EXECUTE THE PROJECT PLAN	PRODUCT VERIFICATION
MANAGE PROJECT PROGRESS	COMPLETE WORK PACKAGES	QUALITY ASSURANCE
PROJECT ARCHIVES	RELEASE RESOURCES	HOLD PROGRESS MEETINGS

Chapter 2
Project Management Framework

Intentionally
left
blank

INTEGRATED CHANGE CONTROL	PROJECT PERFORMANCE MEASURING	PLANNING
PERFORMANCE REPORTING	SCOPE CHANGE CONTROL	DETERMINE QUALITY STANDARDS
QUALITY CONTROL	RISK MONITORING AND CONTROL	EXECUTING
SCHEDULE CONTROL	COST CONTROL	IDENTIFY CHANGES
MANAGE BY EXCEPTION TO THE PROJECT PLAN	ENSURE COMPLIANCE WITH PLANS	CLOSING

Chapter 2
Project Management Framework

Intentionally
left
blank

.

SCOPE VERIFICATION	PROJECT PLAN UPDATES	CONTROLLING
LESSONS LEARNED	UPDATE RECORDS	PROCUREMENT AUDITS
USE WORK AUTHORIZATION SYSTEM	FINANCIAL CLOSURE	END OF PROJECT PERFORMANCE REPORTING
COLLECT HISTORICAL INFORMATION	CREATE RISK MANAGEMENT PLAN	ITERATIONS – GO BACK

Chapter 2
Project Management Framework

Intentionally
left
blank

FORMS OF ORGANIZATION (*Principles of Project Management* pages 11-22, *PMBOK® Guide* pages 18 – 21): Organizational theory describes how a company can be organized to complete its work. PMI® talks about five types of organizational structure. Each type is described in terms of the project manager's level of authority. Many people have commented that they wished they had spent more time studying this topic. Questions on the exam related to organizational theory include:

- Who has the power in each type of organization – the project manager or the functional manager?
- Advantages of each type of organization
- Disadvantages of each type of organization

FUNCTIONAL – This is the most common form of organization. The organization is grouped by areas of specialization within different functional areas (e.g., accounting, marketing and manufacturing). A functional organizational chart might look like this:

NOTE: Many exam questions ask about other forms of organization besides the functional form. Sometimes the reference to the functional form of organization is not even stated. Please see the first practice question at the end of this chapter.

MATRIX – This form is an attempt to maximize the strengths and weaknesses of both the functional and project forms. The team members report to **two bosses:** the project manager and the functional manager (e.g., VP Engineering, etc.). This form may look like this:

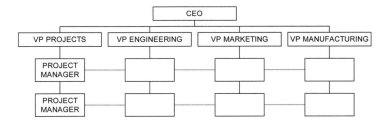

In a strong matrix, power rests with the project manager. In a weak matrix, power rests with the functional manager. In a balanced matrix, the power is shared between the functional manager and the project manager.

A tight matrix has nothing to do with a matrix organization. It simply refers to locating the offices for the project team in the same room. Because it seems close to the other forms of organization, it is often used as a fourth choice for these questions.

PROJECTIZED – All organization is by projects. The project manager has total control of projects. Personnel are assigned and report to a project manager.

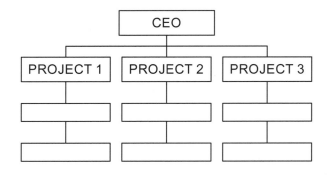

Exercise: Test yourself! You can expect questions about the advantages and disadvantages of each organizational form. Practice by listing your answers in the spaces below.

PROJECTIZED

Advantages	Disadvantages

MATRIX

Advantages	Disadvantages

FUNCTIONAL

Advantages	Disadvantages

Answer: Several potential answers are listed below. Remember that many of the answers should include the phrase "as compared to functional."

PROJECTIZED

Advantages	Disadvantages
Efficient project organization	No "home" when project is completed
Loyalty to the project	Lack of professionalism in disciplines
More effective communications than functional	Duplication of facilities and job functions
	Less efficient use of resources

MATRIX

Advantages	Disadvantages
Highly visible project objectives	Not cost effective because of extra administrative personnel
Improved project manager control over resources	More than one boss for project teams
More support from functional organizations	More complex to monitor and control
Maximum utilization of scarce resources	Tougher problems with resource allocation
Better coordination	Need extensive policies and procedures
Better horizontal and vertical dissemination of information than functional	Functional managers may have different priorities than project managers
Team members maintain a "home"	Higher potential for conflict and duplication of effort

FUNCTIONAL

Advantages	Disadvantages
Easier management of specialists	People place more emphasis on their functional specialty to the detriment of the project
Team members report to only one supervisor	No career path in project management
Similar resources are centralized, companies are grouped by specialties	Project manager has no authority
Clearly defined career paths in areas of work specialization	

PROJECT EXPEDITOR – In this form of organization, the project expeditor acts primarily as a staff assistant and communications coordinator. The expeditor cannot personally make or enforce decisions. This form of organization may look like this:

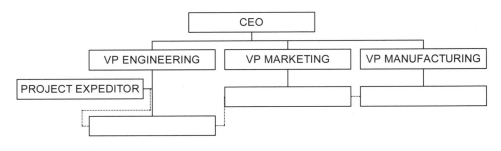

PROJECT COORDINATOR – This form of organization is similar to the Project Expeditor except the coordinator has some power to make decisions, some authority, and reports to a higher-level manager. This form of organization may look like this:

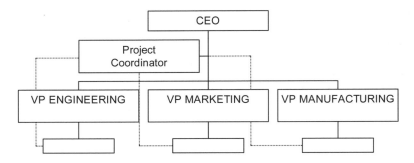

You should understand project expeditor and project coordinator and how they differ from each other.

PROJECT OFFICE (page 21): A formal structure that supports project management within an organization and usually takes one of three forms:
- Providing the policies, methodologies and templates for managing projects within the organization
- Providing support and guidance to others in the organization on how to manage projects, training others in project management or project management software and assisting with specific project management tools
- Providing project managers for different projects and being responsible for the results of the projects. All projects (or projects of a certain size, type or influence) are managed by this office

There is a strong trend to start project offices. To make them work, you should remember three key concepts:
- The role of the project office must be clearly defined
- The commitment of senior management is required
- The project office will not improve your project performance without also using proper project management process and techniques

Practice Exam for the CAPM® and PMP® Exams
Project Management Framework

1. One of the main advantages of a matrix organization is:

   A. Improved project manager control over resources
   B. More than one boss for project teams
   C. Communications are easier
   D. Reporting is easier

2. How is a project expeditor different from a project coordinator?

   A. The project expeditor cannot make decisions
   B. The project expeditor can make more decisions
   C. The project expeditor reports to a higher-level manager
   D. The project expeditor has some authority

3. In a projectized organization the project team:

   A. Reports to many bosses
   B. Has no loyalty to the project
   C. Reports to the functional manager
   D. Will not always have a "home"

4. During which life cycle phase is the detailed project budget created?

   A. Initiating
   B. Before the project management life cycle
   C. Planning
   D. Executing

5. The project charter is created during which life cycle phase?

   A. Executing
   B. Planning
   C. Closing
   D. Initiating

6. A project manager is trying to complete a software development project but cannot get enough attention for the project. Resources are focused on completing process-related work and the project manager has little authority to properly assign resources. What form of organization must the project manager be working in?

   A. Functional
   B. Matrix
   C. Expeditor
   D. Coordinator

7. **The project team has just completed the initial project schedule and budget. The NEXT thing to do is:**

    A. Begin risk identification
    B. Begin iterations
    C. Determine communication requirements
    D. Create a Gantt chart

8. **A project manager has very little project experience but he has been assigned as the project manager of a new project. Because he will be working in a matrix organization to complete his project, he can expect communications to be:**

    A. Simple
    B. Open and accurate
    C. Complex
    D. Hard to automate

9. **A detailed project schedule can be created only after creating the:**

    A. Project budget
    B. Work breakdown structure
    C. Project plan
    D. Detailed risk assessment

10. **The person who should be in control of the project during project planning is the:**

    A. Project manager
    B. Team member
    C. Functional manager
    D. Sponsor

11. **A project team member is talking to another team member and complaining that so many people are asking him to do things. If he works in a functional organization, who has the power to give direction to the team member?**

    A. The project manager
    B. The functional manager
    C. The team
    D. Tight matrix

12. **Who has the MOST power in a projectized organization?**

    A. The project manager
    B. The functional manager
    C. The team
    D. They all share power

13. All of the following are characteristics of a project EXCEPT:

A. Temporary
B. Definite beginning and end
C. Interrelated activities
D. Repeats itself every month

14. All of the following are part of the team's stakeholder management effort EXCEPT:

A. Giving stakeholders extras
B. Identifying stakeholders
C. Determining stakeholders' needs
D. Managing stakeholders' expectations

15. A project manager's boss and the head of engineering discuss a change to a major task. After the meeting, the boss contacts the project manager and tells him to make the change. This is an example of:

A. Management attention to scope management
B. Management planning
C. A project coordinator position
D. A change control system

Project Management Framework Answers

1. **Answer:** A

   Explanation: Remember that if the question doesn't state what it is comparing to, it is comparing to a functional organization.

2. **Answer:** A

   Explanation: The project coordinator reports to a higher level manager and has authority to make some decisions. The project expeditor has no authority to make decisions.

3. **Answer:** D

   Explanation: The main drawback of the projectized organization is that at the end of the project, the team is dispersed but they do not have a functional department (home) to which to return.

4. **Answer:** C

   Explanation: The order of magnitude budget is the only budget that is not created in the planning phase.

5. **Answer:** D

   Explanation: The charter is needed before planning and execution of the work can begin.

6. **Answer:** A

   Explanation: In a functional organization, the project manager has the least support for the project and has little authority to assign resources.

7. **Answer:** C

   Explanation: A Gantt chart (choice D) would have been done during the creation of the schedule so it cannot be the next thing. Iterations (choice B) cannot begin until the risks are identified, qualified, quantified and responses developed. These then create the need to revise the WBS and other parts of the project plan. Communication requirements (choice C) and quality standards are needed before risk (especially risks relating to communication and quality) can be determined (choice A).

8. **Answer:** C

   Explanation: Because a project done in a matrix organization involves people from across the organization, communications are more complex.

9. **Answer:** B

   Explanation: In the project management life cycle, the project budget, project plan and detailed risk assessment come after the schedule. The only answer that could be an input is the WBS.

10. **Answer:** A

    Explanation: PMI® advocates that the project manager be named early in the project, during initiation if possible.

11. **Answer:** B

    Explanation: In a functional organization, the functional manager is the team member's boss and probably also the project manager's boss.

12. **Answer:** A

    Explanation: In a projectized organization, the entire company is organized by projects, giving the project manager the most power.

13. **Answer:** D

    Explanation: Choice D implies that the whole project repeats every month. Generally, the only things that might repeat in a project are some activities. The whole project does not repeat.

14. **Answer:** A

    Explanation: Giving stakeholders extras is gold plating (see the Quality chapter). This is not effective stakeholder or quality management.

15. **Answer:** C

    Explanation: A project coordinator has some authority but management handles important decisions.

WARNING: Do not dismiss this chapter because these questions are generally easy. Framework concepts repeat through all the questions on the exam. It is critical to understand the life cycle game.

Integration Management
(PMBOK® GUIDE Chapter 4)

Integration is currently the hardest knowledge area on the exam, primarily because most people do not understand the project manager's specific duties and do not have the authority described in the *PMBOK® Guide*. Integration is primarily the role of the project manager because the project manager is the only one responsible for seeing the overall "big picture." Integration means putting the pieces of the project together into a cohesive whole while managing tradeoffs among the different project objectives.

Expect up to fourteen questions on the exam! I suggest that you read this chapter lightly the first time through the book and spend more time understanding it the second time.

Hot Topics

- Project manager as integrator
- Project plan execution
- Integrated change control
- Project plan development
- Project plan
- Corrective action
- Historical information
- Project plan updates
- Lessons learned
- Constraints
- Baseline
- Change control system
- Change control board
- Kickoff meeting
- Project plan approval
- Work authorization system
- Change requests
- Configuration management
- Project management information system
- Earned value management
- Project planning methodology

PROJECT MANAGER AS INTEGRATOR: During executing, it is the team members' role to concentrate on completing the tasks, activities and work packages. The project sponsor or senior management should be protecting the project from changes and loss of resources. It is the project manager's role to integrate all the pieces of the project into a whole.

A lack of understanding of these roles can cause many problems on projects. People have difficulty on the exam if they do not understand roles and responsibilities.

CONSTRAINTS (page 110): Constraints are factors that limit the project team's options. A single project may contain cost, time, human resource and other constraints.

HISTORICAL INFORMATION (page 43 and throughout the *PMBOK® Guide*): Historical information (or data) is a record of past projects. It is used to plan and manage future projects, thereby improving the process of project management. Historical information can include:

- Tasks
- WBS
- Reports
- Estimates
- Project plans
- Lessons learned
- Benchmarks
- Risks
- Resources needed
- Correspondence

Because most companies have not kept historical information on their projects, each project is essentially planned, estimated and scheduled from scratch. The creation of a database of historical information is an organizational responsibility that can result in continuous improvement. Assume you have such historical information for the exam.

LESSONS LEARNED (postmortem, throughout the *PMBOK® Guide*): This topic is only briefly mentioned at the end of each chapter in the *PMBOK® Guide*, yet it has great importance in real project management. A lessons learned is a document that talks about what was done right, wrong and what would be done differently if the project could be redone. It should cover three areas:

- Technical aspects of the project
- Project management (how did we do with WBS creation, risk, etc.?)
- Management (how did we do with communications and leadership as a project manager?)

The lessons learned may be created continuously, but the *PMBOK® Guide* only requires it to be created/done during the closeout of each phase of a project. It is required in order for the project to be completed. Continuous improvement in the project management process cannot occur without lessons learned.

The lessons learned from past or ongoing projects are an input into many of the project planning processes for future projects under the title "historical records."

At the very least, the project manager completes the lessons learned. Better yet, the whole project team completes it. Even better, it is completed by the whole team and made available throughout the company. Sometimes a lessons learned is created with sellers involved with the project.

PROJECT PLANNING METHODOLOGY (page 44): Many companies have standard procedures, forms and guidelines for planning projects. These should be followed in planning the project. I know these statements make you laugh, but it is true; we should have standards within our companies. Someday we will. Until then, assume you have procedures, forms and guidelines when you take the exam.

PROJECT MANAGEMENT INFORMATION SYSTEM (PMIS, page 44): This topic shows up frequently on the exam as a choice. A PMIS is an all-encompassing phrase to mean the system set up in advance that keeps the project manager informed of the status of all project tasks. A PMIS is critical to know what is really happening on the project and the real status of the project. It may contain manual and automated tools, techniques and procedures including reporting, meetings, management by walking around, asking questions and using a Gantt chart.

Because there are an infinite variety of possible PMIS', you should keep this general description in mind, but realize that the project manager should set one up in advance of project execution and that having one is of critical importance.

EARNED VALUE MANAGEMENT (page 44): Earned value, described in the Cost chapter, is a technique used to integrate the project scope, schedule and resources as well as to measure and report project performance.

PROJECT PLAN (page 45): Do you really understand what makes up a project plan?

Exercise: Test yourself! List the components of a project plan.

Answer: Did you list the items in a Gantt chart? A Gantt chart is a schedule or status reporting tool; it is not a project plan. A project plan is a multi-page document created by the project manager based on input from the team and stakeholders. It contains mostly charts and tables included in the list below. Once completed, a project plan is used as a day-to-day tool to help manage the project. It is not just a document created for management.

Project charter	Budget
Project management approach	Schedule
Scope statement	Resources
WBS	Change control plan/system
Responsibility chart/assignments	Performance measurement baselines
Network diagram/major milestones	Management plans (scope, schedule, cost, quality, staffing, communications, risk response, procurement)

The project plan is created by the project manager with the help of the team. It should have input from stakeholders and management. Though it may evolve and change over the life of the project, a project plan is designed to be as complete as possible when the project executing phase begins. Project planning is an ongoing effort throughout the life of the project.

PROJECT PLAN DEVELOPMENT (page 42): Project plan development is the process of creating a project plan that is bought-into, approved, realistic and formal. Take the time to reread the last sentence. When you finish the exam and look on your score sheet, this topic could be the reason you do poorly in the area of "Develop a formal and comprehensive project plan." You should spend time here thinking about how to do this in the real world.

Exercise: Test yourself! Make a list of the specific ACTIONS required to create a project plan that meets these criteria.

Answer: If you got most of the answers correct, you are in good shape. If not, think this through. You might find some serious gaps in your project management knowledge. Most people have gaps in this area and do not discover them until they take the exam. To repeat, this exercise is asking what it would take to create a project plan that is bought-into, approved, realistic and formal.

Some of the possible answers to this exercise include:
- Determining a methodology for creating the project plan before it is begun
- Working through iterations of the plan (e.g., changing the work breakdown structure after risk analysis)
- Meeting with resource managers to get the best resources possible and to get management to approve the schedule
- Applying risk reserves to the project schedule and budget to come up with a final project plan
- Analyzing the skills and knowledge of all the stakeholders and determining how you will use them on the project
- Meeting with stakeholders to define their roles on the project
- Looking for the impact on your project from other projects
- Giving team members a chance to approve the final schedule that converts the team's task estimates into a calendar schedule
- Holding meetings or presentations to let management know what project objectives, outlined in the project charter, cannot be met
- Crashing, fast tracking and presenting options to management
- Setting up a control plan including earned value management and project management information systems

PROJECT PLAN APPROVAL: Since the project plan is a formal document that will be used to manage the execution of the project and includes items like project completion dates, milestones and costs, it must receive formal approval by management, stakeholders and the project team. Formal approval means sign-off (signatures). If the project manager has identified all the stakeholders and their needs and objectives, included those needs and objectives in the plan, and dealt with conflicting priorities in advance, project plan approval will be less difficult. A project cannot effectively start without formal approval of the project plan.

BASELINE (page 66, 90): Every time you see the word "baseline" on the exam, think of the original project plan with approved changes. The baseline should be used to monitor the progress of the project, and forecasts of final cost and schedule should be compared to it. The exam can mention cost, time, quality and other baselines. They usually refer to the respective parts of the original project plan. Project baselines may be changed by formally approved changes, but the evolution of the baseline should be documented.

KICKOFF MEETING: A meeting of all parties to the project (customers, sellers, project team, senior management, agencies, functional management, sponsor). It is held at the end of the planning phase just before beginning work on the project. This is a communications and coordination meeting to make certain everyone is familiar with the details of the project and the people working on the project. Topics can include introductions, a review of the project risks, communications plan and meeting schedule.

WORK AUTHORIZATION SYSTEM (page 47): "A formal procedure for sanctioning project work to ensure that work is done at the right time and in the proper sequence." It is also a method to control gold plating, such as the provision of an extra functionality or service. It defines what the task is and is not, and may take the form of a WBS dictionary (see a later description).

CHANGE REQUESTS (page 47): Change requests are identified in project plan execution and handled in integrated change control. They are usually formal documents submitted by anyone on the project after the project has been approved. The project plan is a formal document that needs to be controlled and cannot be changed informally.

PROJECT PLAN EXECUTION: This process involves carrying out the project plan. It makes up the majority of activities in the executing phase of the project and uses up the majority of the project budget.

Exercise: Make a list of the specific ACTIONS required to execute the project plan.

Answer: Project plan execution includes all the efforts necessary to achieve work results and identify change requests. Project plan execution is essentially a guiding, proactive role accomplished by constant referral back to the project plan. Have you included such common mistakes as telling people what to do instead of asking them? Have you included items that should have been done in planning?

Project plan execution may involve the following activities:
- Implementing the project plan
- Completing work packages
- Achieving work results
- Committing project resources in accordance with the project plan
- Managing project progress
- Taking preventative actions
- Guiding, assisting, communicating, leading, negotiating, helping, coaching
- Utilizing your technical knowledge
- Authorizing work using a work authorization system
- Monitoring progress against the project baseline
- Taking corrective action
- Holding team meetings
- Using the project management information system to acquire information
- Managing by exception to the project plan – focusing on looking for exceptions or changes rather than spending time checking up on team members' work or babysitting
- Identifying changes to be handled in integrated change control

Other activities done during the executing phase of the project are not part of project plan execution. These topics are covered in the Communications, Human Resource and Quality chapters and the Life Cycle Game. They consist of:
- Implementing quality assurance procedures
- Communicating project progress
- Producing reports
- Developing the team

It is important to realize that the project is actively managed to the project plan during execution and control. This would imply that the project plan is realistic and can be used to manage the project and measure progress. The project manager keeps the project team and other stakeholders focused on the project plan. Exceptions to plan are looked for, versus spending effort to check up on every team member.

Many people get questions in this area wrong. You may have run into problems with project plan execution on the exam if you score badly under the headings of "Commit project resources," " Implement the project plan," and "Manage project progress" on the actual exam.

TRICK: Keep the phrases "work to the project plan," "be proactive," "adjust," and "guide" in mind as you take the exam to make sure you are thinking along PMI®'s terms.

CHANGE CONTROL BOARD (page 49): A change control board is formed to review change requests to determine if additional analysis is warranted. They also approve or reject project changes. The board may include the project manager, customer, experts, sponsor and others.

CHANGE CONTROL SYSTEM (page 48): A collection of formal, documented procedures, paperwork, tracking systems and approval levels for authorizing changes. A change control system includes both hard (procedures) and soft (management practices) aspects. It may include:

- A change control plan included in the project plan outlining how changes will be managed
- Creation of a change control board to approve all changes (see below)
- Change control procedures (how, who)
- Performance statistics (e.g., time/system, time/drawing)
- Reports (e.g., software output, milestone charts, resource usage)
- Change forms
- Specification reviews
- Demonstrations
- Testing
- Meetings
- Plans for taking corrective action

CORRECTIVE ACTION (page 46 and in the "control" phase of all the project management processes): Any actions done to bring expected future project performance in line with the project plan. Corrective action is accomplished by measuring performance and identification of the root cause of the variation. This is almost impossible if project control systems have not been put in place during planning.

Corrective action is an input to project plan execution and an output from integrated change control and all control processes throughout the *PMBOK® Guide*. Therefore both executing and controlling involve taking corrective action, but only control includes measuring actions needed and taking further corrective action. Corrective action may involve root cause analysis, schedule recovery, cost recovery, changes to risks, changes to quality, etc.

Exercise: What does "take timely corrective action" mean?

| |
| |
| |
| |
| |

Answer: Take timely corrective action means the project manager is looking for deviations, not just waiting for them to be brought to his or her attention. It also means that the project manager does not withdraw from problems or pretend they are not there. The project is managed to the project plan and constantly monitored quantitatively using earned value and other project control tools. Corrective action is very proactive.

Exercise: What does "evaluate the effectiveness of corrective actions" involve?

Answer: Evaluate the effectiveness means the project manager will measure performance after implementing decisions in order to see if the decision produced the desired effects. In other words, project managers frequently say to themselves, "Did the decision I made last week really work?"

In total, the answer to the two exercises should include:

- Identify the need for corrective action
- Take corrective action
- Evaluate the effectiveness of corrective actions
- Measure performance after corrective actions are taken
- Determine the need for further corrective action

Corrective action is emphasized on the exam to a great extent as a choice or as the topic of a question. It will also be listed in two categories on your score sheet, "Take timely corrective action" and "Evaluate the effectiveness of corrective actions."

TRICK: Because this topic is so important, I have a trick for you. Make sure you have the CD-ROM version of the *PMBOK® Guide* and search for the term "corrective action." Seeing how many times and in what contexts it is used will improve your understanding of the topic.

INTEGRATED CHANGE CONTROL (page 47): Integrated change control is the major component of the control phase of the project. I will discuss both control and integrated change control here, as they are intertwined. See the Life Cycle Game for a full list of the different control processes.

Have you noticed that control is the last step of each chapter or knowledge area in the *PMBOK® Guide*? Although it is included only in this chapter, control addresses scope, time, cost, quality and the control of all changes to the project. CONTROL WILL NOT BE REPEATED IN THE OTHER CHAPTERS OF THIS BOOK!

First, it is important for you to discover any gaps in your knowledge. Therefore, I recommend that you spend time with the following exercise before you look at the answer. It is NOT faster to just go directly to the answer. If you want to pass the exam, it is best to follow the flow of this book and complete each exercise as it is presented to you. The more time you spend on each exercise the less time you will study and the higher your score on the exam.

Exercise: Make a list of the specific ACTIONS required to control the project.

Answer: Control is a major hurdle for most exam takers primarily because we do not control our projects. It is therefore the hardest of the five process groups. Spend considerable time here! This section does not require memorization, but rather understanding of what the project manager should be doing in the real world.

The overall focus of integrated change control is to:
- Meet performance baselines
- Make changes
- Coordinate changes across the knowledge areas

Integrated change control may involve the following activities:
- Integrating the changes that result from all the control processes in the *PMBOK® Guide* - the overall focus and control of change
- Taking corrective action
- Working with a change control board
- Managing configuration
- Using and ensuring compliance with the change control system
- Managing changes
- Ensuring compliance and periodically reassessing change management plans
- Controlling all the components of the triple constraint to their baselines
- Exercising judgment to determine what variances are important
- Refining control limits
- Collecting data
- Holding meetings regarding controlling the project
- Handling paperwork
- Negotiating
- Communicating
- Resolving conflict
- Working within policies
- Identifying the root cause of problems
- Issuing updates to the project plan

Other activities done during the control phase of the project are not part of integrated change control. These topics are covered in the Life Cycle Game and the *PMBOK® Guide* and consist of:

SCOPE VERIFICATION (see also the Scope chapter)
- Inspection
- Obtaining formal acceptance of deliverables and the project

SCOPE CHANGE CONTROL
- Measuring performance
- Replanning
- Making changes and adjusting the baseline
- Taking corrective action
- Documenting lessons learned

SCHEDULE CONTROL
- All the items listed for scope change control
- Managing the reserve
- Using earned value

COST CONTROL
- All the items listed for scope change control
- Recalculating the estimate at completion
- Obtaining additional funding when needed
- Managing the budget reserve
- Using earned value

QUALITY CONTROL
- Holding periodic inspections
- Ensuring that authorized approaches and processes are followed
- Identifying the need for corrective action
- Making changes or improvements to work and processes
- Reworking completed work to meet the requirements
- Making decisions to accept or reject work
- Evaluating the effectiveness of corrective actions
- Reassessing the effectiveness of project control plans
- Improving quality

PERFORMANCE MEASURING AND REPORTING
- Continually measuring project performance using variance or trend analysis, earned value, PERT or CPM
- Distributing information
- Holding performance reviews
- Identifying and analyzing trends and variances
- Taking corrective action
- Issuing change requests

RISK MONITORING AND CONTROL
- Responding to risk triggers
- Creating and implementing workarounds
- Implementing contingency plans
- Taking corrective action
- Taking action in accordance with the risk management plan
- Updating lists of risks and risk response plans
- Using risk management procedures
- Issuing change requests

MANAGING CHANGES: The *PMBOK® Guide* says that the project manager must be concerned with:

- Influencing the factors that affect change
- Ensuring that the change is beneficial
- Determining that a change has occurred
- Determining if a change is needed
- Looking for alternatives to changes
- Minimizing the negative impact of changes
- Notifying stakeholders affected by the changes
- Managing changes as they occur

Think about this list for a moment. How does it differ from your projects? Although much can be said about all of these items, the first one is the most confusing. Most people think the project manager's job is simply to make changes. In fact, the project manager should determine all the factors that can cause changes to the project. Then they should proactively use their influence to prevent unnecessary changes and help to discover changes earlier in the project. For example, if the project manager discovers that the scope of work is incomplete, they should try to influence those responsible for completing the scope of work before project planning begins.

Exercise: Test yourself! Describe common changes on projects and determine what you would do to handle each. Because of the wide variety of possible changes, this exercise does not have an answer, but it will help you prepare for questions related to change on the exam.

Common change	How to handle it
Customer says that funds are no longer available.	Would you just stop work? That would not be the best or most ethical choice. Wouldn't it be better to cut the scope of work and try to deliver something of value instead of no value for the funds already expended?

Chapter 3
Integration Management

Common change	How to handle it

The exam has many situational questions, dealing with how to make changes. For example:

> *A functional manager wants to make a change to the project. What is the first thing a project manager should do? Or, a senior manager wants to make a change to the scope of work. What is the best thing to do first?*

The answers are the same in either case. Generally, the team should follow these steps:

1. Evaluate (assess) the impact of the change to the project.
2. Create (compute) alternatives including cutting other tasks, crashing, fast tracking, etc. (described in the Time chapter).
3. Meet with management, sponsor and internal stakeholders.
4. Meet with the customer as necessary.

The process of handling changes is HUGE on the exam. I suggest you go back and reread the last paragraph and make sure you understand that changes are always evaluated first. In most cases, "evaluate" involves considering all components of the triple constraint. "Alternatives" are created based on crashing, fast tracking, re-estimating and playing "what if" using project management software. See the Time chapter for questions about crashing, fast tracking and re-estimating and the Human Resource chapter for questions about roles and responsibilities.

The exam will list steps 3 and 4 as choices. They could be the answer to questions such as "What is the best thing to do?" depending on how the question is written and what exact situation is being described. For example:

> *A change in scope has been determined to have no effect on the triple constraint. What is the BEST thing to do?*

> In this case, evaluation has been done. The answer would be to look for alternatives to adding to the scope of work in case there are unidentified risks, or merely to meet with management (or the sponsor) to let them know about the change and that there will not be any impact. After management has been informed, the customer may be informed by the communication method chosen in advance for such changes.

TRICK: Here is a trick for evaluating questions that deal with who can make or authorize a change. If the change is to the project charter, the person who signed or approved the project charter has to make the final decision. The project manager may provide options.

TRICK: If the change is within the project plan (reserves are available) or the project can be crashed or fast tracked, the project manager can make the decision. They may however, under certain circumstances, get senior managers involved to help protect the project from changes.

TRICK: If the change affects or changes the main objectives of the project plan concerning quality, time, cost and scope, management needs to be involved. The project manager should analyze the situation, crash and fast track, and come up with options. Also see the situations described in the Human Resource chapter, and fast tracking and crashing described in the Time chapter.

PROJECT PLAN UPDATES (page 49): An output to integrated change control is an update to the project plan. Many project managers do not have a thorough understanding of how often and for what reasons the project plan is updated. They also do not control the project to the project plan and so do not know that the plan needs updating. This is a gap to fill before you take the exam. A project plan must exist, be controlled to and formally updated. Changes to the work breakdown structure, network diagram, resources, schedule and cost will always occur, but also need to be controlled. A project plan is progressively elaborated even though the project manager will try to finalize it during planning.

CONFIGURATION MANAGEMENT (page 49): This term has many definitions depending on the industry. For the purposes of the exam, think of this as rigorous change management as it relates to scope. Therefore, it is part of integrated change control.

Practice Exam For the CAPM® and PMP® Exams
Integration Management

Please note, questions on the exam combine terms used in multiple knowledge areas. Therefore, the questions presented in this book will combine topics from all parts of the book. This is especially true of integration questions.

1.   **Effective project integration usually requires an emphasis on:**

    A.   The personal careers of the team members
    B.   Timely updates to the project plan
    C.   Effective communications at key interface points
    D.   Internal control

2.   **The need for ____ is one of the major driving forces for communication in a project.**

    A.   Optimization
    B.   Integrity
    C.   Integration
    D.   Differentiation

3.   **Which of the following describes the BEST use of historical records:**

    A.   Estimating, life cycle costing and project planning
    B.   Risk management, estimating and creating lessons learned
    C.   Project planning, estimating and creating a status report
    D.   Estimating, risk management and project planning

4.   **When it comes to changes, the project manager's attention is BEST spent on:**

    A.   Making changes
    B.   Tracking and recording changes
    C.   Informing management of changes
    D.   Preventing unnecessary changes

5.   **Management's role on a project is BEST described as:**

    A.   Helping to plan tasks
    B.   Helping to prevent unnecessary changes to project objectives
    C.   Identifying unnecessary project constraints
    D.   Helping to put the project plan together

6.   **All of the following are part of an effective change control system EXCEPT:**

    A.   Procedures
    B.   Standards for reports
    C.   Meetings
    D.   Lessons learned

7. **A work authorization system can be used to:**

A. Control who does each task
B. Control what time and in what sequence work is done
C. Control when each task is done
D. Control who does each task and when it is done

8. **A project is plagued by changes to the project charter. Who has the primary responsibility to decide if these changes are necessary?**

A. Project manager
B. Project team
C. Management
D. Stakeholder

9. **Integration is done by:**

A. Project manager
B. Team
C. Management
D. Stakeholder

10. **Which of the following BEST describes the project manager's role as an integrator?**

A. Helping team members become familiar with the project
B. Putting all the pieces of a project into a cohesive whole
C. Putting all the pieces of a project into a program
D. Getting all team members together into a cohesive whole

11. **All technical work is completed on the project. Which of the following remains to be done?**

A. Scope verification
B. Risk response plan
C. Staffing management plan
D. Lessons learned

12. **Company procedures require the creation of a lessons learned. Which of the following is the BEST use of a lessons learned?**

A. Historical information for future projects
B. Planning record for the current project
C. Informing the team about what the project manager has done
D. Informing the team about the project plan

13. **Corrective action is an input to:**

A. Scope control
B. Project plan execution
C. Integrated change control
D. Project plan development

14. A lessons learned is BEST completed by:

    A. Project manager
    B. Team
    C. Management
    D. Stakeholders

15. A particular stakeholder has a reputation for making many changes on projects. What is the BEST approach a project manager can take at the beginning of the project to manage this situation?

    A. Say "no" to the stakeholder a few times to make him change his habits
    B. Get stakeholder involvement in the project as early as possible
    C. Talk to the stakeholder's boss to find ways to direct the stakeholder's activities to another project
    D. Ask that the stakeholder not be included in the stakeholder listing

16. You are a new project manager who has never managed a project before and you have been asked to plan a new project. It would be BEST in this situation to rely on _____ during planning in order to improve your chance of success.

    A. Your intuition
    B. Your training
    C. Historical information
    D. Responsibility chart

17. Which of the following BEST describes a project plan?

    A. A printout from project management software
    B. A Gantt chart
    C. Risk, staff, change control, budget and other plans
    D. The project scope of work

18. During planning, a project manager discovers that part of the scope of work is undefined. What should the project manager do?

    A. Continue to plan the project until the scope of work is defined
    B. Remove the scope of work from the project and include it in the upgrade to the project
    C. Issue a change to the project when the scope is defined
    D. Do what they can to get the scope of work defined before proceeding

19. You are taking over a project and determine the following: Task B has an early finish of day 3, a late finish of day 6, and an early start of day 2. Task L is being done by a hard-to-get resource. The CPI is 1.1 and the SPI is 0.8. Based on this information what would you be more concerned about?

    A. Float
    B. Resources
    C. Cost
    D. Schedule

Integration Management Questions Only For the PMP® Exam

20. The previous project manager for your project managed it without much project organization. There is a lack of management control and no clearly defined project deliverables. Which of the following would be the BEST choice for getting your project better organized?

    A. Adopt a life cycle approach to the project
    B. Develop lessons learned for each phase
    C. Develop specific work plans for each phase of the project
    D. Develop a description of the product of the project

21. You are taking over a project during the planning phase and discover that six individuals have signed the project charter. Which of the following should MOST concern you?

    A. The charter was created during planning
    B. Spending more time on configuration management
    C. Getting a single project sponsor
    D. Determining the reporting structure

22. The project charter for a project was approved for planning and you have just been assigned as project manager. Realizing that planning is an ongoing effort throughout the project life cycle, which processes are you MOST likely to combine?

    A. Scope definition and activity definition
    B. Activity duration estimating and schedule development
    C. Resource planning and cost estimating
    D. Cost estimating and cost budgeting

23. All of the following are part of project plan execution except?

    A. Identifying changes
    B. Using a work breakdown structure
    C. Taking corrective action
    D. Setting up a project control system

24. A project manager is appointed to head a highly technical project in an area with which this person has limited familiarity. The project manager delegates schedule development, cost estimating, selection of tasks, and assignments to work activities to various project team members, and basically serves as an occasional referee and coordinator of activities. The results of this approach are likely to be:

    A. A team functioning throughout the project at a very high level, demonstrating creativity and commitment
    B. A team that initially experiences some amounts of confusion, but that after a period of time becomes a cohesive and effective unit
    C. A team that is not highly productive, but that stays together because of the work environment created by the project manager
    D. A team that is characterized by poor performance, low morale, high levels of conflict and high turnover

25. **You are in the middle of executing a major modification to an existing product when you learn that the resources promised at the beginning of the project are not available. The BEST thing to do is to:**

    A. Show how the resources were originally promised to your project
    B. Replan the project without the resources
    C. Explain what will happen if the resources are not made available
    D. Crash the project

26. **You have been assigned to manage the development of an organization's first website. The site will be highly complex and interactive, and neither your project team nor the client has much experience with website development.**

    The timeline is extremely aggressive. Any delay will be costly for both your firm and the client. You have an executive advocate and have achieved agreement and sign-off on both the project charter and the project plan. Client personnel have been kept fully informed of the project's progress through status reports and regular meetings. The project is on schedule, within the budget, and a final perfunctory review has been scheduled.

    Suddenly you hear that the entire effort may be cancelled because the product developed is totally unacceptable. What is the MOST likely cause of this situation?

    A. A key stakeholder was not adequately involved in the project
    B. The project charter and project plan were not thoroughly explained or adequately reviewed by the client
    C. Communication arrangements were inadequate and did not provide the required information to interested parties
    D. The executive advocate failed to provide adequate support for the project

27. **The project manager has just received a change from the customer that does not affect project time and is easy to complete. What should the project manager do FIRST?**

    A. Make the change happen as soon as possible
    B. Contact the project sponsor for permission
    C. Go to the change control board
    D. Evaluate the other components of the triple constraint

28. **Your company just won a major new project. It will begin in three months and is valued at US $2,000,000. You are the project manager for an existing project. What is the FIRST thing you should do once you hear of the new project?**

    A. Ask management how the new project will use resources
    B. Resource level your project
    C. Crash your project
    D. Ask management how the new project will affect your project

29. **You are a project manager who was just assigned to take over a project from another project manager who is leaving the company. The previous project manager tells you that the project is on schedule, but only because he has constantly pushed the team to perform. What is the FIRST thing you should do as the new project manager?**

    A. Check risk status
    B. Check cost performance
    C. Determine a management strategy
    D. Tell the team your objectives

30. **You are assigned to be the project manager in the middle of the project. The project is within tolerances for the baseline, but the customer is not happy with the performance of the project. What is the FIRST thing you should do?**

    A. Discuss it with the project team
    B. Recalculate baselines
    C. Renegotiate the contract
    D. Meet with the customer

31. **A project manager learns that corrective action was taken by a team member and was not documented. What should the project manager do NEXT?**

    A. Report the violation to the functional manager
    B. Clarify the reasoning behind the team member's action
    C. Add the corrective action to the historical record
    D. Find out who caused the problem

32. **The client demands changes to the product specification that will add two weeks to the critical path. The project manager should:**

    A. Crash the project to recover the two weeks
    B. Fast track the project to recover the two weeks
    C. Consult management before proceeding
    D. Advise the client of the impact of the change

33. **During the project execution, the project manager determines that a change is needed to material purchased for the project. The project manager calls a meeting of the team to plan how to make the change. This is an example of:**

    A. Management by objectives
    B. Lack of a change control system
    C. Good team relations
    D. Lack of a clear work breakdown structure

34. **What should a project manager do FIRST if a team member has added functionality to a product in the project without impacting time, cost or quality?**

    A. Ask the team member how the need for the functionality was determined
    B. Ask the finance department to assess the value of the improvement
    C. Ask the customer to review this and to submit a change request
    D. Ask the team member how they know there is no time, cost or quality impact

35. **A team member notifies you, after the fact, that she has added extra functionality to the project. There was no impact on the cost or schedule. What should be done as a result of this change?**

    A. Inform the customer
    B. Make sure marketing is aware of the change
    C. Understand what functionality was added
    D. Implement change control processes to track the change

36. **A project manager is managing a fixed price contract. She thinks that a large customer-requested change might impact the schedule of the project. What should she do FIRST?**

    A. Meet with the stakeholders
    B. Meet with the team
    C. Renegotiate the reminder of the contract
    D. Follow the change control system

37. **While completing a project, a project manager realizes he needs to decrease project costs. After researching his options, he comes up with the following choices. Which choice would DECREASE project costs?**

    A. Change to component A from component B. Component A costs more to purchase but has a lower life cycle cost than B
    B. Change task A to be completed by resource B instead of resource C. Resource B is a more experienced worker
    C. Move tasks B and H to occur concurrently, and take the risk of a 30% increase in the need for five more resources later
    D. Remove a test from the project plan

Integration Management Answers

1. **Answer:** C

    Explanation: This question is asking for the most important of the choices. Think about what is involved in integration – project plan development, project plan execution and integrated change control. In order to integrate the project components into a cohesive whole (integration), communication is key when one task will interface with another, one team member will interface with another, and any other form of interfacing. Choices B and D are only parts of project control, while integration talks about more than control. Choice A falls under project plan execution and other knowledge areas.

2. **Answer:** C

    Explanation: The project manager is an integrator. This is a question about your role as an integrator and communicator.

3. **Answer:** D

    Explanation: Historical records are not GENERALLY used for life cycle costing (choice A) lessons learned (choice B) or creating status reports (choice C).

4. **Answer:** D

    Explanation: Project managers are proactive beasts. The proactive answer here is preventing unnecessary changes.

5. **Answer:** B

    Explanation: The project plan (choice D) is created by the team and approved by management. Some project constraints (choice C) would come from management but they should be considered necessary. Though management may help with some of the tasks (choice A) it is not their exclusive duty. Since the project objectives are stated in the charter and it is senior management that issues the charter, choice B is the correct answer.

6. **Answer:** D

    Explanation: A change control system consists of the processes and procedures that allow smooth evaluation and tracking of changes. Lessons learned are reviews of the processes and procedures to improve them; they are not part of the system.

7. **Answer:** B

    Explanation: Who does each task (choices D and A) is controlled with the Gantt charts, schedule and responsibility charts. When each task is done (choice C) is controlled by the project schedule. A work authorization system is used to coordinate when and in what order the work is performed so that work and people may properly interface with other work and other people.

8. **Answer:** C

    Explanation: Management issues the charter and so management should help the project manager control changes to the charter. The primary responsibility lies with management.

9. **Answer:** A

    Explanation: Integration is a key responsibility of the project manager, so choice A is the best answer.

10. **Answer:** B

    Explanation: Integration refers to combining tasks, not team members (choice D). Could the project manager smash two team members together and create one big team member? (I just wanted to see if you are still laughing about this PMP® thing!)

11. **Answer:** D

    Explanation: Scope verification (choice A) was done during control. The other plans (choices B and C) were created earlier in the project. But the lessons learned (choice D) needs the input of the team and can only be completed after the work is completed.

12. **Answer:** A

    Explanation: A lessons learned is the result of the project. It can therefore not serve the purpose of choices B or D. Though it could serve the purpose of choice C, the best answer is choice A.

13. **Answer:** B

    Explanation: Corrective action is an output, not an input of most of the control functions (choices A and C). It cannot occur before the project plan is developed (choice D).

14. **Answer:** D

    Explanation: The best answer is stakeholders, as their input is critical for collecting all the lessons learned on each project. Stakeholders include all the other groups.

15. **Answer:** B

    Explanation: We cannot avoid the stakeholder (choices C and D) because he has a stake in the project. A project manager can say "no" (choice A), but this does not solve the root cause. There may be some good ideas within those changes. The only choice that deals with the problem is choice B.

    Changes are not bad! Changes normally come from lack of input at the beginning of the project. If we begin effective communication with this stakeholder early (choice B), we stand a much better chance of discovering their changes during planning when they will have less of an impact on the project.

© 2002 - 1998 Rita Mulcahy, PMP
PHONE: (952) 846-4484 - EMAIL: info@rmcproject.com - WEB: www.rmcproject.com

16. **Answer:** C

Explanation: Because you have no experience, you will have to look at the experience of others. This information is captured in the historical records of previous projects.

17. **Answer:** C

Explanation: The project plan contains more than just a bar or Gantt chart and the project manager's plan for completing the work. It includes all the documentation that went into creating and planning the project, approved by the stakeholders.

18. **Answer:** D

Explanation: This question tests common errors in project management that can never be the correct answer. A project cannot be effectively planned with undefined scope of work (choice A). The best answer would be to try to solve the problem (choice D). If it could not be solved, then it should become part of the risk analysis to be done on the project.

19. **Answer:** D

Explanation: You may not understand this question until you review the rest of the book. Come back to it. This question tries to integrate a lot of information and test your knowledge about what information is relevant to the question. CPI (choice C) is greater than one, so cost is not something to worry about. Most projects have hard-to-get resources (choice B). The question does not give an indication that having hard-to-get resources is a problem. Though some figures to calculate float are provided (choice A), there is no information to say that the float is a problem. SPI is less than one, so choice D is the best answer.

20. **Answer:** A

Explanation: Choice D would help, but not help both control and deliverables for each phase. Choice C would help control each phase, but would not control the integration of the phases into a cohesive whole. Choice B would help improve subsequent phases, but would do nothing for control and deliverables. Effective project management requires a life cycle approach to running the project. Choice A is the only answer that covers both control and deliverables.

21. **Answer:** B

Explanation: This situation implies that there are six areas concerned with this project. In addition to added communications requirements, you should be concerned with competing needs and requirements impacting your efforts on configuration management.

22. **Answer:** A

Explanation: Scope definition consists of subdividing major product deliverables (scope) into smaller, more manageable activities. Activity definition defines the activities that must take place to produce those deliverables.

23. **Answer**: D

    Explanation: A project control system is set up during project planning, not project execution.

24. **Answer:** D

    A project manager must manage a project. If all tasks are delegated, chaos ensues and team members will spend more time jockeying for position than completing tasks.

25. **Answer:** C

    Explanation: Choices B and D are essentially delaying the situation. Instead, the project manager should try to prevent the situation by showing the consequences if the resources are not available (choice C). This is a more effective strategy than saying "but you gave them to me," as in choice A.

26. **Answer:** A

    Explanation: A single high-level executive can end an entire project if he or she is not satisfied with the results even if that person has, by choice, been only tangentially involved in the project. It is critical to ensure that all of the final decision makers have been identified early in a project in order to ensure that their concerns are addressed.

27. **Answer:** D

    Explanation: The other impacts to the project should be evaluated first. Such impacts include time, cost, quality, scope of work and customer satisfaction. Once these are evaluated, the change control board, if one exists, can approve or deny the change.

28. **Answer:** D

    Explanation: As you work on a project, you need to constantly re-evaluate the project goals and how the project relates to other concurrent projects. Taking into account corporate goals, is your project still in line with them? If the other project will impact yours, you need to be proactive and work on options now.

29. **Answer:** C

    Explanation: Before you can do anything else, you have to know what YOU are going to do. Developing the management strategy will provide the framework for all the rest of the choices presented and the other activities that need to be done.

30. **Answer:** D

    Explanation: First you need to find out why the customer is not happy. Then you meet with the team and determine options.

31. **Answer:** C

    Explanation: Such actions should be documented. Since such documents become part of the historical database, choice C is correct.

32. **Answer:** D

Explanation: To handle changes, the project manager must evaluate the impact to the project, look at options and then discuss the impact and options with the stakeholders. There is no way to know if fast tracking (choice B) or crashing (choice A) is the best way to solve this problem. The project manager should take action to evaluate before they go to management with options (choice C). D is the most correct answer.

33. **Answer:** B

Explanation: The project manager is asking how to make a change. The procedures, forms, sign-offs and other similar requirements for handling changes should have already been determined in the change control system (choice B). Because they weren't, the project manager will waste valuable work time trying to figure it out after the fact.

34. **Answer:** D

Explanation: The team members do not have the same view of the project that you as the project manager have. You see the entire project and can better evaluate with their help the impact of changes to the project.

35. **Answer:** C

Explanation: First you need to understand what change has taken place and then determine the impact and options.

36. **Answer:** D

Explanation: Ideally, there is a change control system in place that should be followed to make changes in the project.

37. **Answer**: D

Explanation: Getting tired yet? Get used to answering questions for four hours before you take the exam. Choice A will not decrease project costs, just costs over the life of the project. It will not solve the problem. Choice B will almost always lead to higher costs and choice C could affect costs later, due to the increased risk. Though it may not be the first choice to think of, deleting a test would decrease costs, so it is the best answer. It may also decrease quality, but this is not the question.

Scope Management
(PMBOK® GUIDE Chapter 5)

Scope management covers many important aspects of project management. Many project managers have never completed a project charter or work breakdown structure for their projects and are not familiar with project selection methods. With real-world experience in these areas, scope questions are easy.

Though it is not technically true, many people have mentioned that it seems there are more scope questions than any other topic on the exam. It would be worthwhile to review the project scope management process in the *PMBOK® Guide*, which includes initiation, scope planning, scope definition, scope verification and scope change control. Make certain that you understand the outputs of each.

DEFINITION OF SCOPE MANAGEMENT (page 51): "Includes the processes required to ensure that the project includes all the work and only the work required to complete the project successfully. It is primarily concerned with controlling what is and what is not in the project." This is one of the definitions you should MEMORIZE and understand for the exam.

Scope management means:

- Constantly checking to make sure you are completing all the work

- Saying no to additional work not included in the project or not part of the project charter

- Preventing extra work or gold plating

You should give the customer what they asked for, no more and no less. Giving any extras is a waste of time and adds no benefit to the project. Make sure you understand this approach and why it is a good idea.

PROJECT SELECTION METHODS (page 54): There should be a formal process for selecting projects in all companies in order to make the best use of limited corporate resources. Without such a formal method, projects are often selected not for their value, but for less quantitative reasons such as personal relationships. Two project selection methods frequently on the exam are:

1. Benefit measurement methods (comparative approach)
   - Murder board – a panel of people who try to shoot down a new project idea
   - Peer review
   - Scoring models
   - Economic models
   - Benefit compared to cost

2. Constrained optimization methods (mathematical approach)
   - Linear programming
   - Integer programming
   - Dynamic programming
   - Multi-objective programming

What type of project selection technique is linear programming? The answer is constrained optimization. The exam does not require you to know what each constrained optimization method means.

Although the project manager may not be involved in the selection of one project over another, you need to understand that such a process occurs, as well as the two methods of project selection that can be used.

INITIATING (page 53): Initiating is the first step in the project management process. It includes all the work necessary to create a project charter.

Exercise: Test yourself! Make a list of the specific ACTIONS required to initiate a project.

Answer: Though most people score well in this area of the exam, there are usually a few concepts that everyone does not know. Make sure you go over this list carefully.

Some of the possible answers to this exercise include:
- Select a project
- Collect historical information
- Determine project objectives
- Determine high-level deliverables and estimates
- Document high-level constraints and assumptions
- Determine business need
- Develop the product description
- Define responsibilities of the project manager
- Determine key or high-level resource requirements – what skills may be needed
- Finalize the project charter
- Deal with conflicting high-level goals
- Uncover any existing requirements, goals and assumptions from the stakeholders
- Review or create the high-level scope of work
- Determine process outputs
- Determine what form the charter will take, why, etc.
- Coordinate with stakeholders
- Review policies and procedures
- Ensure compliance with any policies and procedures
- Determine what needs to be controlled
- Define strategy for planning, executing, controlling and closing of the project
- Evaluate alternative approaches to completing the scope of work and project management
- Identify performance criteria that can be used later to measure success
- Write project standards if they do not already exist
- Review resource pools for types of skills available
- Evaluate the need to contract to obtain resources
- Order of magnitude estimating of the project schedule and budget
- Obtain a formal decision from the stakeholders on the charter

You may notice that many of these items (e.g., estimating, assumptions, constraints, etc.) are refined later in the project management process. Who is involved in initiation? There are no standards. For some types of projects, the project manager is the one to initiate a project, in others the project manager is not assigned until after the charter is issued. In any case, the charter is the major output of this process group.

Chapter 4
Scope Management

PROJECT CHARTER (page 54): The exam could include up to five questions that reference a project charter. You should understand what a project charter is and why it is important to the project manager.

Exercise 1: Test yourself! Answer the questions below.

What is included in a project charter?

Exercise 2: Test yourself! Answer the questions below.

What does the charter do for the project manager?

Answer 1: Unfortunately, many companies' project charters require information such as a detailed schedule and a full risk analysis that are not available at the stage of the project management process when the project charter is developed. A project charter is not a project plan! A project charter may look like the following.

Project Charter

PROJECT TITLE AND DESCRIPTION: (What is the project?)

Customer Satisfaction Fix-It Project

Over the last few months the quality assurance department has discovered that many of our customers' orders for our XYZ equipment have taken the customer 10 times longer to place through our computer network than our competitors' networks. The purpose of this project is to investigate the reasons for the problem and propose a solution. The solution will be authorized as a subsequent project. Quality Assurance has detailed records of their findings that can be used to speed up this project.

PROJECT MANAGER ASSIGNED AND AUTHORITY LEVEL: (Who is given authority to lead the project, and can he or she determine budget, schedule, staffing, etc.?)

Alexis Sherman shall be the project manager for this project and have authority to select team members and determine the final project budget. However, Morgan Kolb and Danny Levins are already dedicated to the project because of their expertise in computer networks of this type.

OBJECTIVES: (What numerical criteria related to the triple constraint will be used to measure project success?)

Complete the project no later than September 1, 20XX. Spend no more than £100,000, result in a tested plan to reduce the order time by at least 50%. Have no more than four complaints throughout the project from customers that we are interrupting their day-to-day work.

BUSINESS CASE: (Why is the project being done?)

This project is being completed in order to prevent a further breakdown of customer satisfaction. We expect that improved customer satisfaction will increase revenue to the company in the first year due to a decrease in service calls. As a side benefit, we hope that the project will generate ideas on improving customer satisfaction while fixing this problem.

PRODUCT DESCRIPTION/DELIVERABLES: (What are the specific deliverables are wanted and what will be the end result of the project?)

1. *A report that outlines what can be changed, how much each change will cost and the expected decrease in the time it takes to place an order resulting from each change. Few words are necessary in the report, but it must be created electronically and be agreed to by the heads of Quality Assurance, Customer Satisfaction and Marketing in addition to the project team.*
2. *A list of the interactions with our customers necessary to complete the changes.*
3. *A work breakdown structure, due within two weeks, that outlines the plan for accomplishing the project followed within one further week by a list of risks in completing the project.*

SIGNED AND APPROVED BY:

Samantha Levins, Executive Vice President

SENIOR MANAGEMENT: (A person who is high enough in the organization to warrant everyone on the team reporting to him or her.)

Answer 2: A project charter provides, at a minimum, the following benefits:

- Gives the project manager authority. On the exam, this is the most commonly described benefit or use of the project charter. In most project situations, the project team does not report to the project manager in the corporate structure. This leads to issues of "how to gain cooperation and performance."

- Formally recognizes (authorizes) the existence of the project, or establishes the project. This means that the project does not exist without a project charter.

- Provides the goals and objectives of the project. Most project managers are not provided with the basic information (what is in the project charter) to complete the project. The information provided in the project charter is considered vital to the success of the project. Without the project charter information, it is like being told to get into a car and drive without being told where to go.

The project charter is also:

- Created by a manager who is external and higher in the corporate hierarchy, not the project manager or the team
- Created during initiation
- Broad enough so it does not NEED to change as the project changes
- An output of scope initiation

The *PMBOK® Guide* says that a contract may serve as a project charter for projects under contract, although this may not be as clear or effective as a separate project charter.

The project charter is such an important document that a project cannot be started without one. If the project charter is your target for the project and a definition of how success will be measured, then without a project charter the project and project manager cannot be successful!

CONSTRAINTS (page 55): Factors that limit the team's options such as resources, budget, schedule and scope. Constraints are identified and managed and are inputs to many aspects of project management. Management identifies some constraints, and the stakeholders and the team identify others.

SCOPE STATEMENT (page 56): Provides a basis for a common understanding of the scope among the stakeholders and to determine if the project phase has been completed. Loosely the same as a scope of work or statement of work, the scope statement is an output of scope planning.

SCOPE MANAGEMENT PLAN (page 56): An output of scope planning, this is a document that describes how scope and scope changes will be managed. Most project managers do not spend the time carefully planning all their activities to the extent noted in the *PMBOK® Guide*. Can you think of the benefits of doing so? How about less scope creep, changes and conflict, as well as improved communications and increased customer satisfaction?

MANAGEMENT BY OBJECTIVES (MBO): A management philosophy that says an organization should be managed by objectives. It has three steps:

1.   Establish unambiguous and realistic objectives
2.   Periodically evaluate if objectives are being met
3.   Take corrective action

You should understand what this means for the project manager. If the project is not in line with or does not support the corporate objectives, the project is likely to lose resources, assistance and attention. You should also understand that MBO works only if management supports it.

DELPHI TECHNIQUE (page 132): A method most commonly used to obtain expert opinions on technical issues, scope of work needed, estimates or risks. This is explained in the *PMBOK® Guide* under risk, but it is not a technique exclusively reserved for risk.

To use the Delphi technique, a request for information is sent to experts, the responses they return are compiled, and the results are sent back to them for further review. The Delphi technique has three rules:

1.   Do not get the experts in the same room
2.   Keep the experts' identities anonymous
3.   Try to build consensus

Using the Delphi technique helps reduce bias and undue influence.

THE WORK BREAKDOWN STRUCTURE (WBS, page 59 - 61): Part of activity definition, the WBS is a PMI®-ism. It is a key tool of project management and is completely misunderstood by many people. Check your understanding of the WBS as you read!

Exercise 1: Test yourself! What is a WBS?

| |
| |
| |
| |
| |

Exercise 2: Test yourself! The chart on the right is a segment of a list of tasks on a Gantt chart. The one on the left shows the format of a real, but blank, WBS. Many people think the list in a Gantt chart is the WBS. That is not correct. What is the difference between making a list and completing a real WBS?

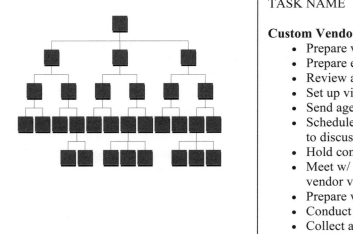

TASK NAME

Custom Vendor Selection
- Prepare visit agenda
- Prepare evaluation forms
- Review agenda with evaluation team
- Set up visits
- Send agenda to vendors
- Schedule conference calls with vendors to discuss agenda
- Hold conference calls with vendors
- Meet w/ evaluation team to discuss vendor visits
- Prepare vendor scoring sheets
- Conduct vendor visits
- Collect and compile evaluation forms
- Select custom vendor finalists

Vendor reference checks
- Request vendor references
- Prepare reference evaluation forms

Answer 1: A WBS is a "deliverable-oriented grouping of project components that organizes and defines the total scope of the project." It breaks the project into smaller and more manageable pieces. Smart project managers understand that they cannot manage a project; they need to manage the pieces. Although the WBS may look like a corporate organizational chart, it is not!

Answer 2: In order to answer questions about the WBS, you must understand the following and have created a WBS in the workplace. The questions that deal with "what do you do in this situation" can be very difficult if you have never completed a WBS for a real project. If you are familiar with the following information and have created a WBS in the workplace, questions that deal with the WBS should be easy.

The picture on the right...

- Represents a summary of the WBS, not the WBS itself
- Does not break down the project into small enough pieces. May include large and small tasks that are greater than the 8 to 80-hour rule of thumb
- May not include all the work (In contrast, the construction of the WBS chart on the left helps to ensure that nothing slips through the cracks)
- Does not allow the team to walk through the project
- Is usually not created by the team
- Does not help to get your mind around the project
- Does not help get team and other stakeholders' buy-in to the project
- Does not show a complete hierarchy of the project, even with indentation
- Does not result in a clear understanding of the project by all the stakeholders

A WBS (on a SUMMARY level) for A Hardware/Software Creation and Installation Project

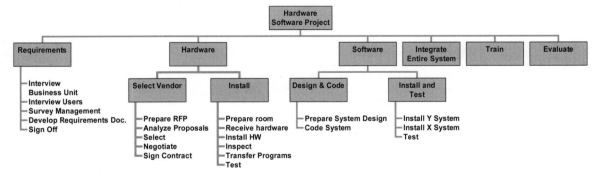

The creation of a WBS has only a few "rules":

- It is created with the help of the team
- The first level is completed before the project is broken down further
- Each level of the WBS is a smaller segment of the level above
- The entire project is included in each of the highest levels. However, eventually some levels will be broken down further than others
- Work toward the project deliverables
- Work not in the WBS is not part of the project
- A WBS can become a template for future projects
- Break down the project into work packages or activities that:
  - Can be realistically and confidently estimated
  - Cannot be logically subdivided further
  - Can be completed quickly
  - Have a meaningful conclusion and deliverable
  - Can be completed without interruption (without the need for more information)

The top level of the WBS is the project title. The first level is most commonly the same as the project life cycle (for a software project - requirement analysis, design, coding, testing, conversion and operation). The second and later levels break the project into smaller pieces. The lowest level the project manager will manage the project to is called the work package, or activity. This work may be broken down again by the person or persons completing the work.

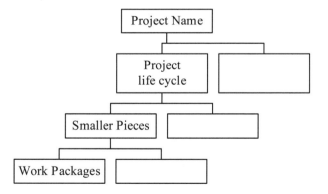

On large projects, the project manager may manage the project only to the work package level (there is no rule of thumb for how large these are, but they could be 300 hours in size), leaving the work packages to be broken into tasks or activity lists by the team members. Other times, the WBS is broken down to the activity level where the activities are between 4 to 40 hours or 8 to 80 hours as a rule of thumb.

The WBS is the foundation of the project. All project planning and project controlling is based on the WBS.

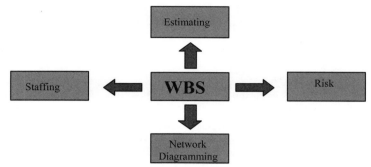

TIP: Know the following. A WBS:
- Is a graphical picture of the hierarchy of the project
- Identifies all the work to be performed – if it is not in the WBS it is not part of the project
- Is the foundation upon which the project is built
- Is VERY important
- Forces you to think through all aspects of the project
- Can be reused for other projects
- Is an output of scope definition

Exercise: Test yourself! What are the benefits of using a WBS?

Answer: The benefits of using a WBS are:
- Helps prevent work from slipping through the cracks
- Provides the project team with an understanding of where their pieces fit into the overall project plan and gives them an indication of the impact of their work on the project as a whole
- Facilitates communications and cooperation between and among the project team and stakeholders
- Helps prevent changes
- Focuses the team's experience on what needs to be done, resulting in a higher quality and an easier project
- Provides a basis for estimating staff, cost and time
- Provides PROOF of need for staff, cost and time
- Gets team buy-in and builds the team
- Helps get your mind around the project
- Helps new team members see their roles

SCOPE DEFINITION AND DECOMPOSITION (pages 57-59): Some students confuse these terms with the WBS. The *PMBOK® Guide* defines scope definition and decomposition as "subdividing the major project deliverables into smaller, more manageable components." The best way to handle these terms is to think of scope definition and decomposition as *what* you are doing, and the WBS as the *tool* to do it.

SCOPE VERIFICATION (page 61-62): "The process of formalizing acceptance of the project scope by the stakeholders." A description of scope verification might include any of the following phrases:
- Reviewing work products and results to ensure that all are completed correctly and satisfactorily
- Conducting inspections, reviews, audits
- Determining whether results conform to requirements
- Determining if work products are completed correctly
- Documenting completion of deliverables
- Gaining formal sign-off

Scope verification is customer feedback on a more detailed basis. It is done at the end of each project phase (in the project life cycle) and during the controlling phase (in the project management life cycle). Scope verification results in formal acceptance by stakeholders, the sponsor and/or the customer.

Scope verification and quality control are generally performed in parallel. The two topics are very similar in that both involve checking for the correctness of work. The difference is focus. Scope verification's primary focus is on customer *acceptance* of the scope of the work while quality control involves analysis of the *correctness* of the work. Note the difference!

Scope verification is also done whenever a project is terminated to verify the level of completion and is an entire step, not just an output, of the scope management process. There can be five questions on the exam that deal with scope verification.

WBS DICTIONARY (page 61, second paragraph): Created with the team members' assistance, a WBS Dictionary is designed to control what work is done and when, to prevent scope creep and to increase understanding of the effort for each task. Sometimes entries are also called task descriptions. They help the project by putting boundaries on what is included in the task (or work package). A WBS Dictionary entry may contain information similar to the following:

WBS DICTIONARY (Task Description)			
Project Name _____	Task No. _____	Date Issued _____	Person Assigned _____
Task description (what work is authorized)			
Quantified objectives (See the description in the project charter)			
Product description (What is the end result of the task or work package?)			
Acceptance criteria (How will the team member be able to check their own work?)			
Deliverables (See the description in the project charter)			
Assumptions			
Resources assigned			
Duration			
Cost			
Due date			
Interdependencies: Before this task _____ After this task _____			
Approved by: Project manager _____ Date: _____			

Chapter 4
Scope Management

Practice Exam for the CAPM® and PMP® Exams
Scope Management

1. A work breakdown structure numbering system allows project staff to:

   A. Systematically estimate costs of work breakdown structure elements
   B. Provide project justification
   C. Identify the level at which individual elements are found
   D. Use it in project management software

2. Which of the following is a chief characteristic of the Delphi technique?

   A. Extrapolation from historical records
   B. Expert opinion
   C. Analytical hierarchy process
   D. Bottom-up approach

3. The work breakdown structure can BEST be thought of as an effective aid for ____ communications.

   A. Team
   B. Project manager
   C. Customer
   D. Stakeholder

4. Which of the following is a KEY attribute of scope verification?

   A. Improved cost estimates
   B. Customer acceptance of project efforts
   C. Improved schedule estimates
   D. An improved project management information system

5. During project execution, a team member comes to the project manager because he is not sure of what work he needs to accomplish on the project. Which of the following documents contain detailed descriptions of work packages?

   A. Work breakdown structure (WBS) dictionary
   B. Scope of work
   C. Budget estimates
   D. Cost estimates

6. During what phase of the life cycle is the project scope statement created?

   A. Initiating
   B. Planning
   C. Executing
   D. Controlling

7. Which of the following is included in a project charter?

   A. Identification of risks
   B. Task estimates
   C. Detailed resource estimates
   D. The business need for the project

8. **As the project becomes more complex, the level of uncertainty in the scope:**

    A. Remains the same
    B. Decreases
    C. Decreases then increases
    D. Increases

9. **A project plan should be realistic in order to be used to manage the project. Which of the following is the BEST method to achieve a realistic project plan?**

    A. Senior manager creates the project plan based on input from the project manager
    B. Functional manager created the project plan based on input from the project manager
    C. Project manager creates the project plan based on input from senior management
    D. Project manager creates the project plan based on input from the team

10. **For which of the following can the work breakdown structure be used?**

    A. Communicating with the customer
    B. Showing calendar dates for each task
    C. Showing the functional managers for each team member
    D. Showing the business need for the project

11. **During a project team meeting, a team member suggests an enhancement to the scope of work that is beyond the scope of the project charter. The project manager points out that the team needs to concentrate on completing all the work and only the work required. This is an example of:**

    A. Change management process
    B. Scope management
    C. Quality analysis
    D. Scope decomposition

12. **When should scope verification be done?**

    A. At the end of the project
    B. At the beginning of the project
    C. At the end of each phase of the project
    D. During planning

13. **Management by objectives works only if:**

    A. It is supported by management
    B. The rules are written down
    C. The project does not impact the objectives
    D. The project includes the objectives in the project charter

14. **The project is mostly complete. However, the customer wants to make a major change to the scope of work. The project manager should:**

    A. Meet with the project team to determine if this change can be made
    B. Ask the customer for a description of the change
    C. Explain that the change cannot be made at this point in the process
    D. Inform management

15. **A project manager new to project management has asked you why they should bother using a work breakdown structure on their project. The BEST response would be:**

    A. Tell them it will prevent work from slipping through the cracks
    B. Tell them that one is not needed
    C. Tell them it is required if the project involves contracts
    D. Tell them it is the only way to identify risks

16. **The process of creating a work breakdown structure results in:**

    A. A project schedule
    B. Team buy-in
    C. A project completion date
    D. A list of risks

17. **To manage a project effectively, work should be broken down into small pieces. Which of the following does NOT describe how far to decompose the work?**

    A. Until it has a meaningful conclusion
    B. Until it cannot be logically subdivided further
    C. Until it can be done by one person
    D. Until it can be realistically estimated

18. **A project manager spends some time determining his company's objectives and how the project fits into them. This is an example of:**

    A. Responsibility charts
    B. Management by objectives
    C. The project's future
    D. The work breakdown structure

19. **A project manager is trying to convince management to use project management and has decided to start with a charter. Why would the charter help the project manager?**

    A. It describes the details of what needs to be done
    B. It lists the names of all team members
    C. It gives the project manager authority
    D. It describes the project's history

20. **A project manager may use _____ to make sure the team clearly knows what work is included in each of their tasks.**

    A. A project scope of work
    B. A project charter
    C. A WBS dictionary
    D. A risk response plan

21. **Linear programming is an example of what type of project selection criteria?**

    A. Constrained optimization
    B. Comparative approach
    C. Benefit measurement
    D. Impact analysis

Scope Management Questions Only For the PMP® Exam

22. A project manager has just been assigned to a new project and has been given the completed project scope. The FIRST thing the project manager must do is:

    A. Create a project plan using the WBS
    B. Confirm that all the stakeholders have had input to the scope of work
    C. Form a team to create the procurement plan
    D. Create a network diagram

23. You have created the project charter, but could not get it approved. Your manager and his boss have asked that the project begin immediately. Which of the following is the BEST thing to do?

    A. Set up an integrated change control process
    B. Show your manager the impact of proceeding without approval
    C. Focus on completing projects that have a signed charter
    D. Start work on only the critical path tasks

24. The engineering department has uncovered a problem with the cost accounting system and has asked the systems department to analyze what is wrong and fix the problem. You are a project manager working with the cost accounting programs on another project. Management has issued a change request to the change control board to add the new work to your project.

    Your existing project has had a CPI of 1.2 and a SPI of 1.3 so you have some room to add work without delaying your existing project or going over budget. However, you cannot see how the new work fits within the project charter for your existing project. After some analysis, you determine that the new work and existing work do not overlap and can be done concurrently. They also require different skill sets. Which of the following is the BEST thing to do?

    A. Create the high-level scope of work and develop the product description
    B. Re-estimate the project schedule with input from the engineering department
    C. Perform scope verification on the new work with the help of the stakeholders
    D. Identify specific changes to the existing work

25. A new project manager is about to begin creating a project scope of work. One stakeholder wants to add many items to the scope of work. Another stakeholder only wants to describe the functional requirements. The project is important for the project manager's company, but a seller will do the work. Which of the following would you advise the project manager to do?

    A. The scope of work should be general to allow the seller to make its own decisions
    B. The scope of work should be general to allow clarification later
    C. The scope of work should be detailed to allow clarification later
    D. The scope of work should be as detailed as necessary for the type of project

26. The construction phase of a new software product is near completion. The next phase is testing and implementation. The project is two weeks ahead of schedule. What should the project manager be MOST concerned with before moving on to the final phase?

    A. Scope verification
    B. Quality control
    C. Performance reports
    D. Cost control

27. A customer has given you a scope of work for a complex, eight month project that has a few unknowns. The customer has asked you to just "get it done" and only wants to see you at the end of eight months when you deliver the finished project. Under these circumstances, which of the following is the BEST thing to do?

    A. Complete the project as requested, but verify its scope with the customer occasionally throughout
    B. Complete the project within eight months without contacting the customer during this time
    C. Ask management to check in with the customer occasionally
    D. Complete the project, but document that the customer did not want contact

28. During project execution, a project team delivers a project deliverable to the customer. However, the customer neither acknowledges the deliverable nor replies to the project manager's requests for verification. What is the BEST thing to do?

    A. Continue with the project
    B. Document the situation
    C. Contact management for help
    D. Call a meeting of the team

29. You are managing a six month project and have held bi-weekly meetings with your project stakeholders. After five-and-a-half months of work, the project is on schedule and budget, but the stakeholders are not satisfied with the deliverables. This situation will delay the project completion by one month. The MOST important process that could have prevented this situation is:

    A. Risk monitoring and control
    B. Schedule control
    C. Scope planning
    D. Scope change control

Scope Management Answers

1. **Answer:** C

   Explanation: The numbering system allows you to quickly identify the level in the work breakdown structure where the specific element is found. It also helps to locate the element in the WBS dictionary.

2. **Answer:** B

   Explanation: The Delphi technique uses experts and builds to consensus; therefore expert opinion is the chief characteristic.

3. **Answer:** D

   Explanation: The term "stakeholder" encompasses all the other choices. In this case, it is the best answer since the WBS can be used (but does not need to be used) as a communication tool for all stakeholders to "see" what is included in the project.

4. **Answer:** B

   Explanation: The goal of scope verification is customer acceptance of project efforts. The other choices all happen during planning, well before when scope verification takes place.

5. **Answer:** A

   Explanation: The lowest level of the work breakdown structure is the activity or work package. The WBS dictionary defines each item in the WBS. Therefore, descriptions of the activities and work packages are in the WBS dictionary. The scope of work is generally a broader description of the project scope.

6. **Answer:** B

   Explanation: The project scope statement must be in accordance with the project charter. Therefore the scope statement must be created in planning (choice B).

7. **Answer:** D

   Explanation: This question may seem simple, but it is really testing if you know what is a correct project charter. Choices A and B do not come until project planning, after the charter. A charter may include the names of some resources (the project manager, for example), but not detail resources (choice C).

8. **Answer:** D

   Explanation: The level of uncertainty in scope increases based on the scale of effort required to identify all the scope. For larger projects it is more difficult to "catch" everything.

9. **Answer:** D

Explanation: If we were to rephrase the question, it is asking, "Who creates the project plan?" The best answer is that project plans are created by the project manager but require input from the team.

10. **Answer:** A

Explanation: A WBS does not show dates or responsibility assignments (choices B and C). Those are included on the Gantt chart and possibly in the communications plan. The business need (choice D) is shown in the project charter.

11. **Answer:** B

Explanation: The team member is suggesting an enhancement that is outside the charter. Scope management involves focusing on doing the work and only the work in the project plan that meets the needs of the charter. The project manager is performing scope management.

12. **Answer:** C

Explanation: The Life Cycle Game shows that scope verification is done during controlling, not closing, so choices A, B and D cannot be correct. The description of scope verification in the Scope chapter also defines it as being done at the end of each phase (the end of design, implementation) making choice C the best answer.

13. **Answer:** A

Explanation: The best answer is the need for management to support the objectives.

14. **Answer:** B

Explanation: Of these choices, the first thing you need to do is determine what is the change (choice B) and then meet with the team (choice A), but only if their input is required.

15. **Answer:** A

Explanation: Though risks should be identified by task or work package, risks can also be identified by interview. Therefore choice D is an incorrect statement and not the best answer. Choice C is not generally true. The WBS is not only needed in order to have a contract, every project must have a WBS. Preventing work from being forgotten (slipping through the cracks) is ONE of the reasons the tool is used.

16. **Answer:** B

Explanation: The WBS is used as input for all of these choices. However, team buy-in (choice B) is a direct result of the WBS creation process, while the other choices require further input to complete. The best answer is B.

17. **Answer:** C

Explanation: The lowest level of the WBS can be a work package that can be broken down further and performed by more than one person.

18. **Answer:** B

Explanation: Management by objectives tries to focus all activities on meeting the company's objectives. If the project's objectives are not in line with the company's objectives, the project may be impacted or cancelled.

19. **Answer:** C

Explanation: The exam will ask questions like this to make sure you know the benefits you should be getting out of the process and tools of project management. Project history (choice D) is found in the lessons learned and other project documents. The names of team members (choice B) are included in responsibility assignment matrix and other documents. The details of what needs to be done (choice A) are found in the WBS dictionary.

20. **Answer:** C

Explanation: Since a risk response plan (choice D) describes risks, it could not be the best answer. A project charter (choice B) does not include a description of each task. The scope of work (choice A) is generally a broad document that does not describe or even mention tasks. Tasks are described in the WBS dictionary. (Do not think of the WBS as a dictionary of terms.)

21. **Answer:** A

Explanation: Constrained optimization uses mathematical models. Linear programming is a mathematical model.

22. **Answer:** B

Explanation: The scope is the basis for making future project decisions and to confirm understanding of the scope among the stakeholders. Since the scope is so important, the project manager must make sure that the needs of all stakeholders are included before continuing the project management process.

23. **Answer:** B

Explanation: The best thing to do would be to evaluate the impact. This is the only choice that prevents future problems – always the best choice. The other choices just pretend the problem does not exist.

24. **Answer:** A

Explanation: How long did it take you to read this question? Expect long-winded questions on the exam. Take another look at the choices before you continue reading. Did you notice that each of the choices occurs during a different phase of the project management process?

This question is essentially asking if the new work should be added to the existing project. There may be many business reasons to try to do this, but from a project management perspective, major additions to the project are generally discouraged. In this case, the question is trying to imply that the new work is a self-contained unit of work, has no overlap with the existing work and needs a different skill set. Therefore, it is generally best to make it a new project.

The first step to answering this question is to realize that the work should be a separate project. The second step is to look at the choices and see which relates to initiating a new project. Choice D is done during executing. Choice C is done during controlling. Choice B sounds like the best choice but only if you did not realize that the new work should be a separate project. Choice B is done during executing. The key words are "develop the product description." Such work is only done during initiation.

25. **Answer:** D

    Explanation: When the seller has more expertise than the buyer, the scope of work would describe performance or function rather than a complete list of work. In any case, the scope of work should be as detailed as possible.

26. **Answer:** A

    Explanation: Scope verification must be done at the end of each phase to verify that the work is completed correctly and satisfactorily and conforms to the requirements.

27. **Answer:** A

    Explanation: It is unethical to ignore scope verification, as it will add risk that the project will not meet the customer's needs. Therefore choice A is the best answer. If this was a real-world situation, one would probably work with the customer to efficiently handle verification so as to cause as little disruption as possible.

28. **Answer:** C

    Explanation: In this case, you need to bring in the bigger guns. Without scope verification at the end of the project phase, you may well be creating the "wrong thing." This is where management can protect the project.

29. **Answer:** C

    Explanation: Choices A, B, and D are all control activities. This situation asks how to prevent the problem. This would have been done in planning, as the project deliverables are defined in scope planning (choice C).

Time Management

(*PMBOK® GUIDE* Chapter 6)

- Schedule development
- Shortening the schedule
  - Crashing
  - Fast tracking
  - Re-estimating
- Network diagrams
  - Dependencies
    - Mandatory
    - Discretionary
    - External
  - Methods to draw
    - Activity-on-arrow (ADM)
    - Activity-on-node (PDM)
- Critical path
- Slack (float)
  - Free slack
  - Total slack
  - Project slack
- Estimating methods
  - PERT
  - CPM
  - Monte Carlo simulation
- Bar (Gantt) charts
- Milestone charts
- Schedule management plan
- Resource leveling
- Lag
- Flowcharts
- Heuristics
- GERT
- Variance analysis

Time management is currently the second-most difficult knowledge area on the exam (after Integration). Many people have not learned and do not use the techniques outlined in this chapter.

In order to answer time management questions correctly, you need a thorough understanding of the process of scheduling a project - Activity Definition, Activity Sequencing, Activity Duration Estimating, Schedule Development and Schedule Control. Review the time management process in the *PMBOK® Guide*.

You should also know manual methods for drawing network diagrams and scheduling. Manual calculations result in you needing to know some things that no longer apply when using software for project management. To make it easier to distinguish these items, I have placed a "memory finger" next to those items you need to just MEMORIZE. They may not make sense, but they are often on the exam.

Also, make sure you realize that there is currently no such thing as project management software. The "project management" software available only helps with limited parts of project management such as scheduling, "what if" scenarios and status reporting functions. Many software programs that do exist suggest planning a project in ways that do not conform to proper project management methods; first make a list of the tasks and then assign them to calendar dates and the project plan is finished. They do not address all aspects of project management and may have changed the basic components of the tools of project management (e.g., Gantt charts.)

Make sure you know the proper process for project management. You do not need to know how to use "project management" software for this exam. Any difference between what is described here and what you already know may be attributed to the adaptations made by your "project management" software.

SCHEDULING TOOLS AND THEIR BENEFITS (page 75-77): Once a network diagram and estimates are completed, it is time to put the information into a schedule. The difference between a time estimate and a schedule is that the schedule is calendar-based. You must be able to answer questions about when to use each of the following:
- Milestone charts
- Flowcharts
- Bar (Gantt) charts
- Network diagrams

Chapter 5
Time Management

Exercise: Test yourself! Fill in the answers to the following questions in the spaces provided.

Under what circumstances would you want to use a network diagram instead of a Gantt chart? In other words, what does a network diagram show that a Gantt chart does not?

Under what circumstances would you want to use a milestone chart instead of a Gantt chart?

Under what circumstances would you want to use a Gantt chart instead of a network diagram?

Answer:

Under what circumstances would you use a network diagram instead of a Gantt chart?	To show interdependencies between tasks
Under what circumstances would you want to use a milestone chart instead of a Gantt chart?	To report to senior management
Under what circumstances would you want to use a Gantt chart instead of a network diagram?	To track progress To report to the team

MILESTONE CHARTS – These are similar to bar charts but only show major events. Remember that milestones have no duration; they are simply the completion of activities. Milestones may include "requirements are complete" or "design is finished" and are part of the inputs for activity sequencing. Milestone charts are good tools for reporting to management and the customer.

FLOWCHARTS (page 98) – Depict workflow and process flow through a system. They are used for quality (see the Quality chapter), engineering and other work.

BAR (GANTT) CHART – Weak planning tools, but effective tools for progress reporting and control.

Gantt charts are not project plans (as described earlier under project plan).

Project management software makes an attempt to draw lines between tasks on a Gantt chart to show interdependencies. However, in their pure form, Gantt charts do NOT show task interdependencies or resources assigned. Remember, you do not have to understand project management software to pass this exam, so ignore this aspect of software when answering these types of questions.

Gantt charts do not help organize the project as effectively as a WBS and network diagram do. They are completed after a WBS and a network diagram in the project management process. A Gantt chart looks similar to this:

ID	Task Name	Duration	Start	Finish	8/18	8/25	September 9/1	9/8	9/15	9/22	October 9/29	10
1	Start	0 days	Mon 8/26/02	Mon 8/26/02		◆ 8/26						
2	D	4 days	Mon 8/26/02	Thu 8/29/02		▨						
3	A	6 days	Mon 8/26/02	Mon 9/2/02		▨▨						
4	F	7 days	Mon 9/2/02	Tue 9/10/02				▨▨				
5	E	8 days	Fri 8/30/02	Tue 9/10/02			▨▨					
6	G	5 days	Wed 9/11/02	Tue 9/17/02					▨▨			
7	B	5 days	Wed 9/11/02	Tue 9/17/02					▨▨			
8	H	7 days	Wed 9/18/02	Thu 9/26/02						▨▨		
9	C	8 days	Fri 9/27/02	Tue 10/8/02							▨▨	
10	Finish	0 days	Tue 10/8/02	Tue 10/8/02								◆

NETWORK DIAGRAMS (PERT, CPM, PDM Charts) –
- Show interdependencies of all tasks
- Show workflow
- Can aid in effectively planning, organizing and controlling the project
- Used for planning the project
- Used for crashing and fast tracking the project in planning and throughout the life of the project

SCHEDULE DEVELOPMENT (page 73): Schedule development is another HUGE source of problems on the exam for many project managers. You will be able to tell if it is one for you by completing the following exercise.

Exercise: Make a list of the specific ACTIONS required to develop a finalized schedule.

Answer: In order to develop a schedule, one needs to define the activities (WBS), put them in order of how the work will be done (activity sequencing), and then estimate the duration of each activity (activity duration estimating). You might have included these in your list but they are not enough. The final project schedule must be bought-into, approved, realistic and formal! What is needed to get it to that level?

- Have the following inputs:
  - Network diagram
  - Duration estimates
  - Resource requirements
  - Resources available
  - Project and resource calendars – when work can be performed and when resources will be available
  - Risk management plan – because it includes a schedule
  - Constraints
  - Assumptions
  - Lags
- Meet with managers to negotiate for resource availability
- Give the team a chance to approve the final schedule. They might have estimated a task, but should also look at the calendar allocation of their estimates to see if they are feasible
- Meetings and conversations to gain stakeholder and management formal approval
- Look for alternative ways to complete the work
- Work with stakeholders' priorities
- Compress the schedule by crashing, fast tracking and re-estimating
- Adjust all the components of the project plan – change the WBS because of risk responses planned
- Simulate the project using Monte Carlo analysis
- Level resources
- Look for interaction with other projects

Think about this carefully before you continue. Then refer to the list of actions for project plan development in Integration. Many of these apply to schedule development as well. Schedule development is described throughout this chapter.

NETWORK DIAGRAM (logic diagram or network logic, page 69): The network diagram shows HOW the project tasks will flow from beginning to end. Once estimates are available for each task, the network diagram also proves your best estimate of how long the project should take to complete. If plotted out against time (or placed against a calendar-based scale), the network diagram would be a time-scaled network diagram. A network diagram is completed after the project charter, project staffing and WBS.

A network diagram is created by putting the project tasks (or work packages) from the lowest practical level of the WBS in their order of completion from project beginning to end. This is called activity sequencing. The resulting diagram may look like the following picture. Some people incorrectly call a network diagram a PERT chart.

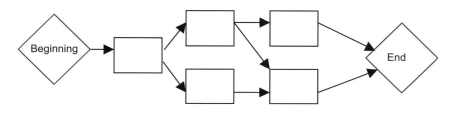

METHODS TO DRAW NETWORK DIAGRAMS – There are two ways to draw network diagrams; activity-on-arrow or activity-on-node. (GERT is a minor item.) Today most of us are used to working with AON. You should, however, understand both methods for the exam and MEMORIZE the following.

ACTIVITY-ON-NODE (AON) OR PRECEDENCE DIAGRAMMING METHOD (PDM) – In this method, nodes (or boxes) are used to represent tasks and arrows show task dependencies. This method adds leads and lags to relationships and:

- There can be four types of relationships between tasks:

  – Finish-to-start – a task must finish before the next can start

  – Finish-to-finish – a task must finish before the next can finish

  – Start-to-start – a task must start before the next can start

  – Start-to-finish – a task must start before the next can finish

- Does not use dummies (described next)

An activity-on-node diagram will show the activities as follows:

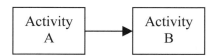

ACTIVITY-ON-ARROW (AOA), ACTIVITY-ON-LINE, OR ARROW DIAGRAMMING METHOD (ADM) – In this method, the arrows are used to represent tasks. The boxes represent task dependencies. This method uses:

- Only finish-to-start relationships between tasks

- May use dummy activities. Dummies are usually represented by a dotted line and are inserted simply to show dependencies between tasks. They do not require work or take time. See the picture below

- According to the exam, PERT and CPM estimating techniques (described later) can only be drawn on an AOA diagram

There are two ways to denote an activity-on-arrow activity. Either the name will be on the arrow, as show at left below, or the activity will be named as shown on the right. You will see an example of this in one of the upcoming exercises.

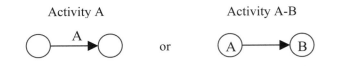

Activity A   or   Activity A-B

Review the following to reduce your confusion. If task D is "determine requirements," task E is "research," and task K is "initial design," then you need a dummy to show that the "initial design" task is dependent upon the "determine requirements" task. However, no work needs to be done between the two tasks. An activity-on-arrow diagram with a dummy is illustrated below.

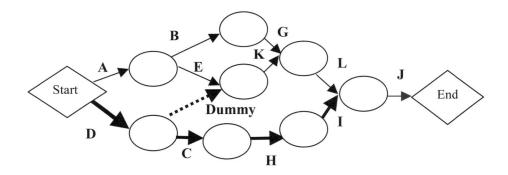

When you take the exam, there is a good chance you will be able to use the same network diagram to answer all the network diagram questions. Look to see if this is true before you spend time redrawing the diagram.

GERT (page 70): A network diagram drawing method that allows loops between tasks. The easiest example is when you have a task to design a component and then test it. After testing, it may or may not need to be redesigned. GERT is only rarely on the exam and when it does appear, it is most often just a choice on the multiple-choice questions.

TYPES OF DEPENDENCIES: The sequence of tasks depends on the following dependencies:
- **MANDATORY DEPENDENCY** (Hard Logic) – Inherent in the nature of the work being done (e.g., you must design before you can construct)

- **DISCRETIONARY DEPENDENCY** (Preferred, Preferential or Soft Logic) – Based on experience, desire or preferences

- **EXTERNAL DEPENDENCY** – Based on the needs or desires of a party outside the project (e.g., government or suppliers)

ESTIMATING: You should understand that people doing the work (not the project manager or senior manager) should create estimates. The role of the project manager is to:
- Provide the team with enough information to properly estimate each task
- Complete a sanity check of the estimate
- Formulate a reserve (more on this later)

Estimates can come from any of the following:
- Guess - Yes, this is okay. (Remember, we are estimating based on a WBS. Estimating a small task by guessing will be more accurate than doing the same for a larger task.)
- Historical information (this is a PMI®-ism, see chapter 1 on recurring themes)
- Actual costs - Labor, material, overhead, risk
- Benchmarks - Comparing your performance to that of another company

ESTIMATING METHODS (page 75): Three main methods are used for estimating the duration of a project; CPM, PERT and Monte Carlo. Please see the Cost chapter for further estimating topics. These topics will show up on your score sheet from the actual exam under the title "Measure project performance continually" in the controlling process group and may be the cause of some questions under the headings, "Refine control limits" and "Evaluate the effectiveness of corrective action" also in the controlling process group.

CPM (Critical Path Method) NOTE: Although this technique may use the words "critical path," it does not refer to finding the "critical path." It refers to estimating based on one time estimate per activity! You should remember that this method:

- Has one time estimate per task
- Has an emphasis on controlling cost and leaving the schedule flexible
- Can be drawn only on an activity-on-arrow (AOA) diagram
- Can have dummies

ESTIMATING USING CPM – When estimating using a one-time estimate (CPM), one estimate per task is received. For example, the person doing the estimating in effect says that the task will take exactly five weeks. This method uses only a most likely time estimate.

PERT (Program evaluation and review technique, page 75) – You should remember that this method:

- Has three estimates per activity
  - Optimistic
  - Pessimistic
  - Most likely
- Can be used to estimate time or cost
- Has an emphasis on meeting schedules with flexibility on costs

Chapter 5
Time Management

- Can be drawn only on an activity-on-arrow (AOA) diagram
- Can have dummies

ESTIMATING USING PERT – PERT is superior to CPM because it requires three time (or cost) estimates per task and uses the distribution's mean instead of the most likely time estimate in CPM. In this form of estimating, the person estimating the task provides an optimistic, pessimistic and most likely estimate for each task. You must MEMORIZE three formulas and know that they can also be used for cost estimates. However, there are only a few questions on the exam on this topic.

PERT formula: $\frac{(P+4M+O)}{6}$	Standard deviation of a task using PERT: $\frac{P-O}{6}$	Variance of a task using PERT: $\left[\frac{P-O}{6}\right]^2$

Exercise 1: Complete the chart using the formulas above. All estimates are in hours.

TASK	O	M	P	PERT OR EXPECTED DURATION	TASK STANDARD DEVIATION	TASK VARIANCE
A	14	27	47			
B	41	60	89			
C	39	44	48			
D	29	37	42			

Answer 1: It is a good practice on the exam to calculate to three decimal places and round to two decimal places when you are ready to check your answer. Remember that square is not times two but a number times itself.

TASK	O	M	P	PERT OR EXPECTED DURATION	TASK STANDARD DEVIATION	TASK VARIANCE
A	14	27	47	28.167	5.500	30.250
B	41	60	89	61.667	8.000	64.000
C	39	44	48	43.833	1.500	2.250
D	29	37	42	36.500	2.167	4.694

Exercise 2: Assuming that the tasks listed above make up the entire critical path for the project, how long should the project take?

Answer 2: This question is provided for understanding and does not represent the complexity of questions on the exam! Most of the questions on the exam relating to PERT are as simple as the ones at the end of this chapter.

The answer is 170.167 hours +/- 10.06 hours at one standard deviation.

170.167 is found by adding the PERT estimates for each of the critical path tasks (in this case all the tasks listed). The +/- 10.06 represents the standard deviation of the estimate (the range of the estimate) and is found by adding the variances of the critical path tasks and taking the square root.

In order to find the standard deviation of a series of items, there is a rule. You cannot add standard deviations; you must convert standard deviations into variances, add the variances and then take the square root of the total to convert back into standard deviation. This calculation means adding 30.250 + 64.000 + 2.250 + 4.694 and taking the square root to find 10.06. Therefore, if we add one standard deviation to the PERT total (for a 68.26% confidence level, see the Quality chapter) the project would not take 170.167 hours, but between 160.107 hours and 180.227 hours. If we add two standard deviations (for a 95.46% confidence level) the project would take between 150.047 hours and 190.287 hours.

MONTE CARLO SIMULATION (page 44, 75 and 139 titled simulation): This method of estimating uses a computer to simulate the outcome of a project based on PERT estimates (optimistic, pessimistic and most likely estimates) and the network diagram, but does not use the PERT formula. The simulation can tell you:

- The probability of completing the project on any specific day
- The probability of completing the project for any specific amount of cost
- The probability of any task actually being on the critical path
- The overall project risk

See the chart on page 142 of the *PMBOK® Guide*. PMI® suggests that Monte Carlo simulation will create a project duration that is closer to reality than CPM or PERT.

Monte Carlo Analysis can also help deal with "path convergence," places in the network diagram where multiple paths converge into one or more tasks, thus adding risk to the project.

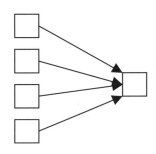

CRITICAL PATH: Once you create a network diagram and estimate tasks, you can find the critical path.

Exercise: Test yourself! What is a critical path and how does it help the project manager?

Answer: The critical path is the longest duration path through a network diagram and determines the shortest time to complete the project. HINT: The easiest way to find the critical path is to add the lengths of time for each path in a network diagram. The path with the longest duration is the critical path.

Although the critical path may change over time, it helps prove how long the project should take and indicates to the project manager which tasks need more monitoring. The critical path almost always has no slack (defined later). Please note that although CPM does stand for "Critical Path Method," a critical path can be found using CPM, PERT or Monte Carlo!

Many critical path-related questions show up on the exam regarding trading off between time, cost, risk and quality to keep the critical path an acceptable length. See crashing and fast tracking, described later.

LAG (page 74): Inserted waiting time between tasks. For example, you must wait three days after pouring concrete before you can construct the frame for a house.

SLACK (FLOAT): The amount of time a task can be delayed without delaying the project. Tasks on the critical path almost always have zero slack. Critical path tasks that are delayed or have dictated dates can result in negative slack.

Slack is extremely useful for a project manager to understand, since it allows for better allocation of resources. Such information also helps team members juggle multiple projects by telling them how much time flexibility they have on each task they are working on.

Slack is found using either LS – ES, or LF – EF. LS is the latest a task can start, ES is the earliest a task can start, LF is the latest a task can finish and EF is the earliest a task can finish. Most project management software will calculate slack for you, but you must be able to understand slack and how to calculate it manually.

The "early" figures are found by calculating length from the beginning of the project to the task, following the dependencies in the network diagram – a "forward pass" through the network diagram. The "late" figures are found by moving in the same way from the end of the project – a "backward pass" through the network diagram. A forward and backward pass can be confusing at first. There are many ways to calculate slack. The exam is only concerned with the answer, not which of the many methods you use to calculate it.

The general definition of slack can be refined further to the following subcategories of slack:

- Free Slack (float) – the amount of time a task can be delayed without delaying the early start date of its successor
- Total Slack (float) – the amount of time a task can be delayed without delaying the project completion date
- Project Slack (float) – the amount of time a project can be delayed without delaying the externally imposed project completion date required by the customer or management, or previously committed to by the project manager

The next few exercises should help you understand this better. As you do them, think about how knowing slack might help you better manage your real-world projects.

Exercise 1: Test yourself by answering the questions below.

You are the project manager for a new project and have figured out the following dependencies.

- Task 1 can start immediately and has an estimated duration of 3 weeks.
- Task 2 can start after task 1 is completed and has an estimated duration of 3 weeks.
- Task 3 can start after task 1 is completed and has an estimated duration of 6 weeks.
- Task 4 can start after task 2 is completed and has an estimated duration of 8 weeks.
- Task 5 can start after task 4 is completed and after task 3 is completed. This task takes 4 weeks.

1. What is the duration of the critical path? _____

2. What is the slack of task 3? _____

3. What is the slack of task 2? _____

4. What is the slack of the path with the longest slack? _____

5. The resource working on task 3 is replaced with another resource that is less experienced. The task will now take 10 weeks. How will this affect the project?

   _____

6. Using the original information, after some arguing between stakeholders, a new task 6 is added to the project. It will take eleven weeks to complete and must be completed before task 5 and after task 3. Management is concerned that adding the task will add eleven weeks to the project. The stakeholder argues that the time will be less than eleven weeks. Who is correct?

   _____

7. Based on the information in number 6 above, how much longer will the project take?

   _____

Answer 1: There are many ways to answer these questions. If you learned another way in your project management training, use it. Here is the simplest way to compute the answers.

1. The length of the critical path is 18. There are two paths here; tasks 1, 2, 4, 5 and tasks 1, 3, 5. Tasks 1, 2, 4, 5 are longest and are therefore the critical path. Their paths add up to 18, so the critical path is 18 weeks long. Follow the dark line on the diagram below.

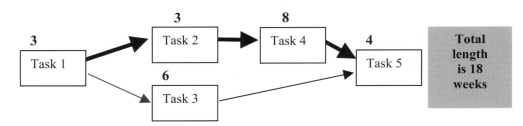

2. Five weeks. Remember to do a forward pass through the network diagram (moving from start to finish) to find the early start and early finish for each task. A backward pass through the network diagram (moving from finish to start) is needed to find the late start and late finish.

   On the forward pass, task 1 will start at the beginning of week 1 and complete at the end of week 3. Task 3 will start at the beginning of week 4 and complete at the end of week 9. Now start the backward pass. Task 5 must end at the end of week 18 and needs to start no later than the beginning of week 15. Task 3 needs to be complete at the end of week 14. So, the latest task 3 can start is at the beginning of week 9. You can use either slack formula to compute slack. LF–EF=14–9=5 or LS–ES = 9–4=5.

   There are many ways to calculate slack. Pick one you learned in project management class that works for you.

3. Zero, it is on the critical path. A task on the critical path almost always has no slack.

4. Five weeks. There are only two paths in this example; tasks 1, 2, 4, 5 and tasks 1, 3, 5. The length of the noncritical path (tasks 1, 3, 5) is 13. The length of the project is 18 so 18 - 13 is 5. The total slack of the path with the longest float is 5.

5. It will have no effect. The length of path tasks 1, 3, 5 was 13. Adding 4 more weeks to the length of task 3 will make that path 17. Since it is shorter than the critical path, the critical path does not change. The length is still 18 weeks because task 3 is not on the critical path.

6. The stakeholder.

7. Six weeks longer. (NOTE: if you answered 24, it means you did not read the question correctly!!!) Follow the dark line in the diagram below.

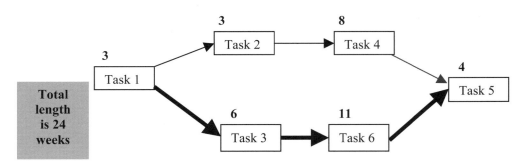

© 2002 - 1998 Rita Mulcahy, PMP
PHONE: (952) 846-4484 - EMAIL: info@rmcproject.com - WEB: www.rmcproject.com

Exercise 2: Considering the following data:

Task	Preceding activity	Estimate in months
Start		0
D	Start	4
A	Start	6
F	D, A	7
E	D	8
G	F, E	5
B	F	5
H	G	7
C	H	8
End	C, B	0

1. What is the duration of the critical path? _____

2. What is the slack of task B? _____

3. What is the slack of task E? _____

4. What is the slack of task D? _____

Answer 2:

1. The critical path (project duration) is 33 months (Start, A, F, G, H, C, End). Here is an easy way to figure it out. List all the paths and put the length next to each one. In this way you are less likely to miss a path.

    D, E, G, H, C = 32
    D, F, G, H, C = 31
    D, F, B = 16
    A, F, G, H, C = 33
    A, F, B = 18

2. 15 months. The project must be completed by month 33 and B takes 5 months. So LF = 33.

    Start, A and F must occur before B can start and they will finish no sooner than the end of month 13. Task B takes 5 months so the earliest B can finish is the end of month 18. So EF = 18.

    Slack = 33 - 18 = 15.

3. 1 month. Task E is not so easy! The project must be completed by the end of month 33. Task E must be completed before G, H and C can start. So LF for E is, 33 - 8 - 7 - 5 or 13.

    Task E must be completed after Task D. So EF is 4 + 8 or 12.

    Slack = LF 13 - EF 12 or 1 month.

4. 1 month. Task D gets even harder! The project must be completed by the end of month 33. Task D must be completed before E, F, G, H, C and B can start. Looking backward through the dependencies, the LF is 33 - 8 - 7 - 5, but then we run into a problem. Normally we would go along the critical path, but look at E and F. E is longer than F so we must go along the path from G to E, making LF 33 - 8 -7 - 5 - 8, or 5.

    EF is easier. There are no predecessors so EF is the end of month 4.
    Slack = 5 - 4 or 1 month.

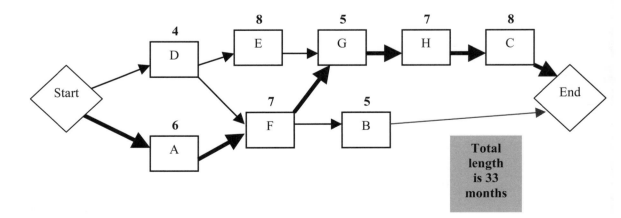

© 2002 - 1998 Rita Mulcahy, PMP
PHONE: (952) 846-4484 - EMAIL: info@rmcproject.com - WEB: www.rmcproject.com

Exercise 3: You can expect more than ten questions on network diagrams, slack and dealing with changes as well as the following topics: crashing and fast tracking. A little more practice is in order. Exam questions could be substantially similar to these or more situational in nature. Please note that the exam may have the picture of a network diagram in a separate window, available at the click of a button.

Considering the following data:

TASK	ESTIMATE In weeks	
Start-A	3	
Start-B	9	
A-C	3	
B-C	Dummy	
B-E	2	
C-D	2	
C-E	1	
E-End	4	
D-End	2	

1. What is the critical path? _____

2. If the duration of Task C-E changes to 2, what is the effect on the project?

   _____

3. What task(s) must be completed before Task C-D begins?

   _____

4. If management tells you to complete the project two weeks early, what is the project float? Does the critical path change?

   _____

Answer 3: Did you realize that this is an AOA diagram? Did you read the questions carefully? Are you reading more into the question than was asked? Are you thinking about what you would do to fix the situation if it were a real project and not just answering the question presented? These are all problems for people taking this exam.

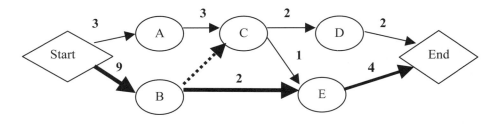

1. The critical path is Start-B, B-E, and E-End. (Sometimes the exam asks for the path, other times for its length.) Use the easy way to figure this out; list all the paths and make sure you see all the paths.

    Start-A, A-C, C-D, D-End = 10
    Start-A, A-C, C-E, E-End = 11
    Start-B, B-C, C-E, E-End = 14
    Start-B, B-C, C-D, D-End = 13
    Start-B, B-E, E-End = 15

2. If C-E changes from 1 to 2, the critical path would be:

    Start-B, B-E, E-End, as well as Start-B, B-C, C-E, E-End

    Yes, you can have more than one critical path. What is the effect on the project? The project is riskier. Make sure you can see the five paths through this network diagram and be able to analyze the diagram completely. Otherwise you will not be able to see the second or the third critical path. TRICK: Always check for a second or more critical path when you answer any questions that change the critical path.

3. Start-A, A-C, and Start-B. The question is really trying to get you to answer Start-B because that is what the dummy is for, to show that dependency. Remember there is no Task C in this AOA drawing and B-C is a dummy, not a task.

4. The project float is -2 and the critical path would not change. This question was about *project* float. Remember project float compares the project length to an external due date. Your difficulty with this question may have been in one of three areas:

    First, you did not realize there is always an assumption on the exam that the project was on time before the situation described. Therefore, asking for a due date two weeks sooner means you are two weeks late.

    Second, you may have assumed you had to do something to fix the problem. This is not what the question asked. It simply said something had happened and asked the status of your project.

    Third, you might not have realized that you can have negative float. You can have negative float if the project is behind an imposed external date, when a task is late, etc.

These are good questions to test your knowledge about critical paths, float, etc.:

- Can there be more than one critical path? Yes, you can have 2, 3 or many critical paths.
- Do you want there to be? No, it increases risk.
- Can a critical path run over a dummy? Yes.
- Why is a dummy included in a network diagram? To show interdependencies of tasks.
- Can a critical path change? Yes.
- Can there be negative float? Yes, it shows you are behind.
- Does the network diagram change when the end date changes? No, not automatically, but the project manager should investigate options such as fast tracking and crashing the schedule to meet the new date and then change the network diagram accordingly.
- Would you leave the project with a negative float? No, you would crash or fast track.

SHORTENING THE SCHEDULE (duration compression, page 75, see also resource leveling, page 76): One of the most common problems projects have is an unrealistic time frame. This can occur during planning when the customer requires a completion date that cannot be met or during project execution when the project manager needs to bring the project back in line with the schedule baseline or to adjust the project for changes. The need to compress the schedule is common on projects and will cover more than 10 questions on the exam. Most project managers are not completely knowledgeable in this area and it shows on their score sheets. To prevent this, let's try an exercise.

Exercise: Based on the network diagram below, what would you do during planning (or executing for that matter, while taking corrective action) to compress the schedule to 30 months?

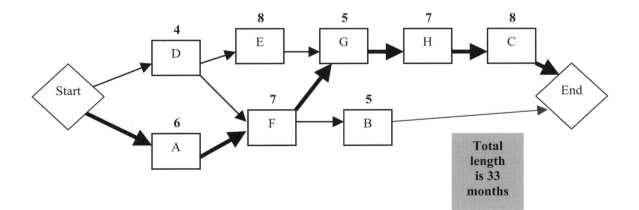

	Option	Method to achieve it
1		
2		
3		
4		
5		
6		
7		
8		
9		

Answer: Did this situation make sense? If it did, you are in good shape. If not, a little study is required. Notice how this effort allows the project manager to proactively deal with reality and take action during the project. The project manager should know whether the project completion date could be met throughout execution! The following answers and methods are explained in the next few pages.

	Option	Method to achieve it
1	Execute H and C in parallel	Fast track
2	Move resources from B to G	Crash
3	Cut task H	Reduce scope
4	Hire consultants to assist	Crash
5	Move more experienced people to tasks on the critical path	Crash
6	Accept a project that meets lower quality standards	Do not get excited. Quality is part of the triple constraint and is an option. In this case it would probably be easier and thus faster to complete.
7	Review assumptions and re-estimate	Now it is time to look at the estimates and see which contain hidden risks. By reducing the risks, the estimate can be lowered and the project finished faster. It is never an option to just cut 10% off of the estimate.
8	Say no, the project must have 33 months	This is not a viable option until after other alternatives are exhausted.
9	Work overtime	Not an option during planning. There are too many other ways to compress the schedule that do not have the negative effects of overtime.

Crashing, fast tracking and re-estimating are ways to shorten the project schedule. This most often happens in two circumstances. First, management says the project duration is too long. Second, a change has been made to the project or the desired completion date changes.

Common errors on the exam relating to schedule compression include the use of overtime or telling the team, "cut 10% off your estimates." Project management does not involve having the team work overtime to complete the project on time because the project manager did not control and adjust along the way. Cutting 10% is just delaying the inevitable, a late project. These are both inappropriate project management techniques because more effective choices exist, as seen above.

WARNING: For questions about changes to the network diagram, make sure you look for subsequent changes in the critical path caused by the changes to the network diagram.

RE-ESTIMATING – Once it is known that the schedule (or budget) must be reduced, a project manager can investigate the task estimates that contain the most unknowns, eliminate or reduce these "risks" and thus decrease the estimate. See the estimating techniques later in this chapter for a further description. Also revisit your list of assumptions as these are prime risks to the project.

CRASHING – Adding more resources to critical path tasks while maintaining scope. This can take the form of moving resources from noncritical tasks or adding extra resources to the task from outside the project. Crashing almost always results in increased costs.

For example, using the diagram from exercise 2 shown, resources could be added to task G or any other task on the critical path (assuming that such a proposition was logical based on the nature of the work).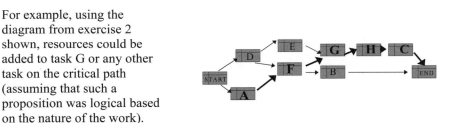
These resources could be acquired from task B or from outside the project.

FAST TRACKING – Doing critical path tasks in parallel that were originally planned in series. Fast tracking often results in rework, usually increases risk and requires more attention to communications.

For example, using the previous network diagram (from Exercise 2) what task would you fast track to shorten the project length? Task H (or any other pair of tasks on the critical path, assuming it is logical due to the nature of the work) could be fast tracked by making it occur at the same time, or in parallel with Task G. Task C could also be fast tracked by having part of it done concurrently with Task H.

Chapter 5
Time Management

In crashing or fast tracking, it is best to see all potential choices and then select the choice or choices that have the least impact on the project. If you have negative project float (the estimated completion date is after the desired date) would your first choice be to tell the customer the date could not be met or to ask for more time? No, the first choice would be to analyze what could be done about it by crashing or fast tracking the project.

But if you have to choose between crashing and fast tracking, what would you do? Adding resources to the project would *generally* cost more than fast tracking. In this case, one would choose fast tracking. However, crashing can also mean *moving* resources around within the project. If making such moves does not add cost, then crashing would be preferable to fast tracking as it would not affect the risk and complexity of the project. Think about this! In the real world, many project managers use the network diagram to manage the day-to-day operations of the project and to make adjustments when changes occur. Therefore, you should expect this to be reflected in the exam by the number of questions on network diagrams, calculations and "what do you do in this situation" type of questions.

Exercise 1: Here is another chance to test yourself on crashing and fast tracking!

1. Imagine that this project has a project float of -3. Which task or tasks presented below would you crash to save three months on the project, assuming that the tasks listed below represent critical path tasks?

2. How much would it cost to crash this project?

Task	Original duration in months	Crash duration in months	Time savings	Original cost in dollars	Crash cost	Extra cost	Cost per month
F	14	12	2	10,000	14,000	4,000	2,000
A	9	7	2	17,000	27,000	10,000	5,000
H	3	2	1	25,000	26,000	1,000	1,000
G	7	6	1	14,000	16,000	2,000	2,000
C	11	8	3	27,000	36,000	9,000	3,000

Answer 1:

1. Tasks F and H. Any time you have negative project float, it means that the project is not going to meet its external deliverable date. The answer, depending on how the question is worded, involves crashing or fast tracking the project and coming up with options, or telling the customer that the date cannot be met.

2. F and H would cost the least, only $5,000.

Exercise 2: Consider the following.

1. Management has told you to get the project completed 2 weeks early. What is the BEST thing for you to do?
    A. Consult the project sponsor
    B. Crash
    C. Fast track
    D. Advise the customer (management) of the impact of the change

2. To handle the situation described in exercise 2, number 1 above, you could assign a more experienced resource to task Start-B in order to get the task done in seven weeks, but it would cost an additional $20,000 to do so. You could eliminate part of Task C-D or E-End and save $5,000 and 1 week of work. You could move work from Task A-C to Task B-E and save $2,000. What is the cost of compressing this project?

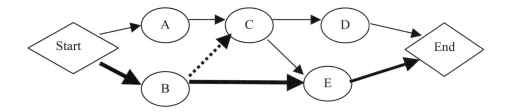

TASK	ESTIMATE In weeks
Start-A	3
Start-B	9
A-C	3
B-C	Dummy
B-E	2
C-D	2
C-E	1
E-End	4
D-End	2

Answer 2:

1. Did you get fooled by the first question? Did you think you had to choose between crashing and fast tracking? There is no information in the first part of this exercise to help you determine which one is better. Therefore, the best choice presented is D, inform the customer of the impact of the change.

    The exam will ask many such questions requiring you to know that you analyze first and then let management, the sponsor, the customer or other parties know the impact of their requests. A project manager does NOT just say yes! They say, for example, "Yes, I would be happy to make the change, BUT the project will be delayed two weeks, I will need two more resources or the project will cost $25,000 more."

2. There is only one viable solution presented that would save the two weeks. That is to assign a more experienced resource to Start-B. Therefore, the crash cost is $20,000.

   Eliminating C-D is not an option as it is not on the critical path. Eliminating E-End would only save one week, not two weeks. Moving work from A-C to B-E moves more work to the critical path and lengthens it, rather than decreasing it.

RESOURCE LEVELING (page 76): Leveling lets schedule and cost slip in favor of having a stable number of resources each month. A little-used tool in project management software, leveling allows you to level the peaks and valleys of resource use from one month to another resulting in a more stable number of resources used on your project.

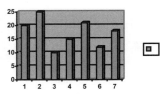

You would level the resources if your project utilized five resources one month, fifteen the next and three the next, or some other up and down pattern that was not an acceptable use of resources. It could also be used if you do not have fifteen resources available and would prefer to lengthen the project, a result of leveling, instead of hiring more resources.

SCHEDULE MANAGEMENT PLAN (page 78): Once the schedule is developed, the project manager can and must put in place a plan for effectively managing the project to the schedule and for managing changes. Such a plan can be formal or informal but is part of the project plan. This plan would include:

- Establishment of a schedule baseline for measuring against during project control
- A plan for how schedule variances will be managed
- Identification of schedule change control procedures
- Identification of performance measures

Does this list make you think? Do you currently do any of this type of activity for your projects? Notice the identification of performance measures. Most project managers just work on the project and hope they meet the deadline. A schedule management plan requires that progress be measured along the way and that the measures of performance are determined in advance. How would you measure schedule performance during the project?

HEURISTICS (page 76): A heuristic means a rule of thumb. (This is the only question I know I got wrong on the exam! Okay, I just wanted to see if you were really reading this.) Several types of heuristics exist; some are scheduling, estimating, planning and resource leveling. One such heuristic is the 80/20 rule that, in quality, suggests that 80% of quality problems are caused by 20% of potential sources of problems.

VARIANCE ANALYSIS (page 80): Comparing actual dates with planned.

Practice Exam for the CAPM® and PMP® Exams
Time Management

1. To control the schedule, a project manager is reanalyzing the project to predict project duration. She does this by analyzing the sequence of activities with the least amount of scheduling flexibility. What technique is she using?

    A. Critical path
    B. Flowchart
    C. Precedence diagramming
    D. Work breakdown structure

2. A dependency that requires that design be completed before manufacturing can start is an example of:

    A. Discretionary dependency
    B. External dependency
    C. Mandatory dependency
    D. Scope dependency

3. Which of the following are GENERALLY illustrated BETTER by bar charts than network diagrams?

    A. Logical relationships
    B. Critical paths
    C. Resource trade-off
    D. Progress or status

4. The estimate for a task is O = 3 days, P = 7 days, M = 4 days. What is the standard deviation for this task?

    A. 5/6 of a day
    B. 2/3 of a day
    C. 1 ½ days
    D. 5 2/3 days

5. A heuristic is best described as a:

    A. Control tool
    B. Scheduling method
    C. Planning tool
    D. Rule of thumb

6. Lag means:

    A. Amount of time a task can be delayed without delaying the project
    B. Amount of time a task can be delayed without delaying the early start date of its successor
    C. Waiting time
    D. The product of a forward and backward pass

7. **Which of the following is the BEST project management tool to use to determine the longest time the project will take?**

    A. WBS
    B. Network diagram
    C. Gantt chart
    D. Project charter

8. **Which of the following is CORRECT?**

    A. A critical path can run over a dummy
    B. There can be only one critical path
    C. The network diagram will change every time the end date changes
    D. A project can never have negative float

9. **What is the duration of a milestone?**

    A. Undefined
    B. Shorter than the activity it represents
    C. There is no duration
    D. Same length as the activity it represents

10. **If the optimistic estimate for a task is 12 days, pessimistic is 18 days, what is the most likely estimate?**

    A. 15 days
    B. 13 days
    C. 16 days
    D. Unknown

11. **If the optimistic estimate for a task is 12 days, pessimistic is 18 days, what is the standard deviation of the task?**

    A. 1
    B. 1.3
    C. 6
    D. 3

12. **Which of the following BEST describes the relationship between standard deviation and risk?**

    A. Nothing
    B. Standard deviation tells you if the estimate is accurate
    C. Standard deviation tells you how unsure the estimate is
    D. Standard deviation tells you if the estimate includes a pad

13. **Monte Carlo analysis is used to:**

    A. Get an indication of the risk involved in the project
    B. Estimate a task's length
    C. Simulate the order in which tasks occur
    D. Prove to management that extra staff is needed

14. The slack of a task is determined by:

A. Performing a Monte Carlo analysis
B. The waiting time between tasks
C. Lag
D. The amount of time the task can be delayed before it delays the critical path

15. A project has three critical paths. Which of the following BEST describes how this affects the project?

A. It makes it easier to manage
B. It increases the project risk
C. It requires more people
D. It makes it more expensive

16. If project time and cost are not as important as the number of resources used each month, which of the following is the BEST thing to do?

A. Perform a Monte Carlo analysis
B. Fast track the project
C. Perform resource leveling
D. Analyze the life cycle costs

17. When would a milestone chart be used instead of a Gantt chart?

A. Project planning
B. Reporting to team members
C. Reporting to management
D. Risk analysis

18. Your project plan results in a project schedule that is too long. If the project network diagram cannot change but you have extra personnel resources, what is the BEST thing to do?

A. Fast track the project
B. Monte Carlo analysis
C. Crash the project
D. Perform a value analysis

19. An activity-on-node diagram is different from an activity-on-arrow diagram because an activity-on-node diagram:

A. Can use PERT
B. Has four relationships among tasks
C. Has only finish-to-finish relationships
D. May use dummy activities

20. Which estimating method uses one time estimate for each task?

A. PERT
B. CPM
C. Monte Carlo
D. Control charts

21. **Which of the following is the BEST thing to do to try to complete a project two days earlier?**

    A. Tell them that the project's critical path does not allow the project to be finished earlier
    B. Tell your boss
    C. Meet with the team and look for options for crashing or fast tracking the critical path
    D. Work hard and see what the project status is next month

22. **In attempting to complete the project faster, the project manager looks at the cost associated with crashing each task. The BEST approach to crashing would also include looking at the:**

    A. Risk impact of crashing each task
    B. Customer's opinion of what tasks to crash
    C. Boss's opinion of what tasks to crash and in which order
    D. Project phase in which the task is due to occur

23. **A project manager is trying to coordinate all the tasks on the project and has determined the following:**

    Task 1 can start immediately and has an estimated duration of one week. Task 2 can start after task 1 is completed and has an estimated duration of four weeks. Task 3 can start after task 2 is completed and has an estimated duration of five weeks. Task 4 can start after task 1 is completed and must be completed when task 3 is completed. Its estimated duration is eight weeks. What is the duration of the critical path for this project?

    A. 10
    B. 11
    C. 14
    D. 8

24. **Based on the data in the question above, if task 4 takes ten weeks, what is the duration of the critical path?**

    A. 10
    B. 11
    C. 14
    D. 8

25. **Which of the following includes asking team members about the time estimates for their tasks and developing agreement on the calendar date for each task?**

    A. Activity sequencing
    B. Schedule development
    C. Scope definition
    D. Initiation

Time Management Questions Only For the PMP® Exam

26. A project manager is in the middle of the executing phase of a very large construction project when he discovers that the time needed to complete the project is longer than the time available. What is the BEST thing to do?

    A. Contact the customer and tell them that their required date cannot be met
    B. Meet with management and tell them that their required date cannot be met
    C. Crash or fast track the project
    D. Plan to crash or fast track the project and present options to management for a decision

27. During planning, you estimate the time needed for each task and then add the estimates to create the project estimate. You commit to completing the project by this date. What is WRONG with this scenario?

    A. The team did not create the estimate and estimating takes too long using that method
    B. The team did not create the estimate and a network diagram was not used
    C. The estimate is too long and should be created by management
    D. The project estimate should be the same as the customer's required completion date

28. During activity definition, a team member identifies an activity that needs to be accomplished. However, another team member believes that the activity is not part of the project as interpreted by the project charter. What is the BEST thing for the project manager to do?

    A. Try to build a consensus of the team
    B. Make the decision about inclusion herself
    C. Ask management
    D. Talk with the project sponsor

29. You are a project manager on a US $5,000,000 software development project. While working with your project team to develop a network diagram, you notice a series of activities that can be worked in parallel but must finish in a specific sequence. What type of activity sequencing method is required for these activities?

    A. Precedence diagramming method
    B. Arrow diagramming method
    C. Critical path method
    D. Conditional diagramming method

30. You are a project manager on a US $5,000,000 software development project. While working with your project team to develop a network diagram, your data architects suggest that quality could be improved if the data model is approved by senior management before moving on to other design elements. They support this suggestion with an article from a leading software development journal. Which of the following BEST describes what this type of input is called?

    A. Mandatory dependency
    B. Discretionary dependency
    C. External dependency
    D. Heuristic

31. Based on the following, if you needed to shorten the duration of the project, what task would you try to shorten?

TASK	ESTIMATE In Weeks
Start-A	1
Start-B	2
Start-C	6
A-D	10
B-E	1
C-E	Dummy
C-F	2
F-End	3
E-End	9
D-End	1

A. Task Start-B
B. Task A-D
C. Task E-End
D. Task C-E

32. You have a project with the following tasks: Task A takes 40 hours and can start after the project starts. Task B takes 25 hours and should happen after the project starts. Task C must happen after task A and takes 35 hours. Task D must happen after tasks B and C and takes 30 hours. Task E must take place after task C and takes 10 hours. Task F takes place after task E and takes 22 hours. Which of the following is TRUE if task B actually takes 37 hours?

A. The critical path is 67 hours
B. The critical path changes to tasks B, D
C. The critical path is A, C, E, F
D. The critical path increases by 12 hours

33. The team has provided the project manager with activity duration estimates. If the project manager is about to start schedule development, which of the following is the MOST important item the project manager needs to adequately develop a schedule?

A. Risk management
B. Corrective action
C. Schedule change control system
D. Change requests

34. A project manager is taking over a project from another project manager while the project is in planning. If the new project manager wants to see what the previous project manager planned for managing changes to the schedule, it would be BEST to look at:

    A. Communications plan
    B. Project plan
    C. Time management plan
    D. Schedule management plan

35. A project manager is using weighted average duration estimates to calculate activity duration. Which type of mathematical analysis is being used?

    A. CPM
    B. PERT
    C. Monte Carlo
    D. GERT

36. The WBS, estimates for each work package, and network diagram are completed. Which of the following would be the NEXT thing for the project manager to do?

    A. Sequence the activities
    B. Verify that they have the correct scope of work
    C. Create a preliminary schedule and get the team's approval
    D. Complete risk management

37. A new product development project has four levels in the work breakdown structure and has been sequenced using the arrow diagramming method. The activity duration estimates have been received. What should be done NEXT?

    A. Create an activity list
    B. Begin the work breakdown structure
    C. Finalize the schedule
    D. Compress the schedule

38. You are a project manager for a new product development project that has four levels in the work breakdown structure, and has been sequenced using the arrow diagramming technique. The duration estimates have been compressed and a schedule created. What time management activity would you do NEXT?

    A. Begin schedule control
    B. Begin resource planning
    C. Analogously estimate the schedule
    D. Gain approval

39. **A team member from research and development tells you that her work is too creative to provide you with a fixed single estimate for the task. You both decide to use the average time the task has taken for past projects to predict the future. This is an example of which of the following?**

    A. Parametric estimating
    B. PERT
    C. CPM
    D. Monte Carlo

40. **A task has an early start of day three, a late start of day thirteen, an early finish of day nine, and a late finish of day nineteen. The task:**

    A. Is on the critical path
    B. Has a lag
    C. Is progressing well
    D. Is not on the critical path

41. **The project is calculated to be completed four days after the desired completion date. You do not have access to additional resources. The project is low risk, the benefit cost ratio is expected to be 1.6, and the dependencies are preferential. Under these circumstances, what would be the BEST thing to do?**

    A. Cut resources from a task
    B. Make more tasks concurrent
    C. Move resources from the preferential dependencies to the external dependencies
    D. Remove a task from the project

42. **A project manager for a small construction company has a project that was budgeted for US $130,000 over a six-week period. According to her schedule, the project should have cost US $60,000 to date. However, it has cost US $90,000 to date. The project is also behind schedule, because the original estimates were not accurate. Who has the PRIMARY responsibility to solve this problem?**

    A. Project manager
    B. Senior management
    C. Project sponsor
    D. Manager of the project office

43. **Your organization is having a difficult time managing all of its projects. You have been asked to help senior management understand this. Which of the following types of reports would help provide summary information to senior management?**

    A. Detailed cost estimates
    B. Project plans
    C. Gantt charts
    D. Milestone reports

Time Management Answers

1. **Answer:** A

    Explanation: There are only two choices related to scheduling: A and C. Choice C, however, is a diagramming technique that deals only with the relationship between tasks, not estimating (schedule flexibility).

2. **Answer:** C

    Explanation: There is no defined term such as a scope dependency (choice D). No mention is made that the dependency comes from a source outside the project, so external (choice B) is not correct. Since the dependency is required, it could not be discretionary (choice A) and therefore must be mandatory. The key word in this question is "requires."

3. **Answer:** D

    Explanation: The bar chart (or Gantt chart) is designed to show a relationship of tasks to time. This is best used when demonstrating progress or status as a factor of time.

4. **Answer:** B

    Explanation: The standard deviation is computed by $(P-O)/6$. Therefore, the answer is $(7-3)/6 = (4)/6 = 2/3$ of a day.

5. **Answer:** D

    Explanation: A heuristic is a rule of thumb. Examples are cost per line of code, cost per square foot of floor space, etc.

6. **Answer:** C

    Explanation: Slack and float (choices A and B) are the time a task can be delayed without impacting the next task or the entire project. CPM (choice D) is an estimating method and not waiting time. Therefore, choice C is the correct answer.

7. **Answer:** B

    Explanation: The charter (choice D) may include any required end dates but not how long the project will take. The Gantt chart (choice C) may show an end date but is not used to determine the end date. The network diagram takes the work packages from the work breakdown structure (choice A) and adds dependencies. The dependencies allow us to look at the various paths throughout the diagram. The longest duration path is the critical path. Choice B is the best answer.

8. **Answer:** A

    Explanation: This question tests your knowledge about a number of topics. You can have negative float (choice D) if you are behind schedule. Choice C uses the word "will." The network diagram may change or it may not, depending on the amount of schedule reserve and the reason for the change to the schedule. There can often be more than one critical path (choice B) but you might adjust to decrease risk and have only one critical path. Only choice A is correct and therefore the best answer.

9. **Answer:** C

   Explanation: A milestone shows the completion of a series of tasks or work packages. Therefore it takes no time of its own. With this in mind, choice C is the best answer.

10. **Answer:** D

   Explanation: PERT uses three separate estimates: optimistic, pessimistic and most likely. If you don't have all three estimates, you cannot compute the PERT estimate.

11. **Answer:** A

   Explanation: The standard deviation is computed by (P-O)/6. Therefore the answer is (18-12)/6 = (6)/6 = 1.

12. **Answer:** C

   Explanation: Choice D cannot be the best answer since there is no such thing as a pad in project management. An estimate might be inflated but it is because of risks, not padding. An estimate can have a wide range (choice B) and still be accurate if the item estimated includes risks. Choice A is not best, as the standard deviation tells you the amount of uncertainty or risk involved in the estimate for the work package or task.

13. **Answer:** A

   Explanation: Monte Carlo can be used to prove things to management (choice D), but its main focus does not deal with staff but with time. Monte Carlo is a simulation (choice C) but it simulates time, not order of tasks. Monte Carlo could help you know that an estimate for a task needs to change, but not what the task estimate should be (choice B). Notice how many choices are half-right? Risk can be assessed using Monte Carlo analysis (choice A). By considering the inputs to the PERT estimates and the network diagram, you can obtain a better overview of the overall project risk.

14. **Answer:** D

   Explanation: Slack is the amount of time a task can be delayed without impacting the end date of the project.

15. **Answer:** B

   Explanation: Though having three critical paths COULD later cost more (choice D) or require more people (choice C) the best answer, or the answer that is definitely and always true, is B. Because you need to manage three critical paths, there is more risk that something could happen to delay the project.

16. **Answer:** C

   Explanation: Fast tracking (choice B) would affect cost and time. Monte Carlo and life cycle costs (choices A and D) do not directly deal with resources. Leveling (choice C) is the only one that will definitely affect resources.

© 2002 - 1998 Rita Mulcahy, PMP
PHONE: (952) 846-4484 - EMAIL: info@rmcproject.com - WEB: www.rmcproject.com

17. **Answer:** C

    Explanation: Risk analysis (choice D) COULD make use of both charts. Team members (choice B) need to see details and so they need a Gantt chart rather than a milestone chart. Project planning (choice A) would use both types of charts. A milestone chart is used instead of a Gantt chart for any situation where you want to report in a less detailed way. Gantt charts can scare people with their complexity and often show too much detail to be worthwhile on a management level. Milestone charts are more effective.

18. **Answer:** C

    Explanation: To answer this question you need to look for the choice that focuses on resource use instead of cost or time. Choice D deals with cost. Choices A and B focus on schedule. Choice C focuses on resources and therefore is the best answer.

19. **Answer:** B

    Explanation: The other choices all apply to activity-on-arrow diagrams.

20. **Answer:** B

    Explanation: Both PERT and Monte Carlo (choices A and C) use three estimates. Control charts (choice D) are not an estimating method.

21. **Answer:** C

    Explanation: This is another question that asks about problem solving. Only choice C relates to "evaluate." Choices B and D do not try to solve the real problem. Choice A is just an untrue statement.

22. **Answer:** A

    Explanation: You may or may not need your customer's (choice B) and your boss's (choice C) input but you will definitely need to include an analysis of risk. Choice A is broader than choice D and therefore is better.

23. **Answer:** A

    Explanation: You need to draw a network diagram for this question.

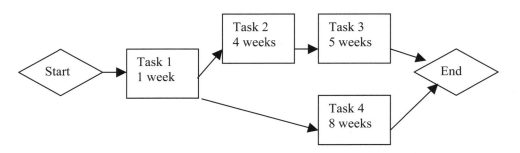

This diagram has two paths: Start, 1, 2, 3, End and Start, 1, 4, End. The length of the first path is ten and the second is nine making the first path critical and the length of the critical path ten. Notice that almost every other answer someone could pick is also listed?

24. **Answer:** B

Explanation: If task 4 now takes 10 weeks instead of 8, the critical path would change to Start, 1, 4, End and be 11 weeks long.

25. **Answer:** B

Explanation: By the time this activity is taking place, initiation, scope definition and activity sequencing would be completed.

26. **Answer:** D

Explanation: This question tests if you know how to solve problems. In other chapters you are told that the first step is to evaluate. That eliminates choices A and B, which are also common errors of inexperienced project managers. Choices C and D are similar, but D is the best choice as it follows the problem solving process. It is most likely that management will need to be involved in making the final choice between the options presented.

27. **Answer:** B

Explanation: Time estimates for the tasks should be created by the team and should not be added. Some may take place concurrently. Therefore choice B must be the correct answer.

28. **Answer:** C

Explanation: This is a clarification of the project charter and therefore must be addressed to the senior manager who issued the charter.

29. **Answer:** A

Explanation: The question implies finish-to-finish relationships between tasks. The arrow diagramming method (choice B) does not support these types of relationships. Choice C is not a diagramming method and choice D is a made up term.

30. **Answer:** B

Explanation: The situation is neither mandatory (choice A) nor driven by an external source (choice C). A rule of thumb (choice D) is something that can be used consistently. This situation is a unique occurrence. The situation is a suggestion or a preferred method so choice B is the best answer.

31. **Answer:** C

Explanation: This is one of the two-stage questions you will find on the exam. In order to answer this question you need to complete two stages. First you need to draw the network diagram and find the critical path, then make a decision. The network diagram would be:

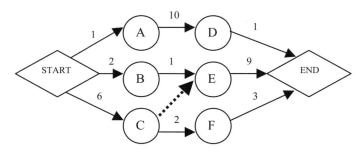

The diagram above has four paths:

Start-A, A-D, D-End	12
Start-B, B-E, E-End	12
Start-C, C-F, F-End	11
Start-C, C-E, E-End	15

The critical path is therefore 15 (Start-C, C-E, E-End) and runs across the dummy (yes that can happen). Without any other information to suggest another alterative, it is best to try to shorten the longest task, E-End, on the critical path.

You may have selected A-D because it is the longest task, but notice that shortening it will not change the length of the project. You may not have understood a dummy and tried to look for the longest path that does not include a dummy. If you did you would have found that Start-B, B-E, E-End and Start-A, A-D, D-End are the same length.

32. **Answer:** C

Explanation: The critical path is A, C, E, F and 107 long. Path BD was 55 long and with the change is now 67 long. Changing task B will have no effect on the critical path.

33. **Answer:** A

Explanation: All the items except choice A are part of schedule control and occur after schedule development.

34. **Answer:** D

Explanation: Answer D is the MOST correct answer. The schedule management plan is an output of schedule development and is the repository for plans for schedule changes.

35. **Answer:** B

Explanation: PERT uses a weighted average to compute activity durations.

36. **Answer:** C

Explanation: Choice A is the same thing as create a network diagram. Choice B is done during controlling, not during planning. Since a schedule is an input to risk management, choice D comes after choice C and so it is not the "next thing to do." The only remaining choice is C.

37. **Answer:** D

Explanation: The question is really asking, "What is done after activity duration estimating?" A and B are done before activity duration estimating. Duration compression occurs before finalizing the schedule and is, therefore, the best answer.

38. **Answer:** D

Explanation: Notice how this question and the one previous seem very similar. This is intended to prepare you for similar questions on the exam. Choice C should have already been done. Choice B is a cost activity not a time activity and this activity should have already been completed. The situation described is within the schedule development process of time management. Choice A is the next time process after schedule development, but schedule development is not finished. Final approval (choice D) of the schedule by the stakeholders is needed before one has a project schedule.

39. **Answer:** A

Explanation: Past history is being used to calculate an estimate. Monte Carlo (choice D) is a simulation of the schedule, not a task. One could use past history to come up with the estimate for CPM or PERT (choices B and C) but the BEST answer is choice A because using past history is a chief characteristic of parametric estimates.

40. **Answer:** D

Explanation: The task described has slack because there is a difference between the early start and late start. A task that has slack is probably not on the critical path. There is no information presented about progress or lag, so Choice D is the best answer.

41. **Answer:** B

Explanation: Cutting resources from a task (choice A) would not save time nor would moving resources in the way described (choice C). Removing a task from the project (choice D) is a possibility, but since the dependencies are preferential and the risk is low, the best choice would be to make more tasks concurrent.

42. **Answer:** A

Explanation: Schedule management is a responsibility of the project manager. This question could have been placed in many different chapters since it relates to cost, integration, human resources and time.

43. **Answer:** D

Explanation: Gantt charts (choice C) are usually only for the team. Project plans (choice B) will have more detail than is necessary for the situation described and may distract from the conversation if used in this situation. Detailed estimates (choice A) have nothing to do with the situation described. The best answer is choice D because milestone reports present the right level of detail for upper management.

© 2002 - 1998 Rita Mulcahy, PMP
PHONE: (952) 846-4484 - EMAIL: info@rmcproject.com - WEB: www.rmcproject.com

Cost Management

(PMBOK® GUIDE Chapter 7)

Hot Topics

- Earned value analysis
  - PV
  - EV
  - AC
  - CPI, SPI
  - BAC
  - EAC
  - ETC
  - VAC
  - CV, SV
- Analogous
- Bottom-up
- Parametric
- Computerized tools
- Inputs to estimating
- Resource planning
- Progress reporting (50/50, 20/80, 0/100)
- Cost management plan
- Order of magnitude
- Budget
- Definitive
- Cost risk
- Project selection methods
- BCR
- NPV
- IRR
- Variable/fixed cost
- Direct/indirect cost
- Payback period
- Opportunity cost
- Present value
- Sunk costs
- Law of diminishing returns
- Working capital
- Straight line/accelerated
- Life cycle cost
- Value analysis

Many people are nervous about questions relating to earned value. To ease your mind, let me tell you that an average of only twelve questions on earned value have been on the exam for the last four years, only an average of six questions have required a calculation. Do you feel better yet? How about this? There are only about five questions that deal with all the accounting standards topics. Remember, you do not have to be an accountant to pass this exam. With a little study, the questions on cost should be easy.

There is a strong connection between cost and time on the exam. Some topics covered here in Cost could easily be moved to the Time chapter. Do not get confused that because a topic is listed here it cannot be used for time estimating, planning and controlling. Earned value is a good example. You should also realize:

- Estimating should be based on a WBS to improve accuracy.

- Estimating should be done by the person doing the work.

- Historical information is a key to improving estimates.

- Costs (and time, scope and resources) should be managed to estimates.

- A cost (and time, scope and resource) baseline should be kept and not changed except for approved project changes.

- Plans should be revised, as necessary, during completion of the work.

- Corrective action should be taken when cost problems (and time, scope and resource problems) occur.

- A project manager should never just accept time or cost requirements from management, but rather analyze the needs of the project, come up with their own estimate and reconcile any differences. Yes, this should be true in the real world!

Think about these! Remember that incorrect project management practices will be listed as choices on the exam. If you do not adequately understand and manage your projects this way, you will have difficulty on the exam and not even know why you scored low.

It would be worthwhile to review the Project Cost Management process in the *PMBOK® Guide*: resource planning, cost estimating, cost budgeting and cost control.

Chapter 6
Cost Management

COST RISK: Sometimes a question on the exam will cross boundaries between risk, procurement and cost. Cost risk is best explained with an example question: "Who has the cost risk in a fixed price contract, the buyer or the seller?" The answer is the seller.

INPUTS TO ESTIMATING (or what do you need before you estimate costs or time): In order to create a good estimate, you need the following before you begin estimating:

- WBS
- Network diagram – Costs cannot be estimated until it is known how the project will flow from beginning to end.
- Schedule – For multi-year projects, the cost of a task is usually different if it is completed in one year compared to another. NOTE: This refers to an overall schedule, not a detailed one. The detailed schedule is created after estimating.
- Historical information
- Resource pool – An understanding of the available resources or the resources assigned.
- Risk management plan – because it includes a budget for risk.
- Risks – An understanding of any risk uncovered to date. Remember, a full risk analysis of the details of the project will not have been completed before costs are estimated.

RESOURCE PLANNING (page 85): The management of resources is as important as managing cost, time, quality and scope. Resources must be planned and coordinated in order to avoid common problems such as lack of resources and resources being taken away from the project. Resource planning may be a more extensive activity than you do on your projects.

Exercise: Describe what activities are involved in resource planning.

Answer: Resource planning involves:
- Review WBS
- Identify potentially available resources
- Review historical information about the use of resources on past or similar projects
- Review organizational policies on resource use
- Solicit expert judgment on what resources are needed and available
- Quantify resource requirement by task
- Develop a plan as to what types of resources are needed, in what numbers, when

COST MANAGEMENT PLAN (page 89): Once costs are estimated, the project manager can and must put in place a plan for effectively managing the project to the cost baseline and manage cost variances. This plan is similar to other management plans (a PMI®-ism). The cost management plan can be formal or informal, but is part of the project plan.

Once again, you can see that such a plan requires thinking about how you will manage in advance. This is a concept that many project managers miss.

COST ESTIMATING (page 86): See the methods listed below.

ANALOGOUS ESTIMATING (Top-Down, page 88) – Top or middle managers use expert judgment or the actual time and cost of a previous, similar project as the basis for estimating the current project. Analogous estimating is a form of expert judgment.

BOTTOM-UP ESTIMATING (page 88) – With this technique, the people doing the work create cost and schedule estimates. Estimates, based on the WBS, are rolled up to get a project total.

PARAMETRIC ESTIMATING – Uses a mathematical model to predict project costs. For example, cost per line of code, cost per linear meter or cost per installation. You should also MEMORIZE the two types of parametric estimates:

- Regression analysis (or scatter diagram, you do not need to know what it is, but a picture of a scatter diagram is shown on the right).

- Learning curve – The 100th room painted will cost less than the first room because of improved efficiency.

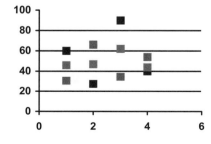

COMPUTERIZED ESTIMATING TOOLS – These are commercially available packages that will help estimate projects in many industries.

Exercise: Answer the questions below in the spaces provided.

What are the advantages of Analogous Estimating?	What are the disadvantages?

What are the advantages of Bottom-Up Estimating?	What are the disadvantages?

Answer: There are many possible answers. The purpose is to get you thinking about the differences so that you can answer any questions on the topic, no matter how they may be worded.

Advantages of Analogous Estimating	Disadvantages
Quick	Less accurate
Tasks need not be identified	Estimates prepared with a limited amount of detailed information and understanding of the project
Less costly to create	Requires considerable experience to do well
Gives the project manager an idea of the level of management's expectations	Infighting at the highest management levels to gain the biggest piece of the pie without knowing what the pie is
Overall project costs will be capped	Extremely difficult for projects with uncertainty

Advantages of Bottom-Up Estimating	Disadvantages
More accurate	Takes time and expense to do this form of estimating
Gains buy-in from the team	Tendency for the team to pad estimates
Based on a detailed analysis of the project	Requires that the project be defined and understood
Provides a basis for monitoring and control	Team infighting to gain the biggest piece of the pie

PROGRESS REPORTING (page 122): A progress report is a useful method to control costs. Many project managers determine how much work has been accomplished by asking team members for an estimate of ***percent complete*** for each task. On projects where work cannot be measured, this estimate is simply a guess. This is time consuming and almost always a complete waste of time because a guess does not provide a confident estimate of the actual percent complete.

If a project has been planned using a WBS, and tasks require about 80 hours of work, we have alternatives to percent complete. Because tasks will be completed faster and more frequently, we can forget percent complete and use one of the following:

50/50 RULE – A task is considered 50% complete when it begins and gets credit for the last 50% only when it is completed.

20/80 RULE – A task is considered 20% complete when it begins and gets credit for the last 80% only when it is completed.

0/100 RULE – A task does not get credit for partial completion, only full completion.

Chapter 6
Cost Management

EARNED VALUE ANALYSIS (page 123): Earned value analysis is a method to measure scope, time and project performance. Many project managers manage their project performance by comparing planned to actual results. With this method, you could easily be on time but overspend according to your plan. A better method is earned value because it integrates cost, time and scope and can be used to forecast future performance and project completion dates. Here is what you need to know.

TERMS TO KNOW:

ACRONYM	TERM	INTERPRETATION
PV	Planned Value	What is the estimated value of the work planned to be done?
EV	Earned Value	What is the estimated value of the work actually accomplished?
AC	Actual Cost	What is the actual cost incurred?
BAC	Budget at Completion	How much did we BUDGET for the TOTAL JOB?
EAC	Estimate at Completion	What do we currently expect the TOTAL project to cost?
ETC	Estimate to Complete	From this point on, how much MORE do we expect it to cost to finish the job?
VAC	Variance at Completion	How much over or under budget do we expect to be at the end of the project?

FORMULAS AND INTERPRETATIONS TO MEMORIZE:

NAME	FORMULA	INTERPRETATION
Cost Variance (CV)	EV - AC	NEGATIVE is over budget, POSITIVE is under budget
Schedule Variance (SV)	EV – PV	NEGATIVE is behind schedule, POSITIVE is ahead of schedule
Cost Performance Index (CPI)	$\frac{EV}{AC}$	We are getting $_____ out of every $1.
Schedule Performance Index (SPI)	$\frac{EV}{PV}$	We are [only] progressing at ____% of the rate originally planned.
Estimate at Completion (EAC) **NOTE:** There are many ways to calculate EAC. The first formula to the right is the one most often asked on the exam.	$\frac{BAC}{CPI}$ AC + ETC AC + BAC - EV $AC + \frac{(BAC - EV)}{CPI}$	As of now, how much do we expect the total project to cost? $ _____. See formulas at left. • Used if no variances from the BAC have occurred or you will continue at the same rate of spending. • Actual plus a new estimate for remaining work. Used when original estimate was fundamentally flawed. • Actual to date plus remaining budget. Used when current variances are thought to be atypical of the future. • Actual to date plus remaining budget modified by performance. Used when current variances are thought to be typical of the future.
Estimate To Complete (ETC)	EAC - AC	How much more will the project cost?
Variance At Completion (VAC)	BAC – EAC	How much over budget will we be at the end of the project?

TRICKS: Make sure you understand and MEMORIZE the following.

1. Notice that EV comes first in every formula. Remembering this one fact alone should help you get about half the earned value questions right. (Aren't you glad you purchased this book?)

2. If it is a variance, the formula is EV minus something.

3. If it is an index, it is EV divided by something.

4. If the formula relates to cost, use AC.

5. If the formula relates to schedule, use PV.

6. For interpretation: negative is bad and positive is good. Thus a –200 cost variance means that you are behind (over) budget.

7. For interpretation: greater than one is good, less than one is bad.

8. One of the earned value questions people often answer incorrectly requires that you differentiate between EAC and ETC and the other terms. The following table may help.

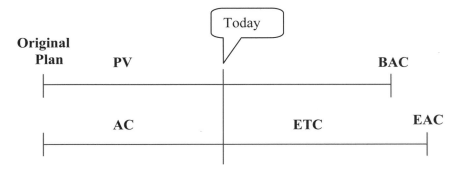

Many people worry about earned value, but there should only be about twelve questions on earned value. Not all of the earned value questions require calculations. Earned value will show up on your score sheet from the actual exam under several titles in the controlling process group, including: "Measure project performance continually," "Refine control limits" and "Evaluate the effectiveness of corrective action."

There is one problem I must tell you about. As of this writing, PMI® has retained some of the old acronyms for earned value on the exam. You should, therefore, know the following until PMI® completely makes the transition to the new terms listed previously.

OLD TERM	OLD ACRONYM	NEW ACRONYM
Budgeted cost of work scheduled	BCWS	PV
Budgeted cost of work performed	BCWP	EV
Actual cost of work performed	ACWP	AC

Still worried about earned value? Not for long. Read the following pages, do the exercises and you might end up appreciating earned value questions over some of the more ambiguous, wordy and confusing questions on this exam.

EARNED VALUE IN ACTION: Earned value is an effective tool for measuring performance and making decisions about corrective action. Following is a sample team meeting conversation on this subject.

Danny, the project manager, calls a meeting of the team and says, "We are six months into this million dollar project and my latest analysis shows a CPI of 1.2 and an SPI of 0.89. This means that we are getting 1.2 dollars for every dollar we put into the project, but only progressing at 89% of the rate originally planned. Lets look for options to correct this problem."

"We could remove me from the project team and replace me with someone less expensive. I must be the most expensive team member," Samantha says.

"Not only would it sadden me to lose you, but your suggestion would improve costs, not schedule. You are the company's best network specialist. Someone else would not be as proficient as you in completing the work."

"We could remove the purchase of the new computers from the project," says Niki. "Or, we could just tell the customer the project will be two weeks late."

"Those are good suggestions, but cancelling the new computers would save us money, not time. We need to focus on time," Danny says. "Nor can we just change the project schedule baseline arbitrarily. That would be unethical."

"Since we are doing well on cost, why don't we bring in another programmer from the IT department to work on this project? We can get the next two tasks completed faster," Jose suggests.

"That sounds like the most effective choice in this situation. Let's see if we can find someone who will improve performance but not cost as much. Thanks for your help," Danny says.

Exercises – Earned Value: The best way to learn this technique is to use it. These exercises are designed to give you a chance to practice calculations AND interpretation. Keep in mind that the Fence exercises are HARDER than the questions on the exam. If you get them right, you should not have to study earned value any more. GOOD LUCK!!!

Exercise: CPI and SPI can be charted each month to show the project trends. Based on the following, what would you be more concerned about, cost or schedule, if you were taking over this project from another project manager?

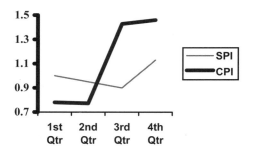

Answer: The answer is schedule. As of today, SPI is closest to 1.

Exercise: The Fence #1

You have a project to build a new fence. The fence is four sided as shown. Each side is to take one day to build and is budgeted for US $1,000 per side.

The sides are planned to be completed one after the other. Today is the end of day three.

Using the project status chart below, calculate EV, etc. When completed, check your answers on the answer sheet on the following page. Interpretation is also important on the exam. Can you interpret what each answer means?

Task	Day 1	Day 2	Day 3	Day 4	Status at the end of Day 3
Side 1	S---------F				Complete, spent $1,000
Side 2		S---------PF	----F		Complete, spent $1,200
Side 3			PS--S---PF		Half done, spent $600
Side 4				PS --------PF	Not yet started

KEY: S – Actual Start, F –Actual Finish, PS - Planned Start, and PF - Planned Finish

What is:	Calculation	Answer	Interpretation of the answer
PV			
EV			
AC			
BAC			
CV			
CPI			
SV			
SPI			
EAC			
ETC			
VAC			

Answer: The Fence #1

What is:	Calculation	Answer	Interpretation of the answer:
PV	1,000 plus 1,000 plus 1,000	3,000	We should have done $3,000 worth of work.
EV	Complete, complete, half done or 1,000 plus 1,000 plus 500	2,500	We have actually completed $2,500 worth of work.
AC	1,000 plus 1,200 plus 600	2,800	We have actually spent $2,800.
BAC	1,000 plus 1,000 plus 1,000 plus 1,000	4,000	Our project budget is $4,000.
CV	2,500 minus 2,800	-300	We are over budget by $300.
CPI	2,500 divided by 2,800	.893	We are only getting 89 cents out of every dollar we put into the project.
SV	2,500 minus 3,000	-500	We are behind schedule.
SPI	2,500 divided by 3,000	.833	We are only progressing at 83% of the rate planned.
EAC	4,000 divided by .893	4,479	We currently estimate that the total project will cost $4,479.
ETC	4,479 minus 2,800	1,679	We need to spend $1,679 to finish the project.
VAC	4,000 minus 4479	-479	We currently expect to be $479 over budget when the project is completed.

NOTE: If your answers differ, check your rounding. It is best to round to three decimal points.

Exercise: The Fence #2

You have a project to build a new fence. The fence is four sided as shown. Each side is to take one day to build and is budgeted for US $1,000 per side. The sides are planned to be completed one after the other. IN THIS CASE, ASSUME THAT THE SIDES HAVE A FINISH-TO-FINISH RELATIONSHIP INSTEAD OF A FINISH-TO-START RELATIONSHIP! Today is the end of day three.

Using the project status chart below, fill in the blanks in the chart and check your answers on the answer sheet on the following page.

Task	Day 1	Day 2	Day 3	Day 4	Status at the end of Day 3
Side 1	S----------F				Complete, spent $1,000
Side 2		S-----F----PF			Complete, spent $900
Side 3		S---	PS---------PF		Half done, spent $1000
Side 4			S----	PS -------PF	75% done, spent $300

KEY: S - Actual Start, F - Actual Finish, PS - Planned Start, PF - Planned Finish

What is:	Calculation	Answer	Interpretation of the answer
PV			
EV			
AC			
BAC			
CV			
CPI			
SV			
SPI			
EAC			
ETC			
VAC			

Answer: The Fence #2

What is:	Calculation	Answer	Interpretation of the answer
PV	1,000 plus 1,000 plus 1,000	3,000	We should have done $3,000 worth of work.
EV	Complete, complete, half done, 75% done or 1,000 plus 1,000 plus 500, plus 750	3,250	We have actually completed $3,250 worth of work.
AC	1,000 plus 900, plus 1,000, plus 300	3,200	We have actually spent $3,200.
BAC	1,000 plus 1,000 plus 1,000 plus 1,000	4,000	Our project budget is $4,000.
CV	3,250 minus 3,200	50	We are under budget by $50.
CPI	3,250 divided by 3,200	1.016	We are getting 1.016 dollars out of every dollar we put into the project.
SV	3,250 minus 3,000	250	We are ahead of schedule.
SPI	3,250 divided by 3,000	1.083	We are progressing at 108% of the rate planned.
EAC	4,000 divided by 1.016	3,937	We currently estimate that the total project will cost $3,937.
ETC	3,937 minus 3,200	737	We need to spend $737 to finish the project.
VAC	4,000 minus 3,937	63	We currently expect to be $63 under budget when the project is completed.

NOTE: If your answers differ, check your rounding. It is best to round to three decimal points.

ACCURACY OF ESTIMATES: When one estimates, the estimate should come with an indication of the range of possible results, especially at the project detail level. The three levels of estimating accuracy you must MEMORIZE for the exam are:

1. **ORDER OF MAGNITUDE ESTIMATE** – This type of estimate is usually made during the initiating phase and is in the range of -25% to +75% from actual.

2. **BUDGET ESTIMATE** – This type of estimate is usually made during the planning phase and is in the range of -10% to +25% from actual.

3. **DEFINITIVE ESTIMATE** – This type of estimate is also made during the planning phase and is in the range of -5% to +10% from actual.

Project managers should watch out for number three. We have already said the project manager should create the project time and cost estimates, not senior management. Most project managers wish this would always be true because they are tired of dealing with unrealistic schedules and estimates. However, project managers should note the difficulty of estimating within -5% and +10% of actual.

ACCOUNTING STANDARDS: Remember that you do not have to be an accountant to pass this exam.

PRESENT VALUE: PLEASE NOTE – Present value is only mentioned one or two times on the exam. You will not have to calculate it, just understand the concept. Present value means the value today of future cash flows and can be found by the formula:

$$PV = \frac{FV}{(1+r)^n}$$

FV = future value
r = interest rate
n = number of time periods

In a simple example, without using the formula, see if you can guess at the following question.

What is the present value of US $300,000 received three years from now if we expect the interest rate to be 10%? Should the answer be more or less than US $300,000?

The answer is less.

I can put an amount of money less than US $300,000 in the bank and in three years have US $300,000. To solve the problem, if you were inclined to do so: $300/(1 + 0.1)^3$ equals, 300/1.331, equals US $225,394.

NET PRESENT VALUE (NPV): This means the present value of the total benefits (income or revenue) less the costs. Let's see if you already have a good understanding of this topic by asking you a question.

You have two projects to choose from. Project A will take three years to complete and has an NPV of US $45,000. Project B will take six years to complete and has an NPV of US $85,000. Which one would you prefer?

The answer is Project B.

The number of years would have been taken into account in the calculation of the NPV. See the sample calculation if you are confused.

To calculate NPV, you need to calculate the present value of both income and revenue figures and then add up the present values. You should not need to calculate NPV for the exam, but you must understand what it means. The following example should help.

Time period	Income/ Revenue	Present value at 10% interest rate	Costs	Present value at 10% interest rate
0	0	0	200	200
1	50	45	100	91
2	100	83	0	0
3	300	225	0	0
TOTAL		353		291

NPV = 353-291 = 62

INTERNAL RATE OF RETURN (IRR): To explain this concept, think of a bank account. You put money in a bank account and expect to get a return of 2% in the USA. You can think of a project in the same way. If a company has more than one project in which to invest, the company may look at the projects' returns and then select the highest one. If you understand this concept, you should do fine on the exam.

IRR does get confusing when you give it a formal definition. DEFINITION: *The rate (read it as interest rate) at which the project inflows (revenues) and project outflows (costs) are equal.* Calculating IRR is complex and requires the aid of a computer. You will not have to perform any IRR calculations on the exam. You will need to understand the definition and be able to answer questions like the following:

You have two projects to choose from; Project A with an IRR of 21% or Project B with an IRR of 15%. Which one would you prefer?

The answer is Project A.

PAYBACK PERIOD: The number of time periods it takes to recover your investment in the project before you start accumulating profit. For example:

You have two projects to choose from; Project A with a payback period of six months or Project B with a payback period of eighteen months. Which one would you prefer?

The answer is Project A.

BENEFIT COST RATIO (BCR): Compares the benefits to the costs of different projects where benefits are the same as revenue, or sometimes referred to as "payback." Remember that revenue is not the same as profit. A BCR of >1 means the benefits are greater than the costs. A BCR of <1 means the costs are greater than the benefits. A BCR of 1 means the costs and benefits are the same.

> *If the BCR of project A is 2.3 and the BCR of project B is 1.7, which project would you select? The answer is A, the project with the higher BCR.*

> *A BCR of 1.7 means?*
> *   A) The costs are greater than the benefits*
> *   B) Payback is 1.7 times the costs*
> *   C) Profit is 1.7 times the costs*
> *   D) Costs are 1.7 times the profit*

> *The answer is B. BCR is talking about revenue (payback) not just the smaller figure of profits.*

OPPORTUNITY COST: The opportunity given up by selecting one project over another. NOTE: This does not require any calculation. See the example below.

> *You have two projects to choose from; Project A with an NPV of US $45,000 or Project B with an NPV of US $85,000. What is the opportunity cost of selecting project B?*

> *The answer is $45,000.*

Exercise: Test yourself! For each row on the following chart, enter the letter of the project you would select if the following information were provided.

	Project A	Project B	Which project would you pick?
Net Present Value	$95,000	$75,000	
IRR	13%	17%	
Payback Period	16 months	21 months	
Benefit Cost Ratio	2.79	1.3	

Answer:

	Project A	Project B	Which project would you pick?
Net Present Value	$95,000	$75,000	A
IRR	13%	17%	B
Payback Period	16 months	21 months	A
Benefit Cost Ratio	2.79	1.3	A

Chapter 6
Cost Management

SUNK COSTS: Expended costs. People unfamiliar with accounting standards might have trouble with the following question:

You have a project with an initial budget of US $1,000,000. You are halfway through the project and have spent US $2,000,000. Do you consider the US $1,000,000 over budget when determining whether to continue with the project?

The answer is no! Be aware that accounting standards say that sunk costs should not be considered when deciding whether to continue with a troubled project.

LAW OF DIMINISHING RETURNS: The more you put into something, the less you get out of it. For example, adding twice as many resources to a task may not get the task done in half the time.

WORKING CAPITAL: Current assets minus current liabilities, or the amount of money the company has to invest, including investment in projects.

PROJECT SELECTION METHODS: The following items were described above and also are considered techniques to help select which projects will be undertaken:
- Present Value
- Net Present Value
- Internal Rate of Return
- Payback Period
- Benefit Cost Ratio

TYPES OF COST: There are several ways to look at costs when creating a budget. Feedback from people taking the exam indicates that it is difficult to differentiate between these types of costs. Therefore, it would be wise to spend time studying these types of costs even though only about three questions on the exam reference them. The examples below should help you answer questions about these types of costs.

A cost can be either variable or fixed:

- **VARIABLE COST** – Any cost that changes with the amount of production or the amount of work. Examples include the cost of material, supplies and wages.

- **FIXED COST** – Costs that do not change as production changes. Examples include set up, rental, etc.

A cost can be either direct or indirect:

- **DIRECT COST** – Costs that are directly attributable to the work on the project. Examples are team travel, team wages, recognition and costs of material used on the project.

- **INDIRECT COST** – Overhead items or costs incurred for the benefit of more than one project. Examples include taxes, fringe benefits and janitorial services.

© 2002 - 1998 Rita Mulcahy, PMP
PHONE: (952) 846-4484 - EMAIL: info@rmcproject.com - WEB: www.rmcproject.com

DEPRECIATION: Large assets (e.g., equipment) purchased by a company lose value over time. Accounting standards call this depreciation. Several methods are used to account for depreciation. The exam asks you what they are. You do not have to perform any calculations. (See, I told you I could make this easy for you!) The following information is all you need to know.

There are two forms of depreciation:

1. **STRAIGHT LINE DEPRECIATION** – The same amount of depreciation is taken each year.

> EXAMPLE: A US $1,000 item with a ten-year useful life and no salvage value (how much the item is worth at the end of its life) would be depreciated at US $100 per year.

2. **ACCELERATED DEPRECIATION** – For the exam you only need to know:

   - There are two forms of accelerated depreciation. You do not have to understand what these two forms mean or do any calculations.
     – Double Declining Balance
     – Sum of the Years Digits
   - Accelerated depreciation depreciates faster than straight line.

> EXAMPLE: A $1,000 item with a ten-year useful life and no salvage value (how much the item is worth at the end of its life) would be depreciated at $180 the first year, $150 the second, $130 the next, etc.

LIFE CYCLE COSTING: This is an interesting concept that slips into the exam every once in awhile. The project we are working on has a life after it is completed. The project manager and the company want the project costs to be as low as possible. However, if the project manager does not consider the life cycle costs, project costs may be low at the expense of greater overall costs for the rest of the life of the project – the operations and maintenance phase. By including this concept on the exam, PMI® is effectively warning us that we should look at and manage life cycle costs instead of just project costs.

VALUE ANALYSIS: (Sometimes referred to as value engineering in the real world.) Find a less costly way to do the same scope of work. It requires the systematic use of techniques to identify the required project functions, assign values to these functions and provide functions at the lowest overall cost without loss of performance. If a team or someone else is looking at decreasing project cost but maintaining the same scope of work, they are performing value analysis.

Chapter 6
Cost Management

1. One common way to compute Completion (EAC) is to take the Budget at Completion (BAC) and:

   A. Divide by SPI
   B. Multiply by SPI
   C. Multiply by CPI
   D. Divide by CPI

2. Estimate at Completion (EAC) is a periodic evaluation of:

   A. Cost of work completed
   B. Value of work performed
   C. Anticipated total cost at project completion
   D. What it will cost to finish the job

3. If Earned Value (EV) = 350, Actual Cost (AC) = 400, Planned Value (PV) = 325, what is Cost Variance (CV)?

   A. 350
   B. -75
   C. 400
   D. -50

4. Rearranging resources so that a constant number of resources are used each month is called:

   A. Crashing
   B. Floating
   C. Leveling
   D. Fast tracking

5. Double declining balance is a form of:

   A. Decelerated depreciation
   B. Straight line depreciation
   C. Accelerated depreciation
   D. Life cycle costing

6. Analogous estimating:

   A. Uses bottom-up estimating techniques
   B. Is used most frequently during the executing phase of the project
   C. Uses top-down estimating techniques
   D. Uses actual detailed historical costs

7. The cost of choosing one project and giving up another is called:

   A. Fixed cost
   B. Sunk cost
   C. NPV
   D. Opportunity cost

© 2002 - 1998 Rita Mulcahy, PMP
PHONE: (952) 846-4484 - EMAIL: info@rmcproject.com - WEB: www.rmcproject.com

8. **The main focus of life cycle costing is to:**

   A. Estimate installation costs
   B. Estimate the cost of operation and maintenance
   C. Consider installation costs when planning the project costs
   D. Consider operation and maintenance costs in making project decisions

9. **Cost performance measurement is BEST done through which of the following:**

   A. Asking for a percent complete from each team member and reporting that in the monthly progress report
   B. Calculating earned value and using the indexes and other calculations to report past performance and forecast future performance
   C. Using the 50/50 rule and making sure the life cycle cost is less than the project cost
   D. Focusing on the amount expended last month and what will be expended the following month

10. **A Cost Performance Index (CPI) of 0.89 means:**

   A. At this time, we expect the total project to cost 89% more than planned
   B. When the project is completed we will have spent 89% more than planned
   C. The project is only progressing at 89% of that planned
   D. The project is only getting 89 cents out of every dollar invested

11. **A Schedule Performance Index (SPI) of 0.76 means:**

   A. We are over budget
   B. We are ahead of schedule
   C. We are only progressing at 76% of the rate originally planned
   D. We are only progressing at 24% of the rate originally planned

12. **Which of the following is not needed in order to come up with a project estimate?**

   A. WBS
   B. Network Diagram
   C. Risks
   D. Change control procedure

13. **Which of the following is a benefit of an analogous project estimate?**

   A. Estimates will be closer to what the work will actually require
   B. It is based on a detailed understanding of what the work requires
   C. It gives the project team an understanding of management's expectations
   D. It helps the project manager determine if the project will meet the schedule

14. **Which of the following is an example of a parametric estimate?**

   A. Dollars per module
   B. Learning bend
   C. Bottom-up
   D. CPM

Chapter 6
Cost Management

15. An order of magnitude estimate is made during which project management phase?

A. Planning
B. Closing
C. Executing
D. Initiating

16. How close to actual costs should a budget estimate be?

A. -75% to +25%
B. -10% to +25%
C. +10% to -25%
D. -5% to +10%

17. Which factors would NOT be considered when choosing between two projects to undertake?

A. NPV
B. BCR
C. Payback period
D. Law of diminishing returns

18. If project A has a Net Present Value (NPV) of US $30,000 and project B has an NPV of US $50,000, what is the opportunity cost if project B is selected?

A. $23,000
B. $30,000
C. $20,000
D. $50,000

19. Which type of cost is team training?

A. Direct
B. NPV
C. Indirect
D. Fixed

20. Project setup costs are an example of:

A. Variable costs
B. Fixed costs
C. Overhead costs
D. Opportunity costs

21. Value analysis is performed to get:

A. More value from the cost analysis
B. Management to buy into the project
C. The team to buy into the project
D. A less costly way of doing the same scope of work

22. Who has the cost risk in a fixed price contract?

A. The team
B. Buyer
C. Seller
D. Management

© 2002 - 1998 Rita Mulcahy, PMP
PHONE: (952) 846-4484 - EMAIL: info@rmcproject.com - WEB: www.rmcproject.com

23. Which of the following represents the estimated value of the work actually accomplished?

   A. EV
   B. PV
   C. AC
   D. ACWS

24. You have four projects from which to choose one. Project A is being done over a six year period and has a Net Present Value (NPV) of US $70,000. Project B is being done over a three year period and has an NPV of US $30,000. Project C is being done over a five year period and has an NPV of US $40,000. Project D is being done over a one year period and has an NPV of US $60,000. Which project would you choose?

   A. Project A
   B. Project B
   C. Project C
   D. Project D

25. Project A has an Internal Rate of Return (IRR) of 21%. Project B has an IRR of 7%. Project C has an IRR of 31%. Project D has an IRR of 19%. Which of these would be the BEST project?

   A. Project A
   B. Project B
   C. Project C
   D. Project D

26. As a project manager, you are presented with the following information on the Net Present Value (NPV) for several potential projects. Which project is your BEST choice?

   A. Project A with an NPV of US $95,000
   B. Project B with an NPV of US $120,000
   C. Project C with an NPV of US $20,000
   D. Project D with an NPV of -US $30,000

27. Your company can accept three possible projects. Project A has a Net Present Value (NPV) of US $30,000 and will take six years to complete. Project B has an NPV of US $60,000 and will take three years to complete. Project C has an NPV of US $90,000 and will take four years to complete. Based on this information, which project would you pick?

   A. They all have the same value
   B. Project A
   C. Project B
   D. Project C

Cost Management Questions Only For the PMP® Exam

28. The seller tells you that your activities have resulted in an increase in their costs. You should:

    A. Issue a change to the project costs
    B. Have a meeting with management
    C. Ask the seller for supporting information
    D. Deny any wrongdoing

29. An analysis shows that you will have a cost overrun at the end of the project. Which of the following should you do?

    A. Evaluate options to crash or fast track the project
    B. Meet with management to find out what to do
    C. Meet with the customer to look for costs to eliminate
    D. Add a reserve to the project

30. A new store development project requires the purchase of various equipment, machinery and furniture. The department responsible for the development recently centralized its external purchase process and standardized its new order system. In which document can these new procedures be found?

    A. Project scope statement
    B. WBS
    C. Staff management plan
    D. Organizational policies

31. Early in the life of your project, you are having a discussion with the sponsor about what estimating techniques should be used. You want a form of expert judgment, but the sponsor argues for analogous estimating. It would be BEST to:

    A. Agree to analogous estimating as it is a form of expert judgment
    B. Suggest life cycle costing as a compromise
    C. Determine why the sponsor wants such an accurate estimate
    D. Try to convince the sponsor to allow expert judgment because it is typically more accurate

32. You've just completed the initiating phase of a small project and are moving into the planning phase when a project stakeholder asks you for the project's budget and cost baseline. What should you tell her?

    A. The project budget can be found in the project's charter, which has just been completed
    B. The project budget and baseline will not be finalized and accepted until the planning phase is completed
    C. The project plan will not contain the project's budget and baseline; this is a small project
    D. It is impossible to complete an estimate before the project plan is created

33. The project manager is allocating overall cost estimates to individual activities or work packages to establish a baseline for measuring project performance. What step is this?

    A. Cost management
    B. Cost estimating
    C. Cost budgeting
    D. Cost control

34. **You are asked to prepare a budget for completing a project that was started last year and then shelved for six months. All the following would be included in the budget EXCEPT?**

    A. Fixed cost
    B. Sunk cost
    C. Direct cost
    D. Variable cost

35. **To accommodate a new project in your department, you need to move resources from one project to another. Because your department is currently working at capacity, moving resources will inevitably delay the project from which you move resources. You should move resources from which of the following projects?**

    A. Project A with a benefit cost ratio of 0.8, no project charter, and four resources
    B. Project B with a net present value of US $60,000, twelve resources, and variable costs between US $1,000 and US $2,000 per month
    C. Project C with an opportunity cost of US $300,000, no project control plan, and an internal rate of return of 12%
    D. Project D with indirect costs of US $20,000 and thirteen resources

36. **A manufacturing project has an Schedule Performance Index (SPI) of 0.89 and a Cost Performance Index (CPI) of 0.91. Generally, what is the BEST explanation for why this occurred?**

    A. The equipment purchased for the project was more expensive than expected
    B. At least one task has taken more time than expected
    C. Less experienced resources were used
    D. The project baseline was changed more than once

37. **Although the stakeholders thought there was enough money in the budget, halfway through the project the Cost Performance Index (CPI) is 0.7. To determine the root cause, several stakeholders audit the project and discover the project cost budget was estimated analogously. Although the task estimates add up to the project estimate, the stakeholders think something was missing in how the estimate was completed. Which of the following describes what was missing?**

    A. Estimated costs should be used to measure CPI
    B. SPI should be used, not CPI
    C. Bottom-up estimating should have been used
    D. Past history was not taken into account

38. **You are a project manager for a large consulting firm. Your superior has just asked you for your input on a decision about which project your company should pursue. Project A has an internal rate of return of 12%. Project B has a predicted Benefit Cost Ratio (BCR) of 1:3. Project C has an opportunity cost of US $75,000. Project D has a payback period of six months. If you had to choose based on this data, which project would you select?**

    A. Project A
    B. Project B
    C. Project C
    D. Project D

Chapter 6
Cost Management

39. You are about to take over a project from another project manager and find out the following information about the project. Task Z has an early start of day 15 and a late start of day 20, task Z is a difficult task, Cost Performance Index (CPI) is 1.1, Schedule Performance Index (SPI) is 0.8, and there are eleven stakeholders on the project. Based on this information, which of the following would you be the MOST concerned about?

A. Schedule
B. Float
C. Cost
D. The number of available resources

40. During the project execution, a large number of changes are made to the project. The project manager should:

A. Wait until all changes are known and print out a new schedule
B. Make changes as needed but retain the schedule baseline
C. Make only the changes approved by management
D. Talk to management before any changes are made

© 2002 - 1998 Rita Mulcahy, PMP
PHONE: (952) 846-4484 - EMAIL: info@rmcproject.com - WEB: www.rmcproject.com

Cost Management Answers

1. **Answer:** D

    Explanation: This question is asking for the formula for EAC, which is BAC/CPI. Notice how you will have to remember the formula to get the questions correct.

2. **Answer:** C

    Explanation: When you look at earned value, many of the terms have similar definitions. This could get you into trouble. Since the EAC means the estimate at completion, choice C must be the best answer. Choice D is the definition of ETC, estimate to complete.

3. **Answer:** D

    Explanation: $CV = EV - AC$

4. **Answer:** C

    Explanation: The key to this question is the phrase "constant number used each month." Only leveling, choice C, has such an effect on the schedule.

5. **Answer:** C

    Explanation: We need to know that double declining balance is a form of depreciation. That eliminates choice D. We also know that double declining balance is a form of accelerated depreciation. Therefore, C is the correct response.

6. **Answer:** C

    Explanation: Here is a case where two answers appear to be correct, C and D. However, you do not need to use historical costs for an analogous estimate. Therefore, C is the most correct answer. Analogous estimating may use management's opinion (choice B), but that opinion relates to the project cost, not task cost.

7. **Answer:** D

    Explanation: Choices A and B are types of costs and do not relate to "giving up another." Choice C is a way to determine today's value of a future cash flow and does not deal with the quoted phrase. The definition of opportunity cost includes the quoted phrase and thus it is the best answer.

8. **Answer:** D

    Explanation: Life cycle costing looks at operating and maintenance costs and balances them with the project costs to try to reduce the cost across its entire life.

9. **Answer:** B

    Explanation: Asking percent complete is not a best practice since it is usually a guess or inaccurate. Often the easiest work is done first on a project, throwing off any percentage calculations of work remaining. It may be a good thing to use the 50/50 rule, as in choice C. But the 50/50 rule is not necessarily included in the progress report and the second part of the sentence is incorrect. The life cycle cost cannot be lower than the project cost as the life cycle cost includes the project cost. Choice D is often done by inexperienced project managers who know of nothing else. Not only does it provide little information, but also it cannot be used to predict the future. Choice B is your best answer since it looks at the past and by using this information future costs can be estimated.

10. **Answer:** D

    Explanation: The CPI is less than one so the situation is bad. Choice D is the best answer.

11. **Answer:** C

    Explanation: Earned value questions ask for a calculation or an interpretation of the results. See the tricks under this topic in this book.

12. **Answer:** D

    Explanation: A change control procedure is not required to obtain estimates, but without the other three, you cannot develop the estimates. You need the WBS to define the tasks, the network diagram to see the dependencies and the risks to determine contingency. NOTE: These are high-level risks, not the detailed risks we identify later in planning.

13. **Answer:** C

    Explanation: Remember that analogous estimates are top-down, high-level estimates. Therefore choices A and B cannot be correct. The project manager needs more than an analogous estimate to determine if the project will meet the schedule (choice D). It is a benefit to know management's expectations of how much the project will cost so that any differences between the analogous estimate and the detailed bottom-up estimate can be reconciled in planning. The best choice is C.

14. **Answer:** A

    Explanation: Parametric estimates use a mathematical model to predict project cost or time.

15. **Answer:** D

    Explanation: Because this estimate has a wide range, it is done during initiating when very little is known about the project.

16. **Answer:** B

    Explanation: This question is designed to determine whether a project manager understands that estimates should be in a range and what are the standard ranges.

17. **Answer:** D

   Explanation: The law of diminishing returns has nothing to do with choosing between projects.

18. **Answer:** B

   Explanation: The opportunity cost is just the value of the project that was not selected - the lost opportunity.

19. **Answer:** A

   Explanation: You are training the team on skills required for the project. The cost is directly related to the project and thus a direct cost.

20. **Answer:** B

   Explanation: A setup cost does not change as production on the project changes. Therefore, it is a fixed cost.

21. **Answer:** D

   Explanation: Notice that you need to know the definition of value analysis to answer this question. Also notice the other choices could be considered correct by someone who does not know the definition.

22. **Answer:** C

   Explanation: If the costs are more than expected under a fixed price contract, the seller must pay those costs. As explained in the procurement chapter, "cost risk" refers to the person who will have to pay for the added cost if costs escalate. Because the price is fixed, the seller will have to pay any increased costs out of their profit. Naturally, this does not include increased PRICE due to change orders. A fixed price contract, and the PRICE, could be changed with change orders.

23. **Answer:** A

   Explanation: It can be confusing to differentiate earned value terms from each other. The definition presented here is for EV or earned value, so choice A is the best choice.

24. **Answer:** A

   Explanation: In using NPV, the number of years is already included in the calculation. You simply pick the project with the highest NPV.

25. **Answer:** C

   Explanation: Remember, the internal rate of return is similar to the interest rate you get from the bank. The higher the rate is, the better the return.

26. **Answer:** B

   Explanation: You should pick the higher number.

Chapter 6
Cost Management

27. **Answer:** D

Explanation: You already incorporate the project length when computing NPV. You would choose the project that provides the most value, in this case the project with the highest NPV.

28. **Answer:** C

Explanation: This is a professional responsibility/procurement/cost question. The situation described involves a claim. The best thing to do would be to get supporting information to find out what happened and take corrective action for the future. After choice C and negotiation, choice A would most likely occur. Choice D is unethical. Choice B is a meeting with YOUR management and should not occur until you have all the information.

29. **Answer:** A

Explanation: The first thing to do is evaluate (choice A). Once that is done, a project manager could meet with management or the customer (choices B and C). A reserve (choice D) is created before costs are incurred, not when they occur.

30. **Answer:** D

Explanation: Procedures for the rental and purchase of supplies and equipment are found in the organizational policies.

31. **Answer:** A

Explanation: This is a tricky question. In order to pick the best answer, you need to realize that analogous estimating is a form of expert judgment. Notice choice C. "Determine why," sounds like a good idea, but look at the rest of the sentence. Analogous estimates are not accurate. Reading every word of this choice helps eliminate it.

32. **Answer:** B

Explanation: The overall project budget (choice A) may be included in the project charter but not the detailed costs. Even small projects (choice C) should have a budget and schedule. It is not impossible to create a project budget before the project plan is created (choice D). It is just not wise, as the budget will not be accurate.

33. **Answer:** C

Explanation: Choice A is too general. The estimates are already created in this example, so the answer is not B. The answer is not D, cost control, because the baseline has not been created. The correct answer is C.

34. **Answer:** B

Explanation: Sunk costs (choice B) are expended costs and the rule is that they should not be considered when deciding whether to continue with a troubled project.

35. **Answer:** A

Explanation: A project without a charter is a project without support. The information provided for the other projects does not justify selecting them. Even the number of resources is not relevant since the number of resources for the new project is not supplied.

36. **Answer:** C

Explanation: To answer this question you need to determine which answer could negatively affect both time and cost. Choice A would most likely affect only cost. Choices B and D would most likely affect only schedule. Less experienced resources will take longer and thus most likely cost more. If you thought choice B was correct, you have incorrectly equated time with cost. Imagine that no work at all was done on the task for a period of time. The task would then take longer but not necessarily cost more.

37. **Answer:** C

Explanation: Actual costs are used to measure CPI, and there's no reason to use SPI in this situation, so choices A and B are not correct. Using past history (choice D) is another way of saying "analogous." The best way to estimate is bottom-up (choice C). Such estimating would have improved the overall quality of the estimate.

38. **Answer:** A

Explanation: This is a question about project selection and could easily be included in other chapters. In order to interpret the information, you need to know what each item is. Based on the information provided there is no reason to recommend or not recommend projects C or D. The BCR for project B is unfavorable. This leaves only project A as providing a clear benefit.

39. **Answer:** A

Explanation: This is one of those questions that combines topics from various knowledge areas. Did you fall into the trap of calculating the float for Z? The amount of float for one task and the number of stakeholders does not tell you anything in this case, so B or D cannot be the best answer. The CPI is greater than one and the SPI is less than one. Therefore, the thing to be most worried about would be schedule.

40. **Answer:** B

Explanation: A project manager must be more in control of the project than choices C and D reflect. Choice A is a common error many project managers make. Instead, the project manager should be controlling the project all during the completion of the project.

Chapter 6
Cost Management

Time and Cost Game

The following game is designed to improve your ability to correctly answer the difficult Time and Cost questions. It is best done verbally with more than one person. The second person can be a spouse, child or someone else studying for the PMP® exam.

Cut out the cards along the lines provided. Try to answer as many questions as you can in 10 minutes. If you answer 10 questions correctly in ten minutes, this should prove to you that you will not have a time problem taking the exam. (The exam allows about 1¼ minute per question.) GOOD LUCK!

- FOR ONE PARTICIPANT: Cover the answers.

- FOR TWO PARTICIPANTS: One person asks the questions and the other answers.

- FOR MORE THAN TWO PARTICIPANTS: One person asks the questions and the others answer. One of those answering should also keep track of the number of correct answers.

Q: What estimating methods can be drawn with an activity-on-line diagram? **A:** PERT and CPM	**Q:** What estimating method would use optimistic time estimates? **A:** PERT	**Q:** "How much work should be done" has what earned value name? **A:** PV
Q: The critical path is? **A:** The longest duration path in the network. The shortest time to complete the project.	**Q:** What is the PERT formula? **A:** $(P + 4M + O)/6$	**Q:** What does the schedule variance tell you? **A:** How much you are behind or ahead of schedule.
Q: What estimating methods use dummy activities? **A:** PERT and CPM	**Q:** What does a finish-to-start relationship mean? **A:** One task must finish before the next can start.	**Q:** What does the estimate at completion tell you? **A:** What we now expect the total project to cost.
Q: Why would you want to crash a project? **A:** To shorten the project duration.	**Q:** Name one of the differences between bar charts and network diagrams. **A:** Bar charts do not show logical relationships between activities.	**Q:** What are sunk costs? **A:** Expended costs.
Q: What does a milestone chart show? **A:** Dates of significant events on the project.	**Q:** What is the duration of a milestone? **A:** Zero	**Q:** What is analogous estimating? **A:** Top-down estimating.

Chapter 6
Cost Management

Intentionally
left
blank

Q: What are fixed costs? **A:** Costs that do not change with project activity.	**Q:** What are direct costs? **A:** Costs incurred directly by the project.	**Q:** What is the earned value name for "how much you have spent to date?" **A:** AC
Q: What is value analysis? **A:** Finding a less costly way to complete the work without affecting quality.	**Q:** What is a management reserve? **A:** An amount of time or money set aside to cover risks.	**Q:** What is the cost variance formula? **A:** EV - AC
Q: Cost risk is greater for the buyer in what type of contract? **A:** Cost Reimbursable	**Q:** What is a heuristic? **A:** Rule of thumb	**Q:** What does present value mean? **A:** The value today of future cash flows.
Q: What is slack? **A:** LS − ES, LF − EF. The amount of time an activity can be delayed without delaying the project.	**Q:** Why would a project manager want to use resource leveling? **A:** To smooth the peaks and valleys of monthly resource usage consumed by the project.	**Q:** What does a BCR of 2.5 mean? **A:** The benefits are 2 ½ times the costs.
Q: A critical path task will generally have how much slack? **A:** Zero	**Q:** What is parametric estimating? **A:** Using mathematical relationships found in historical information to create estimates (e.g., dollars per foot).	**Q:** What is the range of accuracy with a budget estimate? **A:** (-10% to +25%)

Quality Management
(*PMBOK® GUIDE* Chapter 8)

Hot Topics

- Quality planning
- Quality assurance
- Quality control
- Control chart
  - Control limit
  - Assignable cause
  - Rule of seven
  - Specification limits
  - Out of control
- Definition of quality
- Prevention over inspection
- Quality philosophy
- Pareto diagram
- Gold plating
- Definition of quality management
- Total quality management
- Quality control tools
- Quality audits
- Continuous improvement
- Marginal analysis
- Responsibility for quality
- Impact of poor quality
- Cost of conformance and non-conformance
- Normal distribution
- Standard deviation
- 3 or 6 sigma
- Mean
- Variable, Attribute
- Probability
- ISO 9000
- Mutually exclusive
- Statistical independence
- Fishbone diagram
- Benefit/cost analysis
- Benchmarking
- Flowchart
- Just in time
- Design of experiments
- Cost of quality
- Statistical sampling

Quality-related questions can be confusing because PMI® may espouse a quality philosophy that is different from that of your company. Also, many of the topics on the exam are not in the *PMBOK® Guide*. Read the *PMBOK® Guide* Quality chapter and this chapter carefully and MEMORIZE the definitions provided. Many students report that the definitions are extremely important for the exam. There may be fifteen questions that relate to control charts and definitions.

QUALITY PHILOSOPHY: This is listed as a separate item to make certain you notice it. You must understand PMI®'s approach to quality because it is different from what most people have learned. PMI®'s philosophy can be illustrated in the definitions of quality, gold plating and prevention over inspection.

DEFINITION OF QUALITY: Quality is defined as *conformance to requirements and fitness of use.* MEMORIZE this phrase to help you answer about four questions. It means the project must produce what it said it would produce and what it produces must satisfy real needs.

The definition of quality ties into what was mentioned in Framework under the definition of stakeholder. The project manager should perform careful and accurate needs analysis at the beginning of the project to ensure stakeholder satisfaction. These requirements become the foundation of the scope of work.

The project manager's role during the project is to simply complete what has been committed to. Notice that quality is NOT giving the customer extras. PMI®'s philosophy is that quality is doing what you said you were going to do.

GOLD PLATING: PMI® does not recommend giving the customer extras (e.g., extra functionality, higher-quality components, and extra scope of work or better performance). Gold plating adds no value to the project. Often, such additions are included based on the project team's impression of what the customer would like. This impression may not be accurate. Considering that only 26% of all projects succeed, project managers would be better off spending their time seeing that projects conform to requirements.

PREVENTION OVER INSPECTION: Prevention over inspection and the quality philosophy flow through many of the questions on the exam. Many years ago, the main focus of quality was on inspection (e.g., check production after items are produced). The cost of doing so (cost of nonconformance, mentioned later) is so high that it is better to spend money on preventing problems. QUALITY MUST BE PLANNED IN, NOT INSPECTED IN! This is part of PMI®'s quality philosophy and frequently comes up on the exam.

MARGINAL ANALYSIS: Optimal quality is reached at the point where the incremental revenue from improvement equals the incremental cost to secure it.

DEFINITION OF QUALITY MANAGEMENT (page 95): "The processes required to ensure that the project will satisfy the needs for which it was undertaken." This can also mean the same thing as completing the project with no deviations from the project requirements. In the *PMBOK® Guide*, quality management includes quality planning, quality assurance and quality control.

CONTINUOUS IMPROVEMENT or KAIZEN: Small improvements in products or processes to reduce costs and ensure consistency of performance of products or services. These two words are taken to mean the same thing on the exam, however, in Japan this is just a word, not a quality movement. Kaizen means Kai (alter) and Zen (make better or improve). In the United States and most of Western Europe, improvements are thought of as BIG improvements. In Japan, improvements are thought of as small improvements.

JUST IN TIME (JIT): This is an approach to decrease the amount of inventory that a company carries, thereby decreasing the investment in inventory. A just in time philosophy directs a company to improve quality (forces attention to quality) because extra materials are not available.

ISO 9000: A standard created by the International Standards Organization (ISO) to help ensure that organizations have quality procedures and that they follow them. Many people think that ISO 9000 tells you what quality should be or describes a recommended quality system. This is not correct.

TOTAL QUALITY MANAGEMENT (TQM): A philosophy that encourages companies and their employees to focus on finding ways to continuously improve the quality of their business practices and products.

MUTUALLY EXCLUSIVE: Two events are said to be mutually exclusive if they cannot both occur in a single trial. For example, flipping a coin once cannot result in both a head and a tail.

STATISTICAL INDEPENDENCE: The probability of one event occurring does not affect the probability of another event occurring (e.g., the probability of rolling a six on a die is statistically independent from the probability of rolling a five on the next roll).

PROBABILITY: The likelihood that something will occur, usually expressed as a percent.

NORMAL DISTRIBUTION: A normal distribution is the most common probability density distribution chart that is in the shape of a bell curve and is used to measure variations.

STANDARD DEVIATION (or sigma): A measure of how far you are from the mean (the dotted vertical line) not the median. (Remember $(P - O)/6$ is the PERT formula for standard deviation using optimistic, pessimistic and most likely estimates.)

3 OR 6 SIGMA: Sigma is another name for standard deviation. 3 or 6 sigma represents the level of quality that a company has decided to try to achieve. At 6 sigma, only 1 out of 10,000 doors produced will have a problem. At 3 sigma, 27 out of 10,000 will have a problem. Therefore, 6 sigma represents a higher quality standard than 3 sigma. 3 or 6 sigma are also used to calculate the upper and lower control limits in a control chart, described later.

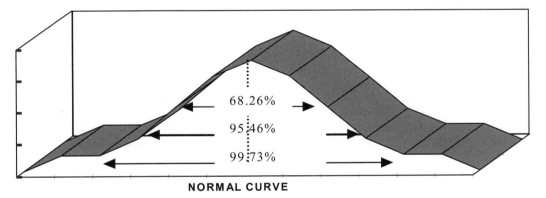

NORMAL CURVE

You should MEMORIZE:
- Half the curve is above the mean (with a positive value) and half the curve is below the mean (with a negative value). The left side of the mean is negative and the right side positive.
- +/- 1 sigma is equal to 68.26%
- +/- 2 sigma equals 95.46%
- +/- 3 sigma equals 99.73%
- +/- 6 sigma equals 99.99%

RESPONSIBILITY FOR QUALITY: The entire organization has responsibilities relating to quality. Therefore, read questions on this topic carefully. Determine to whom in the organization the question refers. PMI® is notorious for questions that seem ambiguous. The project manager has the ultimate responsibility for the quality of the product of the project, but each team member must check his or her work – self-inspection. Senior management has the ultimate responsibility for quality in the organization as a whole. It is not acceptable for a team member to simply complete the work and then turn it over to the project manager or their manager for checking. Work should meet the project requirements and testing should be done whenever appropriate before submission.

IMPACT OF POOR QUALITY: If you have poor quality, you have:
- Increased costs
- Low morale
- Lower customer satisfaction
- Increased risk

Increases in quality can result in increased productivity and cost effectiveness and decreased cost risk.

COST OF CONFORMANCE AND COST OF NONCONFORMANCE: PMI® and Deming (an expounder of quality philosophy) say that 85% of the costs of quality are the direct responsibility of management. Specifically, these costs are:

COST OF CONFORMANCE	COST OF NONCONFORMANCE
Quality training	Rework
Studies	Scrap
Surveys	Inventory costs
	Warranty costs

TRICKS FOR UNDERSTANDING THE DIFFERENCE BETWEEN QUALITY PLANNING, ASSURANCE, AND CONTROL: One of the major concerns people have while studying is how to understand the difference between quality planning, quality assurance and quality control. In addition to understanding these terms by reading this chapter, the following table will really help.

	Quality Planning	Quality Assurance	Quality Control
	Plan	Implement, check overall	Measure details
Tricks to understand the difference	What quality standards should we use on the project? How will we meet those standards?	What lessons can we find to improve quality – quality audit? Let's take the outputs of quality control measurement and see if we will meet the overall quality standards. Are our quality standards still appropriate?	Let's measure (test) the number of errors in this program. Let's measure schedule performance. Did we meet the specific quality standard?
Mostly done during	Planning	Executing	Controlling

TRICK: It is easier to determine if something is part of quality control (e.g., relates to one of the quality control tools) than to determine if it is part of one of the other quality processes. Therefore, always eliminate quality control first when you have questions on the exam that require you to differentiate between quality planning, assurance and control.

QUALITY PLANNING (page 97): In addition to the previous chart, quality planning is done concurrently with other project planning and includes:

- Identifying quality standards relevant to the project and determining how to satisfy them

- **BENCHMARKING** (page 98) – Looking at past projects to determine ideas for improvement and to provide a measure of quality performance

- **BENEFIT/COST ANALYSIS** (page 98) – Considering the benefits versus the costs of quality requirements

- **FLOWCHART** (page 99, 100) – Showing how a process or system flows from beginning to end and how the elements interrelate. It is used in quality planning to analyze potential future quality problems and determine quality standards. It is used in quality control to analyze quality problems. A fishbone diagram is an example of a flowchart.

- **DESIGN OF EXPERIMENTS** (page 99) – The use of experimentation or "what if" to determine what variables will improve quality.

- **COST OF QUALITY** (page 99) – Looking at how the costs of conformance and nonconformance to quality will cost the project and creating an appropriate balance. Costs of quality include prevention costs, appraisal costs and failure costs.

- **FISHBONE DIAGRAM** (Cause-and-Effect, Ishikawa, page 98) – This is a quality planning tool if used to determine what will define quality on the project (i.e., look toward the future). See also quality control.

QUALITY ASSURANCE (page 101): Quality assurance is primarily done during the executing phase of the project. In addition to the previous chart, quality assurance includes:

- The process of evaluating overall performance on a regular basis to provide confidence that the project will satisfy the relevant quality standards

- Re-evaluating quality standards, methods and procedures used on the project

- **QUALITY AUDITS** (page 101) – A structured review of quality activities that identifies lessons learned

Chapter 7
Quality Management

QUALITY CONTROL (page 102): Quality control is done during the controlling phase of the project and its focus is on the correctness of work. In addition to the chart above, quality control includes:

- The process of monitoring (inspecting, checking for correctness) specific project results to determine if they comply with relevant quality standards and to identify ways to eliminate causes of unsatisfactory performance

- Performance of the measurement or process, using quality control tools or checking the work. This usually involves using the following terms:

    VARIABLE: The characteristic you want to measure (e.g., size, shape, weight).

    ATTRIBUTE: The measurement (inches, pounds) that will tell if the sample is acceptable. Attributes can be subjective or objective and are the specific characteristics for which a product is built.

- **QUALITY CONTROL TOOLS** – The following is a list of all the control tools. Some will be described later.
    - Inspection – Checking the quality after work is completed
    - Pareto diagram
    - Fishbone diagram
    - Checklists
    - Statistical sampling
    - Control charts
    - Flowcharting – Described under quality planning
    - Trend analysis – Examining project results over time to evaluate performance

    PARETO DIAGRAM (page 103, 105): Projects always run into problems. Many project managers will attempt to resolve each problem that arises. However, this may not be the best use of the project manager's time. It might be worthwhile to graph the types of problems and the frequency of their occurrence in order to figure out which problem occurs more frequently and should be prevented. A Pareto diagram performs this function.

    The diagram is based on the 80/20 rule – 80% of the problems will come from 20% of the work. See *PMBOK® Guide* page 105 for a picture of a Pareto chart. Understand the following phrases:
    - The chart presents the information being examined in its order of priority and helps focus attention on the most critical issues
    - Prioritizes potential "causes" of the problems
    - Separates the critical few from the uncritical many

FISHBONE DIAGRAM (Cause-And-Effect, Ishikawa, page 98): The diagram illustrates how various causes and sub-causes relate to create potential problems. It looks like the bones of a fish. This is an example of one form of flowchart. The exam has used the following three phrases to describe this diagram. You should MEMORIZE these:

1. A creative way to look at the causes or potential causes of a problem

2. Helps stimulate thinking, organizes thoughts and generates discussion

3. Can be used to explore the factors that will result in a desired future outcome

The following, and *PMBOK® Guide* page 99, are illustrations of fishbone diagrams.

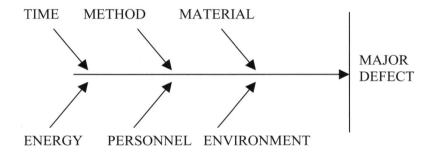

CHECKLIST: Contains a list of items to inspect or a picture of the item to be inspected with space to note any defects found.

STATISTICAL SAMPLING (page 103): Inspecting by choosing only part of a population - a sample. For example, we will study only 5% of the tables made to determine if we have met the quality standards for all the tables. It is best to take a sample of a population if studying the entire population would:

*   Take too long
*   Cost too much
*   Be too destructive
*   When we believe there are not many defects

CONTROL CHART (page 103): PMI® says that control charts are "graphic displays of the results, over time, of a process ... used to determine if the process is 'in control'." A manufacturer of doors knows that production can never be exact. The measurement of each door should, however, be within a range of normal and acceptable limits. A control chart helps monitor production and other processes to see if the process is within these limits and therefore if a problem exists.

To create a control chart, samples are taken, variables measured and attributes found. The attributes (size, for instance) are plotted on the chart (the small squares shown on the control chart exercise). The following can be found on a control chart:

UPPER AND LOWER CONTROL LIMITS – The acceptable range of variation of a process often shown as two dashed lines on a control chart. Every process is expected to have some variation - each door manufactured will not be exactly the same size. The acceptable range, between the upper and lower control limits, is determined by the organization's quality standard (e.g., 3 or 6 sigma). Data points within this range are generally thought of as "in control," excluding the rule of seven, and are an acceptable range of variation. Data points outside this range mean the process is out of control.

MEAN – A line in the middle of the control chart that shows the middle of the range of acceptable variation of the process.

SPECIFICATION LIMITS – Specification limits represent the customer's expectations or contractual requirements for performance and quality. Specification limits are characteristics of the measured process and are not inherent. Therefore, they can appear either inside or outside of the control limits. In other words, specification limits are not calculated based on the control chart, but are inputs from the customer. Specification limits will be outside the control limits on the control chart if the project can meet the specification limits. If the project cannot meet the specification limits, they will be within the control limits on the control chart. For the purposes of the exam, think of them as solid lines *outside* the upper and lower control limits on the chart.

OUT OF CONTROL – The process is out of a state of statistical control under either of two circumstances:
- A data point falls outside of the upper or lower control limit, or
- Non-random data points that are still within the upper and lower control limits, such as the rule of seven.

Think of "out of control" as a lack of consistency and predictability in the process.

RULE OF SEVEN – Is a rule of thumb or heuristic. It refers to non-random data points grouped together in a series that total seven on one side of the mean. The rule of seven tells you that although none of these points are outside of the control limits, they are not random and the process is out of control. This type of situation should be investigated and a cause found.

ASSIGNABLE CAUSE – A data point, or rule of seven, that requires investigation to determine the cause of the variation.

Exercise: Much of what is tested on control charts is not in the *PMBOK® Guide*. Find all examples of each item listed on one or both of the control charts shown on this page and place each item number next to its location on the chart. If you are unsure, take a guess and then review the control chart descriptions on the following page. These pictures represent two different control charts.

When you are able to pick out all the items in a control chart on the exercise, you should be ready to answer questions about control charts on the exam.

NOTE: The questions on the exam relating to control charts do not use pictures, but may ask questions that are easier to answer if you can picture a control chart in your mind. Because many people have excellent visual memory, this exercise is designed to make sure you understand control charts and can answer questions about them.

Exercise: Find the following on the charts below:

1. Upper control limit
2. Lower control limit
3. Assignable cause
4. The process is out of control
5. Normal and expected variation in the process
6. Rule of seven
7. Specification limits
8. Three sigma
9. Six sigma
10. Normal distribution curve

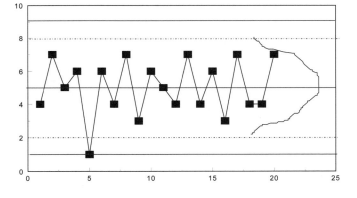

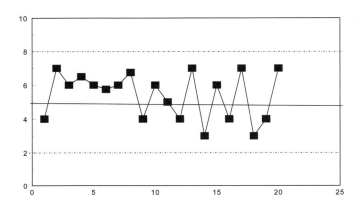

Answer:

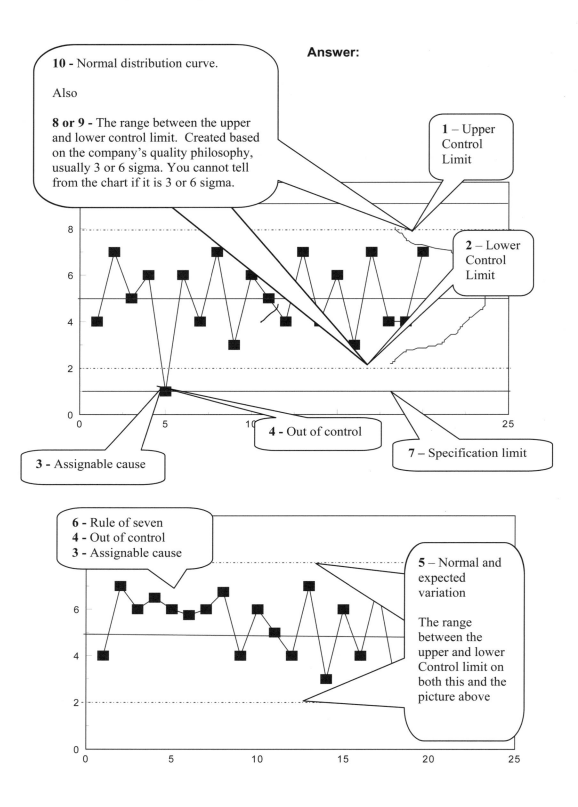

10 - Normal distribution curve.

Also

8 or 9 - The range between the upper and lower control limit. Created based on the company's quality philosophy, usually 3 or 6 sigma. You cannot tell from the chart if it is 3 or 6 sigma.

1 – Upper Control Limit

2 – Lower Control Limit

3 - Assignable cause

4 - Out of control

7 – Specification limit

6 - Rule of seven
4 - Out of control
3 - Assignable cause

5 – Normal and expected variation

The range between the upper and lower Control limit on both this and the picture above

Practice Exam for the CAPM® and PMP® Exams
Quality Management

1. When a product or service completely meets a customer's requirements:

    A. Quality is achieved
    B. The cost of quality is high
    C. The cost of quality is low
    D. The customer pays the minimum price

2. To what does the following sentence refer? "The concept of optimal quality level is reached at the point where the incremental revenue from product improvement equals the incremental cost to secure it."

    A. Quality control analysis
    B. Marginal analysis
    C. Standard quality analysis
    D. Conformance analysis

3. Who is ultimately responsible for quality management in the project?

    A. Project engineer
    B. Project manager
    C. Quality manager
    D. Team member

4. A project manager has been overwhelmed with problems on his project. He would like to identify the root cause of the problem in order to determine where to focus his attention. Which of the following tools would be BEST for the project manager to use?

    A. Pareto chart
    B. Conflict resolution techniques
    C. Fishbone diagram
    D. Trend analysis

5. A team is using a fishbone diagram to help determine what quality standards will be used on the project. What part of the quality management process are they in?

    A. Control
    B. Assurance
    C. Planning
    D. Variable analysis

6. Which of the following BEST describes the results of an increase in quality?

    A. Increased productivity, increased cost effectiveness, decreased cost risk
    B. Increased productivity, decreased cost effectiveness and increased cost risk
    C. Increased productivity, increased cost effectiveness and increased cost risk
    D. Increased productivity, decreased cost effectiveness and decreased cost risk

7.   From the project perspective, quality attributes:

A. Determine how effectively the performing organization supports the project
B. Provide the basis for judging the project's success or failure
C. Are specific characteristics for which a product is designed and tested
D. Are objective criteria that must be met

8.   Quality is:

A. Meeting and exceeding the customer's expectations
B. Adding extras to make the customer happy
C. Conformance to requirements and fitness of use
D. Conformance to management's requirements

9.   All the following are not examples of quality assurance EXCEPT?

A. Inspection
B. Team training
C. Pareto diagram
D. Fishbone diagram

10. Pareto diagrams help the project manager:

A. Focus on the most critical issues to improve quality
B. Focus on stimulating thinking
C. Explore a desired future outcome
D. Determine if a process is out of control

11. A control chart helps the project manager:

A. Focus on the most critical issues to improve quality
B. Focus on stimulating thinking
C. Explore a desired future outcome
D. Determine if a process is functioning within set limits

12. Testing the entire population would:

A. Take too long
B. Provide more information than wanted
C. Be mutually exclusive
D. Show many defects

13. All of the following are examples of the cost of nonconformance EXCEPT?

A. Rework
B. Quality training
C. Scrap
D. Warranty costs

14. Standard deviation is a measure of how:

A. Far the estimate is from the highest estimate
B. Far the measurement is from the mean
C. Correct the sample is
D. Much time remains in the project

15. What percentage of the total distribution are 3 sigma from the mean equal to?

A. 68.26%
B. 99.9%
C. 95.4%
D. 99.7%

16. All of the following are examples of a variable EXCEPT?

A. Size
B. Shape
C. Pounds
D. Weight

17. A control chart shows seven data points in a row on one side of the mean. What should be done?

A. A design of experiments
B. Adjust the chart to reflect the new mean
C. Find an assignable cause
D. This is the rule of seven and can be ignored

18. You are managing a project in a just in time environment. This will require more attention, because the amount of inventory in such an environment is generally:

A. 45%
B. 10%
C. 12%
D. 0%

19. An Ishikawa diagram helps to:

A. Put information in its order of priority
B. Explore past outcomes
C. Show team responsibilities
D. Show functional responsibilities

20. In planning your project, which would generally have the highest priority; quality, cost or schedule?

A. Cost is most important, quality next, and then schedule
B. Quality is more important than cost and schedule
C. Schedule is most important, quality next, and then cost
D. It is situational and must be decided by the project objectives

21. A project manager is using a cause-and-effect diagram with the team to determine how various factors might be linked to potential problems. In which step of the quality management process is the project manager involved?

A. Quality analysis
B. Quality assurance
C. Quality control
D. Quality planning

22. A project manager and team from a firm that designs railroad equipment are tasked to design a machine to load stone onto railroad cars. The design allows for 2% spillage, amounting to over two tons of spilled rock per day. In which of the following does the project manager document quality control, quality assurance and quality improvements for this project?

    A. Quality management plan
    B. Quality policy
    C. Control charts
    D. Project plan

Quality Management Questions Only For the PMP® Exam

23. During a team meeting, the team adds a specific area of extra work to the project because they have determined it would benefit the customer. What is wrong in this situation?

    A. The team is gold plating
    B. These efforts shouldn't be done in meetings
    C. Nothing. This is how to meet or exceed customer expectations
    D. Nothing. The project manager is in control of the situation.

24. The project team has created a plan describing how they will implement the quality policy. It addresses the organizational structure, responsibilities, procedures and other information about plans for quality. If this changes during the project, WHICH of the following plans will also change?

    A. Quality assurance
    B. Quality management
    C. Project
    D. Quality control

25. You are a project manager for a major information systems project when someone from the quality department comes to see you about beginning a quality audit of your project. The team, already under pressure to complete the project as soon as possible, objects to the audit. You should explain to the team that the purpose of a quality audit is:

    A. Part of an ISO 9000 investigation
    B. To check if the customer is following its quality process
    C. To identify lessons learned that can improve performance on the project
    D. To check the accuracy of costs submitted by the team

26. You are in the middle of a major new facility construction project. The structural steel is in place and the heating conduits are going into place when senior management informs you that he is worried that the project will not meet the quality standards. What should you do in this situation?

    A. Assure senior management that during quality planning it was determined the project would meet the quality standards
    B. Analogously estimate future results
    C. Form a quality assurance team
    D. Check the results from the last quality management plan

27. You are asked to select tools and techniques to implement a quality assurance program to supplement existing quality control activities. Which of the following would you choose?

   A. Quality audits
   B. Statistical sampling
   C. Pareto diagrams
   D. Trend analysis

28. The new software installation project is in progress. The project manager is working with the quality assurance department to improve everyone's confidence that the project will satisfy the quality standards. Which of the following MUST they have before they start this process?

   A. Quality problems
   B. Quality improvement
   C. Quality control measurements
   D. Rework

29. The project you are working on has an increase in cost effectiveness, increased productivity and increased morale. What might be the reason for these changes?

   A. Project goals are in line with those of the company
   B. Increased quality
   C. Management's focus on cost containment
   D. Rewards presented for individual efforts

30. A project manager has just taken over the project from another project manager during the executing phase. The previous project manager created a project budget, determined communications requirements and went on to complete work packages. What should the new project manager do NEXT?

   A. Coordinate performance of work packages
   B. Identify quality standards
   C. Begin risk identification
   D. Execute the project plan

31. A project is facing a major change to its project deliverables. If the project manager is involved in determining which quality standards are relevant to the change, the project manager must be involved in:

   A. Quality management
   B. Quality assurance
   C. Quality planning
   D. Quality control

32. A project team member comes to the project manager during project execution to tell him that they feel the project cannot meet its quality standards. The project manager calls a meeting of the affected stakeholders to work through the problem. Which step of the quality management process is the project manager in?

    A. Quality assurance
    B. Quality analysis
    C. Quality control
    D. Quality planning

33. At the end of a project, a project manager determines that the project has added four areas of functionality and three areas of performance. The customer has expressed satisfaction with the project. What does this mean in terms of success of the project?

    A. The project was an unqualified success
    B. The project was unsuccessful because it was gold plated
    C. The project was unsuccessful because the customer being happy means they would have paid more for the work
    D. The project was successful because the team had a chance to learn new areas of functionality and the customer was satisfied

Quality Management Answers

1. **Answer:** A

    Explanation: As a general rule, one cannot say that quality (as defined in the question) is either of high or low cost (choices B and C) or that it provides the minimum price (choice D). It does give the customer what the customer wanted, which may not be the lowest or highest cost. Therefore, the best answer is A.

2. **Answer:** B

    Explanation: Know the term so you will be able to answer questions that deal with this concept. Choices A, C and D may sound good, but they are made-up terms.

3. **Answer:** B

    Explanation: Though each person working on the project should check their own work as part of any project, the project manager ultimately has the responsibility for quality on the project as a whole.

4. **Answer:** C

    Explanation: Trend analysis (choice D) does not deal with root causes, it deals more with predicting the future. Though the project manager is troubled, there is nothing to use conflict resolution techniques with (choice B) because the real problem has not been identified. A Pareto chart (choice A) might help the project manager decide which problems to focus on, but does little to find the root cause of a problem. The best choice is C.

5. **Answer:** C

    Explanation: The key phrase here is "will be used." The team is looking to the future of what quality will be on the project and therefore must be in quality planning, choice C.

6. **Answer:** A

    Explanation: Quality should produce a decrease rather than an increase in cost risk as a result of less rework, so choices B and C can be eliminated. Quality should also provide increased cost effectiveness due to less rework. This eliminates Choice D and makes the best answer A.

7. **Answer:** C

    Explanation: Quality attributes are the measurements that determine if the product is acceptable. They are based on the characteristics of the product for which it was designed.

8. **Answer:** C

    Explanation: The common definition in use today is "meeting and exceeding expectations." However, PMI® states that C is the correct answer. Be sure to wear your PMI® hat for the test.

9. **Answer:** B

   Explanation: Choice A is done as part of quality control. Choices C and D are done as part of quality planning or control (depending on how they are used). This leaves only choice B, which must be the best answer, as team training could be taken to mean that all parties are trained on the quality requirements for the project. Watch out for "double-negative" questions like this on the exam!

10. **Answer:** A

    Explanation: Choice D relates to control charts. Choices B and C relate to fishbone diagrams. Only choice A relates to Pareto diagrams.

11. **Answer:** D

    Explanation: Choice D relates to control charts. Choices B and C relate to fishbone diagrams. Choice A relates to Pareto diagrams.

12. **Answer:** A

    Explanation: The length of time it takes to test a whole population is one of the reasons to take a sample.

13. **Answer:** B

    Explanation: All the other choices are costs of nonconformance to quality.

14. **Answer:** B

    Explanation: Standard deviation is the measurement of a range around the mean. Choice B must therefore be the best answer.

15. **Answer:** D

    Explanation: Memorize the numbers for 1-, 2-, 3- and 6-sigma.

16. **Answer:** C

    Explanation: A variable is something that will be measured. Choice C is an attribute; what unit the variable will be measured in.

17. **Answer:** C

    Explanation: The rule of seven applies here. If you have seven data points in a row on the same side of the mean, statistically, the mean has shifted, calling for action to correct the problem.

18. **Answer:** D

    Explanation: With just in time, supplies are delivered when you need them and not before. Therefore, you have little or no inventory.

19. **Answer:** B

Explanation: Notice that the choices for this question include the definitions for many of the control tools. Such questions can easily confuse you if you do not remember why you use each of the tools. Choices C and D refer to the many responsibility charts and therefore cannot be the best answer. Choice A refers to the function of a Pareto chart.

20. **Answer:** D

Explanation: This question is asking about overall importance of quality. The triple constraint may be prioritized differently on each project but they are generally of equal importance. In other words, do not dismiss quality.

21. **Answer:** D

Explanation: The key words here are "potential problems." They are looking into the future and, therefore, must be in quality planning.

22. **Answer:** A

Explanation: Choices B and C are components of a quality management plan. The quality management plan is part of the project plan. The best answer is the quality management plan.

23. **Answer:** A

Explanation: This is an example of gold plating. You should provide ONLY what the customer asked for in the scope statement. The team does not know if their change will provide benefit to the customer. Focus efforts on conforming to requirements.

24. **Answer:** C

Explanation: The plan described is the quality management plan. Since this plan is included in the project plan, changing the quality management plan will also change the project plan.

25. **Answer:** C

Explanation: PMI®'s definition of an audit is different from what we are used to. An audit is a structured review of quality activities to identify lessons learned. These lessons are used for process improvement.

26. **Answer:** C

Explanation: The quality management plan (choice D) does not provide results. Choice A is not productive since it does not solve the problem. An analogous estimate (choice B) looks at past history of other projects. This would not be appropriate to determine how the current project is going. Quality assurance (choice C) helps to determine if the project will satisfy the relevant quality standards.

27. **Answer:** A

Explanation: Choice A is a structured review of quality management activities performed to identify lessons learned that can be applied to this and other projects. The other choices are tools and techniques that apply to quality control rather than quality assurance.

28. **Answer:** C

    Explanation: This question is similar to others in this book, but not exactly the same. You may also see this occur on your exam. Carefully read the questions. Though quality problems (choice A) MAY lead to quality assurance efforts, they are not a MUST. Choice B is an output of quality assurance, not an input. Choice D is an output of quality control. That leaves only choice C which is an input to quality assurance.

29. **Answer:** B

    Explanation: As you increase quality there will be associated benefits for the project. Some of these benefits are increased productivity, increased cost effectiveness, decreased cost risk and improved morale.

30. **Answer:** B

    Explanation: Since the previous project manager did not finish planning, choice D should not be the next activity. Risk identification (choice C) sounds like a good choice, however, choice B occurs before choice C. Performance of work packages (Choice A) is done after planning. The best answer is B.

31. **Answer:** C

    Explanation: Although quality planning usually occurs during planning, it can occur during executing when there is a change.

32. **Answer:** A

    Explanation: The team should re-evaluate whether the quality standards are valid. This is part of the quality assurance process.

33. **Answer**: B

    Explanation: Gold plating a project wastes time and probably cost. It makes the project unsuccessful.

Human Resource Management

(*PMBOK® GUIDE* Chapter 9)

- Role of:
  - PM
  - Stakeholder
  - Senior management
  - Sponsor
  - Functional manager
  - Team
- HR responsibilities for project managers
- Problem solving process
- Staffing management plan
- Powers of the project manager
  - Formal
  - Reward
  - Penalty
  - Expert
  - Referent
- Conflict resolution techniques
  - Confronting
  - Compromising
  - Withdrawal
  - Smoothing
  - Forcing
- Maslow's hierarchy
- McGregor's X and Y
- Herzberg
- Responsibility chart
  - Responsibility matrix
  - Resource histogram
  - Resource Gantt chart
- Team building
- Leadership styles
- Arbitration
- Perquisites
- Fringe benefits
- Expectancy theory
- Halo effect
- War room

These are probably the easiest questions on the exam, but you will want to be careful about roles and responsibilities. PMI® splits human resources into administrative and behavioral management topics. Most of the answers to human resource questions should come from your everyday knowledge and work experience. You are required to understand that people must be compensated for their work (I am serious, this question has appeared on the exam) and that people should be rewarded.

ROLES AND RESPONSIBILITIES (page 110): A project manager must clearly show the roles and responsibilities of all stakeholders, team members and management, and may use a responsibility matrix to do so. Roles and responsibilities are discussed throughout this book. There is an effort in this chapter to summarize all the roles from previous chapters because I have seen some people fail the exam solely because they did not know what a project manager was, at least not the kind of project manager the *PMBOK® Guide* defines. People have also had problems differentiating between what the team and management should be doing. TRICK: Here is a fast and effective way to review these topics. After you try the following exercises search for the words "project manager," "team," "management," "stakeholder" and "sponsor" on a CD-ROM version of the *PMBOK® Guide*. This will take awhile, as these words are mentioned many times, but seeing the contexts in which they are used will improve your understanding of roles and responsibilities.

Exercise: Test yourself! Describe the role of the project sponsor.

Exercise 2: Test yourself! Describe the role of senior management.

Exercise 3: Test yourself! Describe the role of the team.

© 2002 - 1998 Rita Mulcahy, PMP
PHONE: (952) 846-4484 - EMAIL: info@rmcproject.com - WEB: www.rmcproject.com

Exercise 4: Test yourself! Describe the role of all the stakeholders combined.

Exercise 5: Test yourself! Describe the role of the functional manager.

Exercise 6: Test yourself! Describe the role of the project manager.

Answers:

THE ROLE OF THE PROJECT SPONSOR (pages 62, 74, 125, 130): The *PMBOK® Guide* defines this person as the one who provides the financial resources for the project. WARNING: This may be different than the role of the sponsor in your organization. ANOTHER WARNING: In most instances the customer fulfills the role of the sponsor as well as customer. Carefully read over the role of the sponsor in the *PMBOK® Guide*. In practice, the sponsor:

- Along with the customer, the sponsor formally accepts the product of the project (formal acceptance) during scope verification and administrative closure.
- Along with the customer and the other stakeholders, the sponsor may provide key events, milestones and deliverable due dates.
- Along with the customer, the sponsor's threshold for risks should be taken into account.
- The sponsor does *not* sign the project charter! That is the role of senior management.

THE ROLE OF SENIOR MANAGEMENT: Management is anyone senior to the project manager in the organization(s). In some situations the word "senior management" is a catchall phrase to include the sponsor, functional managers and anyone higher in the performing organization than the project manager.

Management has a unique role on projects that cannot be fulfilled by anyone else. Unfortunately, many managers do not realize that project management is a profession and a science that requires unique efforts from management. Management must have at least an overview understanding of the tools and techniques of project management. It is important for management to know that they are the only ones who can:

- Help organize work into appropriate projects
- Provide the project team with time to plan
- Encourage the finalization of requirements and scope by the stakeholders
- Determine the priorities between the triple constraint components
- Set priorities between projects
- Issue the project charter
- Identify many risks
- Protect the project from outside influences
- Help evaluate tradeoffs during crashing, fast tracking and re-estimating
- Determine the reports needed by management to manage the project
- Approve the final project plan during project plan development
- Resolve conflicts that extend beyond the project manager's control

Chapter 8
Human Resource Management

THE ROLE OF THE TEAM: Generally it is the team's role to help plan what needs to be done (WBS) and create time estimates for their tasks. During project execution, the team members simply complete work packages or tasks and help look for changes from the project plan. More specifically, the team may help:

- Make some project decisions
- Create the work breakdown structure
- Identify constraints and assumptions
- Identify and manage stakeholders
- Attend project team meetings
- Create the change control system
- Identify dependencies
- Provide cost and time estimates
- Determine reserves
- Review project performance reports
- Determine and measure corrective action
- Determine the definition of quality on the project and how it will be met

THE ROLE OF THE STAKEHOLDERS (pages 16, 44, 49, 54, 56, 119, 121): The role of stakeholders and proper management of them run throughout the exam. Stakeholders should be involved in planning the project and managing it more extensively than you might be doing on your projects. (Stakeholders is a PMI®-ism.) For example, lets look at a more complete list of stakeholders and how they are involved in the project. They must first be identified and their communications needs determined. Stakeholders:

- Are distributed information during the life of the project
- Have their knowledge and skills assessed
- Are notified of project plan changes
- Use expert judgment throughout the project and especially in the creation of the contents of the project charter and the scope statement
- Are involved in:
    - Project plan development
    - Approving project changes and being on the change control board
    - Scope verification
    - Identifying constraints
    - Risk management
- Information needs are considered and analyzed throughout the project processes as part of stakeholder analysis
- Are listed in the project team directory
- Are considered in team development
- Have presentations made to them
- Receive performance reports
- Have their risk tolerances identified and incorporated into the risk management process
- Become risk owners

THE ROLE OF THE FUNCTIONAL MANAGER (throughout): The individual who manages and "owns" the resources in the IT, engineering, public relations, marketing and other departments and generally directs the technical work of individuals from their functional area that are working on the project. The amount of involvement of the functional manager depends on the form of organizational structure. In a matrix organization, this responsibility to direct the work of individuals is shared with the project manager. In a projectized organization, the project manager does all of the directing. The project manager does little directing in a functional organization. To avoid conflict, the project manager and functional manager must coordinate their respective needs regarding the use of resources to complete project work.

The specific activities performed by the functional manager vary greatly based on the type of organizational structure and the type of project. They MAY include:

- Assigning specific individuals to the team and negotiating with the project manager regarding resources
- Participating in the initial planning until work packages or tasks are assigned
- Involved in go, no-go decisions
- Approving the final schedule during schedule development
- Approving the final project plan during project plan development
- Assisting in planning corrective action
- Assisting with problems related to team member performance
- Improving their staff utilization
- Letting the project manager know of other projects that may impact the project

THE ROLE OF THE PROJECT MANAGER (throughout): The individual responsible for managing the project. Many people have failed the exam due to a lack of understanding of what is the project manager's role. That role is described throughout this book. The project manager's level of authority can vary depending on the form of organization. On this exam, such authority generally means that the project manager:

- Is assigned to the project as early as possible
- Must have the authority and accountability necessary to accomplish the work
- Must be able to deal with conflicting or unrealistic scope, quality, schedule, risk and other requirements
- Is the only one who can integrate the project components into a cohesive whole that meets the customer's needs
- Is proactive
- Must have the authority to say "no" when necessary
- Is held accountable for project failure
- Understands professional responsibility
- Is in charge of the project, but not necessarily the resources
- Does not have to be a technical expert
- Leads and directs the project planning efforts
- Assists the team and stakeholders during project execution
- Maintains control over the project by measuring performance and taking corrective action
- Performs most of the activities outlined in this book

Exercise: Test yourself! This exercise is designed to cut down to the essence of the situational questions on the exam dealing with roles and responsibilities and to help you discover any incorrect procedures you may be following. You will probably disagree with a few of my answers, either because you read something into the question other than what was intended (a bad habit you should discover before you take the exam), or you have an error in your project management knowledge.

Considering the previous comments, write the initials of the key person responsible to solve each of the problems in the following chart. The choices are: team members (T), project manager (PM), Sponsor (SP), functional manager (FM), senior management or someone higher in the organization than the project manager (SM). HINT: Since most projects are managed in matrix forms of organizations, keep matrix organizations in mind when considering these situations.

	Situation	Key person
1	Two project team members are having a disagreement	
2	There is a change to the overall project deliverable	
3	A functional manager is trying to pull a team member off the project to do other work	
4	The project manager does not have the authority to get things done	
5	There are not enough resources to complete the project	
6	The team is unsure of what needs to happen when	
7	A task needs more time and will cause the project to be delayed	
8	A task needs more time without causing the project to be delayed	
9	A team member is not performing	
10	The team is not sure who is in charge of the project	
11	There is talk that the project may no longer be needed	
12	Senior management provides an unrealistic schedule requirement	
13	The team is in conflict over priorities between tasks	
14	The project is behind schedule	
15	A team member determines that another method is needed to complete the task within its scope of work	
16	The project is running out of funds	
17	Additional work is added to the project that will add cost and was not identified as part of the risk management process	

Answer: If you got many of the answers wrong, you should reread the roles and responsibilities topic and the exact wording of the situations presented here. With such a brief description, you could easily have thought the question meant something different than I intended. This is planned to give you more experience interpreting questions on the exam. The exercise is meant to make you think. You may also have preferred the word "decide" or the words "make the final decision" in place of "solve" in some of these questions. Think!

	Situation	Key person
1	Two project team members are having a disagreement – *The people involved in the conflict must solve it themselves.*	T
2	There is a change to the overall project deliverable – *This is a change to the project charter. Only senior management can approve changes to the project charter.*	SM
3	A functional manager is trying to pull a team member off the project to do other work – *The project manager must give the team member enough information (e.g., Gantt chart, network diagram, project plan, risks) so that they can manage their own workload. Because the word "trying" is used, we know that this situation is occurring at the present time. If the question had used the words "has pulled" the answer would be project manager. Read situational questions carefully.*	T
4	The project manager does not have the authority to get things done – *It is senior management's role to give the project manager authority in the form of a project charter.*	SM
5	There are not enough resources to complete the project – *Senior management and functional management control resources.*	SM/FM
6	The team is unsure of what needs to happen when – *It is the project manager's role to take the individual tasks and task estimates and combine them into the project schedule.*	PM
7	A task needs more time and will cause the project to be delayed – *Notice the word "will." This means the evaluation by the team is completed and there is no available reserve since the project completion date is most likely included in the charter. Any such changes are changes to the project charter and require senior management involvement.*	SM
8	A task needs more time without causing the project to be delayed – *It is the project manager's role to manage the project time and cost reserves to handle any such eventuality.*	PM
9	A team member is not performing – *Senior management and functional management control resources.*	SM/FM
10	The team is not sure who is in charge of the project – *Senior management designates the project manager in the project charter.*	SM
11	There is talk that the project may no longer be needed – *It is senior management's role to protect the project from changes, including such a large change.*	SM/SP
12	Senior management provides an unrealistic schedule requirement – *Although it is often the senior manager's fault that this occurs, only they can make a change to the project charter (including schedule requirements). The project manager must provide evidence that the schedule is unrealistic.*	SM
13	The team is in conflict over priorities between tasks – *It is the project manager's role to settle any such conflicts and to provide a project network diagram and critical path. It is senior management's role to set priorities among projects.*	PM

	Situation	Key person
14	The project is behind schedule – *Only the project manager can control the overall project schedule. During project execution, the team focuses on completing their tasks.*	PM
15	A team member determines that another method is needed to complete the task within its scope of work – *The team member has control over his tasks as long as he meets the time, quality, cost and scope of work objectives set up with the project manager. The team member must keep the project manager informed of these changes so the project manager can integrate them into the rest of the project and look for any impacts.*	T
16	The project is running out of funds – *It is the sponsor's role to provide funding for the project.*	SP
17	Additional work is added to the project that will add cost and was not identified as part of the risk management process – *The fact that the change was not identified in the risk management process and is additional work means it was not included in the original project budget (or the budget reserve). Therefore, the sponsor must be involved in providing additional funds.*	SP

HUMAN RESOURCE RESPONSIBILITIES FOR PROJECT MANAGERS: Read this list carefully for PMI®-isms, especially if you have never realized that these are the project manager's responsibilities. A project manager has some human resource responsibility:

- Creating a project team directory (page 114)
- Negotiating with resource managers for the best resources (page 113)
- Creating project job descriptions for team members and other stakeholders (page 112)
- Understanding the team's and other stakeholders' needs for training related to their work on the project and making sure they get the training (page 112)
- Creating a formal plan for team, management and other stakeholders; how they will be involved in the project and what roles they will perform - a staffing management plan (page 111)

RESPONSIBILITY CHART (pages 110 - 112 with illustrations): PMI® advocates that all roles and responsibilities on the project be clearly assigned and closely linked to the project scope definition. Many types of charts may be used for this purpose. For the exam, you should understand what is shown on each chart. For example:

A responsibility matrix does not show _____.

Answer – when people will do their jobs (time).

1. **RESPONSIBILITY MATRIX** (page 111) – This chart cross-references team members with the tasks they are to accomplish. For example:

TASK	TEAM MEMBER			
	Nicole	Morgan	Riki	Alexis
A	P		S	
B		S		P

KEY- P = Primary responsibility, S = Secondary responsibility
It may also cross-reference team members and issues. For example:

Issue	TEAM MEMBER			
	Nicole	Morgan	Riki	Alexis
Invoicing	P		S	
Hardware		S		P

2. **RESOURCE HISTOGRAM** (page 112) – Is a graph that shows the number of resources used each month and is displayed in a bar chart format. A picture is shown in the *PMBOK® Guide.*

3. **RESOURCE GANTT CHART** – Shows WHEN staff is allocated to tasks.

STAFFING MANAGEMENT PLAN (page 111): After stakeholders are identified, a plan for managing the project staff must be put into place later in the planning stage. Described in the Human Resource section of the *PMBOK® Guide* and closely aligned with Roles and Responsibility assignment, this topic is often missed in the real world.

Exercise: Describe what needs to be done in order to set up a staffing management plan.

Answer:
- Identify all project stakeholders
- Identify their needs, expectations and objectives
- Determine the roles of each stakeholder on the project
- Determine the skills and knowledge of each stakeholder
- Assess the overall impact of stakeholders on the project
- Determine how stakeholders should be managed

HALO EFFECT: The tendency to rate high or low on *all* factors due to the impression of a high or low rating on *some* specific factor. This can mean, "You are a great programmer. Therefore, we will make you a project manager and also expect you to be great."

TEAM BUILDING (TEAM DEVELOPMENT pages 114 -116): Questions related to team building are very easy and most people can answer them based on their own experience. Make sure you know:

- It is the job of the project manager to "enhance the ability of stakeholders to contribute as individuals as well as enhance the ability of the team to function as a team"
- Project managers should incorporate team building activities into all project activities
- Team building requires a concerted effort and continued attention throughout the life of the project
- The WBS is a team building tool
- Team building should start early in the life of the project

POWERS OF THE PROJECT MANAGER (*Principles* page 75): Many people have told me that they find it surprising that this topic is on the exam. In fact it is not surprising. Project managers almost always have difficulty getting people to cooperate and perform, especially if they are working in a matrix organization. Therefore, it is important for the project manager to understand what they can do to get people to perform. These are the "powers."

- FORMAL (legitimate) – Power based on your position. "Do the work because I have been put in charge!"
- REWARD – Giving rewards. "I understand that you have been wanting to participate in the acceptance testing of this project. Because of your performance, I will assign you as part of that team!"
- PENALTY (coercive) – Being able to penalize team members. "If this does not get done on time, I will remove you from the group going to Hawaii for the customer meeting!"
- EXPERT – Being the technical or project management expert. "We should listen to what the project manager suggests. She is the world authority on this technology!"
- REFERENT – Based on the project manager's personality or knowledge or referring to the authority of someone in a higher position. "The vice president has put this project at the top of his list! We will do the work on this project first."

NOTE: PMI® says that the best forms of power are EXPERT and REWARD. Penalty is the worst choice. PMI® also says that FORMAL, REWARD and PENALTY are powers derived from the project manager's position in the company. EXPERT power is earned on your own.

LEADERSHIP STYLES: Project management is heavily dependent on managing people. Therefore the project manager must determine the most appropriate leadership style for the needs and phases of the project. Some of the choices are:

- Directing – Telling others what to do
- Facilitating – Coordinating the input of others
- Coaching – Instructing others
- Supporting – Providing assistance along the way
- Autocratic – Making decisions without input

- Consultative – Inviting ideas from others
- Consensus – Problem solving in a group with decision-making based on group agreement

Studies disagree on which styles should be used during the different parts of the project management life cycle. However, there is a general consensus that a project manager needs to provide more direction at the beginning of the project (only he knows what must be done to plan the project). Then during the executing phase, the project manager needs to do more coaching, facilitating and supporting. Carefully read any such questions.

Watch out for consensus. Many project managers believe that all decisions need to be made with the project team. This is not always the case. During project execution, a project manager should have enough information about the project to make many decisions on their own. The first or best choice when a problem or issue arises may not be to call a meeting of the team.

CONFLICT MANAGEMENT: There can be many situational questions on the exam that involve conflict regarding scope, resources and competing objectives. Remember to connect this section with the Professional Responsibility chapter.

Many people naturally withdraw from conflict and just hope it will go away. Others have very low authority in the real world and therefore cannot effectively manage conflict. As a result, they have problems with conflict-related questions on the exam. A project manager should be proactive, look for problems and conflicts and then deal with them before their impact on the project expands! Watch out for this as you answer questions on the actual exam!

Although many of us think conflict is bad, it actually presents opportunity for the project to improve. This is another situation where the understanding of many project managers differs from accepted research. Read this carefully and make sure your basic thinking is on the new side and not the old.

Changing Views of Conflict	
Old	**New**
Conflict is dysfunctional and caused by personality differences or a failure of leadership.	Conflict is an inevitable consequence of organizational interactions.
Conflict is to be avoided.	Conflict can be beneficial.
Conflict is resolved by physical separation or the intervention of upper management.	Conflict is resolved through identifying the causes and problem solving by the people involved and their immediate manager.

Conflict is unavoidable because of the:

- Nature of projects trying to address the needs and requirements of many stakeholders
- Limited power of the project manager
- Necessity of obtaining resources from functional managers

Conflict can be avoided through the following techniques:
- Informing the team of:
  - Exactly where the project is headed
  - Project goals and objectives
  - All key decisions
  - Changes
- Clearly assigning tasks without ambiguity or overlapping responsibilities
- Making work assignments interesting and challenging

Many project managers think that the main source of conflict on a project is personality differences. They may be surprised to learn that this is rarely the case. It only becomes personal if the root cause of the problem is not resolved. The following describes the seven categories of conflict in order of frequency. MEMORIZE the top four:
- Schedules
- Project priorities
- Resources
- Technical opinions
- Administrative procedures
- Cost
- Personality

CONFLICT RESOLUTION TECHNIQUES (*Principles* page 161): Following are the primary conflict resolution techniques. Do you know which is the best or the worst? Many people skip this topic in favor of more analytical aspects of project management. They then have difficulty with the complexity of the situational questions related to this topic on the actual exam, especially questions about conflicting needs covered under Professional Responsibility. Do not make the same mistake!

Conflict is best resolved by those involved in the conflict. The project manager should generally try to resolve problems and conflict as long as he or she has authority over those in conflict or the issues in conflict. If not, senior management or functional managers may be called in to assist. There is one exception. In instances of professional responsibility (breaking laws, policies, ethics) the project manager must go over the head of the person in conflict.

TRICK: When you have questions on the exam relating to this topic, make sure you first think, "Who generally has authority over the situation described in this question?" Another good phrase to remember is, "What resolution of this problem would best serve the customer's interests?"

The following are the main conflict resolution techniques you will need to know for the exam. Make sure you notice that some have more than one title and know both.

- **CONFRONTING (PROBLEM SOLVING**) – Solving the real problem.

  "It seems that the real problem here is not a lack of communication, but a lack of knowledge of what needs to be done and when. Here is a copy of the project schedule. It should let you understand what you need to know."

  "Mary, you say that the project should include the purchase of new computers and Steve, you say that the project can use existing equipment. I suggest we

perform the following test on the existing equipment to determine if it needs to be replaced."

- **COMPROMISING** – Finding solutions that bring some degree of satisfaction to both parties.

  "Let us do a little of what both of you suggest."

  "Mary, what if we get new computers for the design tasks on the project and use the existing computers for the monitoring functions?"

- **WITHDRAWAL (AVOIDANCE)** – Retreating or postponing a decision on a problem. Since PMI® stresses dealing with problems, this is rarely the BEST choice for resolving conflict.

  "Let's deal with this issue next week."

  "Since we can not decide on the purchase of new computers, we will have to wait until our meeting next month."

- **SMOOTHING** – Emphasizing agreement rather than differences of opinion.

  "Let's calm down and get the job done!"

  "Mary and Steve, both of you want this project to cause as little distraction to your departments as possible. With that in mind, I am sure we can come to an agreement on the purchase of equipment and what is best for the project."

- **FORCING** – Pushing one viewpoint at the expense of another.

  "Do it my way!"

  "We have talked about new computers enough. I do not want to get the computers and that is it!"

NOTE: The exam may ask you which technique is best or worst. PMI® recommends problem solving as the best choice, followed by compromising. Forcing is the least preferable option.

PROBLEM SOLVING: Even though a project manager spends a great deal of time and energy preventing problems, there are still problems that need to be solved. You should expect more than ten questions that require you to solve a cost, time, human resources or other problem.

TRICK: When you get to one of these questions ask yourself, "What is the real problem behind the situation presented?"

Make sure you understand the process of solving problems as outlined below. This process may also be used with stakeholders to find a fair resolution to conflicting objectives. See more about this in the Professional Responsibility chapter.

- Define the cause of the problem, not just the symptoms of the problem
- Analyze the problem
- Identify solutions
- Implement a decision
- Review the decision and confirm that the decision solved the problem

WAR ROOM: The project team is located in one room. It is used to create a project identity for the project team and management in a matrix organization.

EXPECTANCY THEORY: Employees who believe that their efforts will lead to effective performance and who expect to be rewarded for their accomplishments remain productive as rewards meet their expectations.

ARBITRATION: The hearing and resolution of a dispute performed by a neutral party.

PERQUISITES (perks): The giving of special rewards to some employees such as assigned parking spaces, corner offices and executive dining.

FRINGE BENEFITS: The "standard" benefits formally given to all employees such as education benefits, insurance and profit sharing.

MOTIVATION THEORY: Years ago, I was surprised that the exam included questions about theories of motivation until I realized that this is an important topic for gaining cooperation. Here are three theories you need to understand for the exam.

> **MCGREGOR'S THEORY OF X AND Y** – McGregor believed that all workers fit in one of two groups, X and Y. The exam uses many different ways to describe each of these theories. It can be confusing to determine which answer is the correct or even what the choices are saying. For all of you with visual memory, I will provide you with a foolproof method to answer any question on these theories.

> > **THEORY X** – Based on the picture, take a guess as to what theory X is.

> > People need to be watched every minute. People are incapable, avoid responsibility and avoid work whenever possible.

> > **THEORY Y** – Based on the picture, take a guess as to what theory Y is.

> > People are willing to work without supervision and want to achieve. People can direct their own efforts.

MASLOW'S HIERARCHY OF NEEDS – Maslow's message is that people do not work for security or money. They work to contribute and to use their skills. Maslow calls this "self-actualization." He created a pyramid to show how people are motivated and said that one cannot ascend to the next level until the levels below are fulfilled.

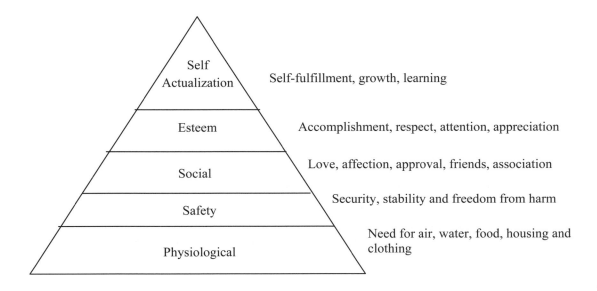

HERZBERG'S THEORY – This theory deals with hygiene factors and motivating agents.

> **HYGIENE FACTORS** – Poor hygiene factors may destroy motivation, but improving them, under most circumstances, will not improve motivation. Hygiene factors are not sufficient to motivate people. Examples of these are:
> - Working conditions
> - Salary
> - Personal life
> - Relationships at work
> - Security
> - Status

> **MOTIVATING AGENTS** – What motivates people is the work itself, including such things as:
> - Responsibility
> - Self-actualization
> - Professional growth
> - Recognition

> The lesson to project managers - motivating people is best done by rewarding them and letting them grow. Giving raises does not do it. Many project managers initially disagree with this statement until they have a chance to think about it. Besides, the project manager may not have any influence over pay raises if the team members do not report to the project manager in the organizational structure.

Chapter 8
Human Resource Management

Practice Exam for the CAPM® and PMP® Exams
Human Resource Management

1. All of the following are forms of power derived from the project manager's position EXCEPT:

   A. Formal
   B. Reward
   C. Penalty
   D. Expert

2. The highest point of Maslow's hierarchy of needs is called:

   A. Physiological satisfaction
   B. Attainment of survival
   C. Need for association
   D. Esteem

3. The "halo effect" refers to the tendency to:

   A. Promote from within
   B. Hire the best
   C. Move people into project management because they are good in their technical field
   D. Move people into project management because they have had project management training

4. An obstacle to team building in a matrix organization is that the:

   A. Team organization is technically focused
   B. Team members are borrowed resources and can be hard to motivate
   C. Teams are too centralized
   D. Teams are too large and therefore very hard to handle

5. All of the following are typical concerns of matrixed team members EXCEPT:

   A. Wondering who will handle their evaluations
   B. Serving multiple bosses
   C. Developing commitment
   D. Computing fringe benefits when working on multiple projects

6. Which of the following conflict resolution techniques will generate the MOST lasting solution?

   A. Forcing
   B. Smoothing
   C. Compromise
   D. Problem solving

7. Which type of organization is BEST for managing complex projects involving cross-disciplinary efforts?

   A. Projectized
   B. Functional
   C. Line
   D. Matrix

8. The MOST common causes of conflict on a project are schedules, project priorities and:

    A. Personalities
    B. Resources
    C. Cost
    D. Management

9. What conflict resolution technique is a project manager using when he says, "I cannot deal with this issue now!"

    A. Problem solving
    B. Forcing
    C. Withdrawal
    D. Compromising

10. What does a responsibility Gantt chart show that a responsibility matrix does not?

    A. Time
    B. Tasks
    C. Interrelationships
    D. The person in charge of each task

Human Resource Questions Only For the PMP® Exam

11. You have just been assigned as project manager for a large telecommunications project. This one-year project is about halfway done. The project team consists of five sellers and twenty of your company's employees. You want to understand who is responsible for doing what on the project. Where would you find such information?

    A. Responsibility matrix
    B. Resource histogram
    C. Gantt chart
    D. Project organization chart

12. During project planning in a matrix organization, the project manager determines that additional human resources are needed. From whom would he request these resources?

    A. Project manager
    B. Functional manager
    C. Team
    D. Project sponsor

13. A project manager must publish a project schedule. Activities, start/end times and resources are identified. What should the project manager do NEXT?

    A. Distribute the project schedule according to the communications plan
    B. Confirm the availability of the resources
    C. Refine the project plan to reflect more accurate costing information
    D. Publish a Gantt chart illustrating the timeline

14. During every project team meeting, the project manager asks each team member to describe the work he or she is doing, and the project manager assigns new tasks to team members. The length of these meetings has increased because there are many different tasks to assign. This could be happening for all the following reasons EXCEPT:

    A. Lack of a WBS
    B. Lack of a responsibility matrix
    C. Lack of resource leveling
    D. Lack of team involvement in project planning

15. You are a project manager leading a cross-functional project team in a weak matrix environment. None of your project team members report to you functionally and you do not have the ability to directly reward their performance. The project is difficult, involving tight date constraints and challenging quality standards. Which of the following types of project management power will likely be the MOST effective in this circumstance?

    A. Referent
    B. Expert
    C. Penalty
    D. Formal

16. A team member is not performing well on the project because she is inexperienced in system development work. There is no one else available who is better qualified to do the work. What is the BEST solution for the project manager?

    A. Consult with the functional manager to determine project completion incentives for the team member
    B. Obtain a new resource more skilled in development work
    C. Arrange for the team member to get training
    D. Allocate some of the project schedule reserve

17. A project manager has just found out that a major subcontractor for her project is consistently late delivering work. The project team member responsible for this part of the project does not get along with the subcontractor. To resolve the problem, the project manager says, "You both will have to give up something to solve this problem." What conflict resolution mode is she using?

    A. Confrontation
    B. Compromise
    C. Smoothing
    D. Communicating

18. A project has several teams. Team C has repeatedly missed deadlines in the past. This has caused team D to have to crash the critical path several times. As the project leader for team D, you should meet with the:

    A. Manager of team D
    B. Project manager alone
    C. Project manager and management
    D. Project manager and the team C leader

19. On his first project assignment as project manager, the project manager encounters disagreements among highly technical team members. How would the project manager BEST deal with the conflict?

    A. He should listen to the differences of opinions, determine what is the best choice, and implement that choice
    B. He should postpone further discussions, meet with each individual, and determine the best approach
    C. He should listen to the differences of opinions, encourage logical discussions, and facilitate an agreement
    D. He should help the team focus on agreeable aspects of their opinions and build unity by using relaxation techniques and common focus team building

20. A project manager has just been hired and is trying to gain the cooperation of others. What is the BEST form of power for gaining cooperation under these circumstances?

    A. Formal
    B. Referent
    C. Penalty
    D. Expert

21. A project manager is trying to settle a dispute between two team members. One says the systems should be integrated before testing, and the other maintains each system should be tested before integration. The project involves over thirty people, and twelve systems need to be integrated. Senior management is demanding that integration happen on time. What is the BEST statement the project manager can make to resolve the conflict?

    A. Do it my way
    B. Let's calm down and get the job done
    C. Let's deal with this again next week after we all calm down
    D. Let's test one system after integration and one before integration and see if there are any differences

22. A project is in the middle of project execution when a stakeholder suggests a major new change. This change will cause the third major overhaul of the project. At the same time the project manager discovers that a major task was not completed because a team member's boss moved them to another project that had a higher priority. Which of the following is the best person for the project manger to address these issues with?

    A. Team
    B. Sponsor
    C. Customer
    D. Senior management

23. Instructions for the construction of the concrete footings were poorly translated between the different languages in use on the project. Which of the following is the BEST thing for the project manager to do?

    A. Call the team together for a meeting to determine what to do
    B. Do nothing, the work is now done and the problem has gone away
    C. Ask management for help
    D. Fix the problem himself

Chapter 8
Human Resource Management

Human Resources Management Answers

1. **Answer:** D

   Explanation: When someone is given the job of project manager they will have formal, reward and penalty power. But just having the position does not make the project manager either a technical or project management expert.

2. **Answer:** D

   Explanation: This question is asking which of the FOLLOWING is the highest. Self-actualization is not listed, so the next best choice is esteem.

3. **Answer:** C

   Explanation: Just because a person is good in their technical field does not mean they will also be a good project manager.

4. **Answer:** B

   Explanation: Team members are harder to motivate if their loyalty is to their functional organization rather than to the project team.

5. **Answer:** D

   Explanation: In a matrix organization, each team member has the project manager and the functional manager that they report to. Team members may therefore be worried about choices A, B and C. Since the same fringe benefits are given to all employees no matter what work they do, choice D is the exception.

6. **Answer:** D

   Explanation: Problem solving normally takes more time but it gets buy-in from everyone, generating a more lasting solution.

7. **Answer:** D

   Explanation: The key words here are "cross-disciplinary." When a project crosses functional lines, a matrix organization is needed.

8. **Answer:** B

   Explanation: Know the top four sources so you can answer questions such as this one. Don't be fooled because "personalities" is on the list. It is last.

9. **Answer:** C

   Explanation: Delaying the issue is called withdrawal.

10. **Answer:** A

Explanation: Time is shown in a schedule or Gantt chart. The responsibility assignment matrix maps specific resources against the tasks from the WBS.

11. **Answer:** A

Explanation: The responsibility "assignment" matrix maps who will do the work, whereas the resource histogram (choice B) shows the number of resources used in each time period. In its pure sense, a Gantt chart (choice C) shows only task and calendar date. An organizational chart (choice D) shows who reports to whom.

12. **Answer:** B

Explanation: Did you forget that in a matrix organization the functional manager controls the resources?

13. **Answer**: B

Explanation: The project schedule remains preliminary until resource assignments are confirmed.

14. **Answer**: C

Explanation: Resource leveling refers to maintaining the same number of resources on the project for each time period. Leveling has nothing to do with assigning tasks or managing meetings.

15. **Answer**: B

Explanation: Per PMI®, reward and expert are the best sources of power. Reward is not listed as a choice.

16. **Answer**: C

Explanation: The job of the project manager includes providing or obtaining project-specific training for team members. This kind of training is a direct cost of the project.

17. **Answer:** B

Explanation: The act of both parties giving something defines compromise.

18. **Answer:** D

Explanation: Those having the problem should resolve the problem, in PMI®'s view. In this case, the two team leads need to meet and, because it is impacting the project, the project manager needs to participate.

19. **Answer:** C

Explanation: Problem solving and compromising are the two most important conflict resolution techniques. A key general management skill includes conflict management.

20. **Answer:** A

    Explanation: Generally, the best forms of power are reward or expert. The project manager has not had time to become a recognized expert in the company and reward is not a choice. This leaves formal power as the only logical choice.

21. **Answer:** D

    Explanation: Choice D is an example of compromising – one of the best choices for resolving conflict.

22. **Answer:** D

    Explanation: It is senior management's role to prevent unnecessary changes and to set priorities between projects. The situation described in this question implies that such work is not being done and the project manager must therefore go to the root of the problem, senior management.

23. **Answer:** D

    Explanation: This may seem like a communications question, but it is really about roles and responsibilities. The real problem is that the communications plan has not been adequate to prevent the problem. The communications plan is the project manager's responsibility. The team should not be involved in all the project management work. During project execution, their focus should be on completing work.

Communications Management
(PMBOK® GUIDE Chapter 10)

Communications questions are generally very easy. However, many students comment that the number of communications questions on the exam surprises them. Remember; although there may be only 10 questions from the material in this chapter on the exam, there are many other communications questions addressed in other parts of the book. For example, a WBS is a communications tool (see the Scope chapter) and actions planned to mitigate risks should be communicated (in the Risk chapter).

Lack of communication is high on most project managers' lists of common project problems. Therefore, it is important that a project manager has some background in proper communication techniques so that they can improve their own communications. Read and understand the following, but note that none of the lists and bullet points, except the communications model, needs to be MEMORIZED.

Hot Topics

- Administrative closure
  - Product verification
  - Financial closure
  - Lessons learned
  - Update records
  - Performance reporting
  - Project archives
  - Formal acceptance
  - Release resources
- Communications planning
- Communications management plan
- Information distribution
- Communications methods
  - Formal/informal written
  - Formal/informal verbal
- Communication channels
- Meetings
- Communications blockers
- Communications model
  - Nonverbal
  - Paralingual
  - Active listening
  - Effective listening
  - Feedback
- Control of communications

COMMUNICATIONS PLANNING (page 119): Communications planning involves "determining the information and communications needs of the stakeholders." This is, once again, a very proactive approach. PMI® is saying that this requires a well thought-out plan, and therefore project managers must think about this and put a formal written plan together.

Communications can take place in many ways including face-to-face, by telephone, fax, email or meetings. It is important to MEMORIZE that 90% of the project manager's time is spent communicating.

Do not expect all direct questions on the exam such as, "How much time does a project manager spend communicating?" Some questions on the exam can connect two topics that you might not have seen connected before.

Which skill is most important for a project manager?

    A. Team building
    B. Negotiating
    C. Communicating
    D. Technical expertise

The answer is C, communicating.

COMMUNICATIONS MANAGEMENT PLAN (page 120): This is another area of common project management errors. Most project managers do not know what this is, do not realize it should be in writing for most projects, nor realize that the individual needs of each stakeholder must be taken into account. If you have communications problems on your project, you are not spending enough time in this area.

Chapter 9
Communications Management

A communications management plan is an output of communications planning. This plan is created by the project manager and becomes part of the project plan. The purpose of this plan is to inform all stakeholders how and in what form communications will be handled on the project. The creation of a communications management plan involves an analysis of the needs of each individual stakeholder. It may include:

- What information needs to be collected and when
- Who will receive the information
- Methods used to gather and store information
- Limits, if any, on who may give direction and to whom
- Reporting relationships
- Listing of contact information for all stakeholders
- Schedule for distribution of each type of communication

INFORMATION DISTRIBUTION (page 121): Implementing the communications management plan by distributing information to project stakeholders through reports, presentations and informal and formal communications. Read over this description in the *PMBOK® Guide*! Many people do not realize the extent of the information that must be distributed.

Exercise 1: Test yourself! What information needs to be distributed on a project?

Answer 1: There can be many answers to this question, depending on the nature of the project. Your answer should include:

- Status
- Problems
- Updated project plans or components of the project plan
- Successes
- Team member performance
- Meeting schedule
- New risks uncovered
- The date of the next milestone completion party

Exercise 2: Test yourself! Who does information need to be distributed to?

Answer 2:

- Internal to the project
- External to the project
- Management
- Sponsor
- Team
- Team members' managers
- Other project managers
- Project manager
- Other stakeholders

COMMUNICATIONS MODEL: Many of my students think that understanding the communications model is trivial. However, they begin to realize its importance when they note how many communication problems project managers have on projects. If communications are not working, one solution is to review what and how you are communicating – look at the communications model.

The communications model looks like a circle with three parts: the sender, the message and the receiver. Each message is encoded by the sender and decoded by the receiver based on the receiver's education, experience, language and culture. PMI® advocates that the sender encode a message carefully, determine the communications method (listed below) used to send it, and confirm that the message is understood. The receiver should decode the message carefully and confirm that the message is understood.

Chapter 9
Communications Management

The following terms sometimes show up on the exam:

- **NONVERBAL** – about 55% of all communications are nonverbal (e.g., based on physical mannerisms).

- **PARALINGUAL** – means the pitch and tone of your voice. This also helps to convey a message.

- **ACTIVE LISTENING** – The receiver confirms that she is listening, confirms agreement and asks for clarification.

- **EFFECTIVE LISTENING** – Watching the speaker to pick up physical gestures and facial expressions, thinking about what you want to say before responding, asking questions, repeating and providing feedback.

- **FEEDBACK** – Saying things like, "Do you understand what I have explained?" usually asked by the sender.

COMMUNICATIONS METHODS (page 121): In order to have clear, concise communications, the project manager must handle communications in a structured manner by selecting the form of communication that is best for the situation. Communications occur internal and external to the core project team and vertical and horizontal within the organization. A decision regarding whether the communication needs to be formal or informal, written or verbal, needs to be made for each instance of communication. Questions on communications methods should be easy if you understand the following chart:

Communications Method	When used
Formal written	Complex problems, project plans, project charter, communicating over long distances
Formal verbal	Presentations, speeches
Informal written	Memos, email, notes
Informal verbal	Meetings, conversations

Exercise: Test yourself! What is the best form of communication in the following situations?

Situation	Communications Method
Memos	
Project plans	
Communicating over long distances	

Situation	Communications Method
Meetings	
Presentations	
Conversations	
Complex problems	
Email	
Notes	
Speeches	
Project charter	

Answer: Imagine these as situational questions. Exam questions may have more words but they will boil down to straightforward situations like the ones described below.

Situation	Communications Method
Memos	Informal written
Project plans	Formal written
Communicating over long distances	Formal written
Meetings	Informal verbal
Presentations	Formal verbal
Conversations	Informal verbal
Complex problems	Formal written
Email	Informal written
Notes	Informal written
Speeches	Formal verbal
Project charter	Formal written

Chapter 9
Communications Management

CONTROL OF COMMUNICATIONS: The exam may also ask:

- Can the project manager control all communications? The answer is no! That would be impossible.
- Should the project manager try to control communications? Yes, otherwise changes, miscommunications, unclear directions and scope creep can occur.
- What percent of the project manager's time is spent communicating? About 90%.

COMMUNICATION BLOCKERS: Phrases such as "what is your game plan," "getting down to the nitty-gritty," or even "zero in on problems" can cause miscommunication with people from other cultures. So can such comments as "What a bad idea!" The exam has often had one or two questions that ask, "What can get in the way of communications?" The answer may include:

- Noise
- Distance
- Improper encoding of messages
- Saying "that is a bad idea"
- Hostility
- Language
- Culture

MEETINGS: The project manager may have many different types of meetings. Meetings are a problem in the real world because many project managers manage by doing everything in meetings and most meetings are not efficient.

Expect questions about the following rules for meetings (but then we already know these and follow them, don't we)?

- Set a time limit and keep to it
- Schedule recurring meetings in advance
- Meet with the team regularly, but not too often
- Have a purpose for each meeting
- Create an agenda with team input
- Distribute agendas beforehand
- Stick to the agenda
- Let people know in advance their responsibilities
- Bring the right people together
- Chair and lead the meeting with a set of rules
- Assign deliverables and time limits for all tasks that result from meetings
- Document and publish meeting minutes

COMMUNICATION CHANNELS: Communications grow at a greater than linear rate (exponentially) and are represented by the following formula: $(N \times (N-1))/2$ where N equals the number of people. The same formula could be written as $(N^2-N)/2$. You should understand this formula. The intent is for the project manager to realize that communications are complex and need to be managed but cannot be controlled.

TRICK: Anytime you see a formula containing the letter "N," even if it looks slightly different than the formula above, that formula represents communications channels.

Sample question: *If a team of four people adds one more person to the team, how many more channels of communication are there?*

Answer: *Four more channels of communication.* There were six communication channels. Using the formula above, there are now ten. The question asks how many MORE so the answer is 10 – 6, or four.

PERFORMANCE REPORTING (pages 122-124): Reports should provide the kinds of information and the level of detail required by stakeholders. Reports are communication tools and may include:
- Status report – describing where the project now stands
- Progress report – describing what has been accomplished
- Trend report – examining project results over time to see if performance is improving or deteriorating
- Forecasting report – predicting future project status and performance
- Variance report – comparing actual results to planned
- Earned value – integrating scope, cost and schedule measures to assess project performance. This report makes use of the terms described under cost (e.g., PV, EV, AC, etc.)

ADMINISTRATIVE CLOSURE (page 125): Completing the closure of the project as stated in the project plan. This will include administrative activities such as collecting and finalizing all the paperwork needed to complete the project and technical work to verify that that product of the project is acceptable. Administrative closure and contract closeout make up 14 questions on the exam!

Closure is done:
- When a project ends
- When a project (or contract) is terminated before the work is completed
- At the end of each project phase (e.g., Design, Engineering, Implementation)

All projects must be closed out no matter the circumstances under which they stop, are terminated, or complete. If the project involves contracts, contract closeout should occur before administrative closure. Remember these for the exam!

Exercise: What activities are done during closure?

Answer: Did you include contract closeout activities? If so, see the Procurement chapter. Let's just concentrate on administrative closure here. These activities include:

- **PRODUCT VERIFICATION:** Checking to see if all the work was completed correctly and satisfactorily. Was the product of the project the same as what was requested? Did the product of the project meet the needs of the stakeholders?

- **FINANCIAL CLOSURE:** Making final payments and completing cost records.

- **LESSONS LEARNED:** An analysis of what went right and wrong on the project and what would be done differently if the project could be done over again. Though the *PMBOK® Guide* lists this topic as an output of most controlling processes and also as part of closing, exam questions require you to know that it is done during closing.

- **UPDATE RECORDS:** Updating project records and adding the new skills acquired to team members' human resource records.

- **FINAL PROJECT PERFORMANCE REPORTING:** Analyzing and documenting the success and effectiveness of the project.

- **PROJECT ARCHIVES:** At the end of each project, a concerted effort must be made to put all files, letters, correspondence and other records of the project into an organized file which is stored for use on future projects.

The following are the results or outputs of administrative closure:

- **PROJECT ARCHIVES**

- **LESSONS LEARNED**

- **PROJECT CLOSURE/FORMAL ACCEPTANCE**: Once administrative closure is completed and formal sign-off that the products of the project are acceptable is received from the customer, other stakeholders and/or the sponsor, the project is closed. Expect many questions on the exam that provide you with situations and require you to determine if the project is closed.

- **RELEASE RESOURCES**: All human resources are released back to their functional areas and other resources are transferred to appropriate departments.

Practice Exam for the CAPM® and PMP® Exams
Communications Management

1. Extensive use of ___ communication is most likely to aid in solving complex problems.

   A. Verbal
   B. Written
   C. Formal
   D. Nonverbal

2. The work breakdown structure can be an effective aid for communication in which situation(s)?

   A. Internal within the project team
   B. Internal within the organization
   C. External with the customer
   D. Internal and external to the project

3. Conflict resolution techniques that may be used on a project include confronting, smoothing, forcing and:

   A. Withdrawing
   B. Directing
   C. Organizing
   D. Controlling

4. The MOST likely result of communication blockers is that:

   A. The project is delayed
   B. Trust level is enhanced
   C. Conflict occurs
   D. Senior management is displeased

5. Communications are often enhanced when the sender ___ the receiver.

   A. Speaks up to
   B. Uses more physical movements when talking to
   C. Talks slowly to
   D. Shows concern for the perspective of

6. Formal written correspondence with the customer is required when:

   A. Defects are detected
   B. The customer requests additional work not covered under contract
   C. The project has a schedule slippage that includes changes to the critical path
   D. The project has cost overruns

7. A project manager has a problem with a team member's performance. What is BEST form of communication for addressing this problem?

   A. Formal written communication
   B. Formal verbal communication
   C. Informal written communication
   D. Informal verbal communication

8. **Communications under a contract should tend toward:**

   A. Formal written communications
   B. Formal verbal communications
   C. Informal written communications
   D. Informal verbal communications

9. **The project status report is an example of which form of communication?**

   A. Formal written communication
   B. Formal verbal communication
   C. Informal written communication
   D. Informal verbal communication

10. **When a project manager is engaged in negotiations, nonverbal communication skills are of:**

    A. Little importance
    B. Major importance
    C. Importance only when cost and schedule objectives are involved
    D. Importance only to ensure you win the negotiation

11. **A large, one-year telecommunications project is about halfway done when you take the place of the previous project manager. The project involves three different sellers and a project team of 30 people. You would like to see the project's communications requirements and what technology is being used to aid in project communications. Where will you find this information?**

    A. The project plan
    B. The information distribution plan
    C. The Gantt chart
    D. The communications management plan

12. **Contract closeout is similar to administrative closure in that they both involve:**

    A. Product verification
    B. Kickoff meetings
    C. Quality assurance activities
    D. Creation of the scope verification plan

13. **An output of administrative closure is the creation of:**

    A. Project archives
    B. A project charter
    C. A project plan
    D. A risk analysis plan

14. **All of the following are part of administrative closure EXCEPT?**

    A. Lessons learned
    B. Formal acceptance
    C. Reduced resource spending
    D. Benefit/cost analysis

15. A project is not completed until?

A. The work is completed
B. Formal acceptance is received
C. The customer is satisfied
D. Lessons learned are completed

Communications Management Questions Only For the PMP® Exam

16. You have been working on a very large software development project that has made use of over 230 people. Finally, all the scope of work is completed. It would be BEST to?

A. Throw a party for the team members
B. Make sure the project is integrated with other projects
C. Begin to focus on your other projects
D. Report on the performance of the project

17. You provide a project cost estimate of the project to the project sponsor. He is unhappy with the estimate, because he thinks the price should be lower. He asks you to cut 15% off the project estimate. What should you do?

A. Start the project and constantly look for cost savings
B. Tell all the team members to cut 15% from their estimates
C. Inform management of the tasks to be cut
D. Look for resources with low hourly rates

18. Project information has been distributed according to the communications plan. Some project deliverables have been changed. Those changes were made according to the change control plan. One stakeholder expressed surprise to the project manager upon being informed of a previously published change to a project deliverable. All stakeholders received the communications containing notification of the change. What should the project manager do?

A. Determine why the stakeholder did not receive the information and let him know when it was published
B. Ask the functional manager why the stakeholder did not understand his responsibility
C. Review the communications plan and make revisions, if necessary
D. Address the situation in the next steering committee meeting so others do not miss published changes

19. A project team has members in five different locations with varying information systems. The project manager works with the project team to determine how stakeholders should be managed. These methods are detailed in which document?

A. Overall project plan
B. Scope statement
C. Communications management plan
D. Staffing management plan

20. Halfway through a large, one-year project, you take the place of the previous project manager. The project involves four different sellers and a project team of 40 people. Where will you find information regarding the project's communications requirements and what technology is being used to aid in project communications?

    A. Information distribution plan
    B. Project plan
    C. Communications management plan
    D. Gantt chart

21. As the project manager, you are preparing your methods for quality management. In your project management system, you are looking for a method that can demonstrate the relationship between events and their resulting effects. You want to use a method to depict the events that cause a negative effect on quality. Which of the following is the BEST choice for accomplishing your objective?

    A. Histogram
    B. Pareto chart
    C. Ishikawa diagram
    D. Control chart

22. A project manager had a complex problem to solve and made a decision about what needed to be done. A few months later, the problem resurfaced. Most likely what did the project manager not do?

    A. Proper risk analysis
    B. Confirm that the decision solved the problem
    C. Have the project sponsor validate the decision
    D. Use an Ishikawa diagram

23. Communication is the key to the success of a project. As the project manager, you have three stakeholders with whom you need to communicate. As such, you have six channels of communication. A new stakeholder has been added that you also need to communicate with. How many communications channels do you have now?

    A. 7
    B. 10
    C. 12
    D. 16

24. Two people are arguing about what needs to be done to complete a task. If the project manager wants to know what is going on, she should pay MOST attention to:

    A. What is said
    B. What is being discussed according to those arguing
    C. Physical mannerisms
    D. The pitch and tone of the voices

25. A project manager has a project team consisting of people in four countries. The project is very important to the company, and the project manager is concerned about its success. The length of the project schedule is acceptable. What type of communications method should he/she use?

    A. Informal verbal
    B. Formal written
    C. Formal verbal
    D. Informal written

26. The project status meeting is not going well. Everyone is talking at the same time, there are people who are not participating and many topics are being discussed at random. Which of the following rules for effective meetings is NOT being adhered to?

    A. Courtesy and consideration of each other
    B. Schedule meetings in advance
    C. Have a purpose for the meeting
    D. Create and publish an agenda

27. You have just been assigned as project manager for a large manufacturing project. This one-year project is about halfway done. It involves five different sellers and twenty members of your company on the project team. You want to quickly review where the project now stands. Which of the following reports would be the MOST helpful in finding such information?

    A. Task status
    B. Progress
    C. Forecast
    D. Communications

28. A project manager has just reached the end of a project. Which of the following documents will the project manager need for closure of the project?

    A. Documents that describe the project status
    B. Trend analyses
    C. Change requests
    D. Documents that describe the product of the project

29. A team member is visiting the manufacturing plant of one of the suppliers. Which of the following is the MOST important thing to be done in any telephone calls the project manager might make to the team member?

    A. Ask the team member to repeat back what the project manager says
    B. Review the list of contact information for all stakeholders
    C. Ask the team member to look for change requests
    D. Review the upcoming meeting schedule

Communications Management Answers

1. **Answer:** B

   Explanation: Written communication allows your words to be documented, and they will go to everyone in the same form. When there are complex problems, you want everyone to receive the same thing.

2. **Answer:** D

   Explanation: The work breakdown structure allows communication up and down the organization as well as outside the project.

3. **Answer:** A

   Explanation: There is always the option to simply postpone dealing with the issue until later. This is withdrawing.

4. **Answer:** C

   Explanation: The major result of communication barriers and miscommunication as a whole, is conflict.

5. **Answer:** D

   Explanation: Understanding the receiver's perspective allows you to direct the communication to meet their needs.

6. **Answer:** B

   Explanation: Everything that we do is more formal in a contract environment than in other project activities. Because B deals with contracts, it is the best answer.

7. **Answer:** D

   Explanation: The best choice is D. If informal verbal communication does not solve the problem, choice A is the next best choice. This does not mean that you do not keep records of the problem, but this question is asking about communication between two parties.

8. **Answer:** A

   Explanation: When we talk about contracts, everything that we do is more formal than in other project activities. Records are also important, thus the need for written communication.

9. **Answer:** A

   Explanation: The project status needs to be known by many people. Therefore, it is best to make this type of communication written so that it can be transmitted to many people. It is also formal in that it is an official report of the project. Therefore choice A is the best answer.

10. **Answer:** B

Explanation: Nonverbal communication carries 55% of the message you send. With this much at stake, nonverbal communication is of major importance.

11. **Answer:** D

Explanation: Although the information is found as a sub-plan to the project plan (choice A), the communications management plan (choice D) is the best answer because it directly answers the question.

12. **Answer:** A

Explanation: A scope verification plan (choice D) is created earlier in the project and used during controlling, not closing. Quality assurance (choice C) occurs during executing, and kickoff meetings (choice B) during planning. All types of closure must make sure that the actual product of the project meets the requirements for the product. Therefore choice A is the best answer.

13. **Answer:** A

Explanation: You have not seen the term risk analysis plan (choice D) in this book so it is unlikely to be the best answer. The project plan and project charter (choices B and C) are products of earlier steps in the project management life cycle.

14. **Answer:** D

Explanation: Benefit/cost analysis (choice D) is done earlier in the project to help select between alternatives. All the other choices are done during closing. Therefore choice D must be the best answer.

15. **Answer:** B

Explanation: A project is not complete until administrative closure is completed and formal acceptance is received. The best choice here is B.

16. **Answer:** D

Explanation: Notice how this question is similar to number 15? Though all the choices seem like a good idea, there is only one BEST. Usually these questions can be reworded to, "What do you do next?" In this case, the project manager cannot move on until the project is actually completed. That means that administrative closure must occur. The only choice that relates to administrative closure is choice D. Integrating (choice B) is a great idea but not all projects have another project with which to integrate. Once administrative closure is done, then throw a party!

17. **Answer:** C

Explanation: This is a major problem on any project when management does not understand project management. Why cut all tasks, as in choice B? One should only look at the critical path tasks. Choice A is not correct because the project manager must deal with the cost problem during planning, not wait until later.

18. **Answer:** C

Explanation: Choice A cannot be correct because he may have received the communication but forgotten or not understood it. Choices B and D do not address the root cause of the problem. The problem presented here shows that there is something missing in the communications plan. The best answer is to review the communications plan in order to prevent future problems and find any instances of similar problems.

19. **Answer:** D

Explanation: A concerted effort must be made to determine how to best use stakeholders on the project. The management of this asset is defined in the staffing management plan. The staffing management plan becomes part of the project plan.

20. **Answer:** C

Explanation: Although the information is found as a sub-plan to the project plan (choice B), the communications management plan (choice C) is the best answer.

21. **Answer:** C

Explanation: Ishikawa diagrams (also called cause-and-effect diagrams) and all reports and diagrams are communication tools. This question asks you to pick the most appropriate communication tool. The Ishikawa is more appropriate than the Pareto chart (choice B) since you are trying to determine the causes. Once causes are known and you have data on occurrences, the data can be displayed in a Pareto chart.

22. **Answer:** B

Explanation: The final steps of problem solving include: implement a decision, review it and confirm that the decision solved the problem.

23. **Answer:** B

Explanation: Did you realize that the project manager is part of the communication channels? Therefore, there are actually four stakeholders to begin with and six channels of communication. The question is asking how many total channels of communication do you have with a team of five people. The formula is (N x (N-1))/2 or (5 x 4)/2 = 10. The formula is (Nx(N-1))/2 or (5x4)/2 = 10.

24. **Answer:** C

Explanation: Choice C refers to nonverbal communication, which represents 55% of communication.

25. **Answer:** B

Explanation: Because of the differences in culture and the distance between team members, you need to have formal written communications.

26. **Answer:** D

Explanation: Choice A is not a "rule" for effective meetings. Since there is no indication in the situation that the meeting was not scheduled in advance (choice B) or that there isn't a purpose (choice C), these cannot be the best answers. "Discussed at random" implies no agenda (choice D). If an agenda is issued beforehand, people will be following the outline and should not need random discussions.

27. **Answer:** B

Explanation: The key word is quickly. The progress report will summarize project status. The task status (choice A) is too detailed for a quick look. A forecast report (choice C) only looks into the future.

28. **Answer:** D

Explanation: Product verification is accomplished in the closing phase. To do the verification, you need the original description to compare to the results. Choice C is not correct since they are only requests and not approved changes.

29. **Answer:** A

Explanation: Questions like this can drive one crazy. Although it asks for the most important thing, there are many choices that are reasonably correct. In questions like these, look for the most immediate need. In this case, the team member is in a manufacturing environment. That means that communications will most likely be blocked by noise. In order to have the issue at hand taken care of, the communication, it is BEST for the project manager to use choice A.

Risk Management
(PMBOK® GUIDE Chapter 11)

This can be a hard topic on the exam. Many people assume that risk management means simply completing a list. They have never had training in real risk management. The topic is also difficult in that this chapter has been completely rewritten in the 2000 edition of the *PMBOK® Guide*. I suggest that you read the entire chapter in the *PMBOK® Guide*.

It is important to understand that project risks can be substantially decreased. Some studies quote a 90% decrease in project problems through the use of risk management. Risk management is a very proactive task. Through the process of risk management, we change from the project being in control of the project manager to the project manager being in control of the project.

You do not have to be a risk management expert to pass risk questions on the exam, nor will this chapter make you an expert. It will provide the overview necessary for the exam, but you should realize that there are more tools and techniques to real-world risk management.

Although the exam does not require memorization of *PMBOK® Guide* definitions, knowing some definitions in risk can help you find answers to exam questions. You should MEMORIZE the definitions, the process of risk management and what happens when in the process.

DEFINITION OF A RISK OR RISK EVENT: "A discrete occurrence that may affect the project for good or bad." NOTE: Do not forget that there can be good risks, sometimes called opportunities!

DEFINITION OF UNCERTAINTY: "An uncommon state of nature, characterized by the absence of any information related to a desired outcome."

RISK FACTORS: When looking at risk, one should determine:
- The probability that it will occur (what)
- The range of possible outcomes (impact or amount at stake)
- Expected timing (when) in the project life cycle
- Anticipated frequency of risk events from that source (how often)

Chapter 10
Risk Management

RISK AVERSE: Someone who does not want to take risks.

RISK TOLERANCES (page 129): The amount of risk that is acceptable (tolerance level). For example, "a risk that affects our reputation will not be tolerated," or "a risk of a two week delay is okay, but nothing more."

DEFINITION OF RISK MANAGEMENT (page 127): "The processes involved with identifying, analyzing and responding to risk. It includes maximizing the results of positive events and minimizing the consequences of adverse events."

INPUTS TO RISK MANAGEMENT (page 129): What is needed in order to begin the risk process.

Exercise: Test yourself! Explain why each of the following inputs to risk management are needed before one can adequately perform the risk management process.

Project background information	
Historical information	
Past lessons learned	
Project charter	
Scope statement	
Team	

Stakeholders	
WBS	
Network diagram	
Cost and time estimates	
Staffing plan	
Organizational policies and templates	
Procurement plan	
Stakeholder risk tolerances	

PHONE: (952) 846-4484 - EMAIL: info@rmcproject.com - WEB: www.rmcproject.com

Chapter 10
Risk Management

Answer: There can be many answers. Here are some possible ones.

Project background information	Detailed enough information about the project, what other companies are doing, articles and other such information will help you identify more risks
Historical information	Will tell you risks from past projects
Past lessons learned	Will tell you what past teams would do if they could do their projects again Will help you identify, mitigate and manage risks on your project
Project charter	Helps you see if the overall project objectives are generally risky or not Helps identify risks based on what is and what is not included
Scope statement	Tells you the complexity of the project and helps you compare your team's knowledge and experience to what is required
Team	The project manager cannot identify all the risks alone. A group approach and the ability to split up risk management activities make the risk management process more accurate and timely.
Stakeholders	They will be able to see risks that the team cannot. Their involvement helps continue proper stakeholder management.
WBS	Risks are identified by task as well as by project
Network diagram	Shows path convergence (where paths converge) and thus helps to better analyze the risks of each task
Cost and time estimates	High-level time and cost requirements help identify time and cost risk. They are an input to risk management when they are high level and an output of risk management at the detail level
Staffing plan	Helps you understand what resources are available
Organizational policies and templates	Provide a foundation or standardization for your risk activities
Procurement plan	There is a strong connection between contracts (or procurement) and risk. One of the ways to mitigate risk may be to have certain terms and conditions added to a contract or to have the entire risky work outsourced. You would give it to someone for whom it is less risky, and thus less costly
Stakeholder risk tolerances	Knowing where and how much risk tolerance stakeholders have helps identify the impact of risks and which risk mitigation technique you would use

RISK MANAGEMENT PROCESS (page 127): This is an important topic. You must MEMORIZE what happens when, how the risk management process works on a real project and how it relates to the project life cycle. The risk management process includes six steps:

1. Risk Management Planning
2. Risk Identification
3. Qualitative Risk Analysis
4. Quantitative Risk Analysis
5. Risk Response Planning
6. Risk Monitoring And Control

STEP 1: **RISK MANAGEMENT PLANNING** (page 129): Defined as "deciding how to approach and plan the risk management activities for a project." The project manager, team, customer, stakeholders, experts and others will review any templates and procedures that exist for risk management, determine how risk management will be handled on the current project and develop the risk management plan. Therefore, risk management should be adjusted to the size, complexity, experience, skill level, etc., of the project and not done with just a standardized checklist.

RISK MANAGEMENT PLAN (page 130): Defines how the risk process will be structured and performed during the project life cycle. This is a new step in the 2000 edition of the *PMBOK® Guide*.

A risk management plan may include:
- Methodology
- Roles and responsibilities – non-team members may be included
- Budgeting for the risk management process
- Timing – how often the risk process will be performed throughout the project
- Scoring and interpretation
- Thresholds – a method to determine which risks will and will not be acted upon
- Reporting formats
- Tracking

Because a risk management plan contains budgets and schedules, it is an input to schedule development and cost budgeting.

OUTPUTS FROM RISK PLANNING (page 130):
- Risk management plan – described above

STEP 2: **RISK IDENTIFICATION** (page 131): Defined as "determining which risks might affect the project and documenting their characteristics." All stakeholders as well as experts from other parts of the company or outside the company may be involved in identifying risks. Sometimes, the core team will begin the process and then the other members will become involved, making risk identification an iterative process.

Smart project managers begin looking for risks as soon as a project is first discussed. However, the major risk identification effort occurs during planning. Risk identification cannot be completed until a WBS has been created and the project team knows "what is the project." Because risk identification can occur during the initiating and planning phases, the exam has often said that risk identification happens at the *onset* of the project. Risks may be identified at the beginning of the project, during each project phase and before approval of a major scope change. Risks may also be identified during all phases of the project including initiating, planning, executing, controlling and closing. In other words, although the major risk identification effort occurs at the onset of the project, risks should continue to be identified throughout the project.

RISK CATEGORIES (sources of risk, page 131): Risk categories are lists of common categories of risk (sources of risk) experienced by the company or on similar projects. Such a list may be an input to risk identification, but using such a list of categories is not the entire risk identification process. The categories help analyze and identify risks on each project. Expect the phrases "sources of risk" and "risk categories" to be used interchangeably on the exam.

There are many ways to classify or categorize risk. The *PMBOK®* refers to:
- Technical, quality or performance risks
- Project management risks
- Organizational risks
- External risks

A prior version of the *PMBOK® Guide* included another way to classify risks that still shows up on the exam from time to time.
- External – Regulatory, environmental, government, market shifts
- Internal – Time, cost, unforeseen conditions, scope changes, inexperience, poor planning, people, staffing, materials, equipment
- Technical – Changes in technology
- Unforeseeable – Only a small portion of risks (some say about 10%) are actually unforeseeable

If you look at categories of risk as "where do risks come from," sources of risk might be different than the list above. Here I have included some examples to help you understand what is a risk.
- Schedule risk - *"The hardware will arrive later than planned causing a delay in task XYZ of three days."*
- Cost risk - *"Because the hardware may arrive later than planned, we may need to extend our lease on the staging area at a cost of $20,000."*
- Quality risk - *"The concrete may not dry before winter weather sets in causing us to not meet our quality standard of concrete strength."*
- Performance or scope of work risk - *"We might not have correctly defined the scope of work for the computer installation. If that proves true we will have to add tasks at a cost of $20,000."*
- Resources risk - *"Riki is such an excellent designer that he may be called away to work on the new project everyone is so excited about. If that occurs we will have to use someone else and our schedule will slip between 100 to 275 hours."*
- Customer satisfaction (stakeholder satisfaction) risk - *"There is a chance that the customer will not be happy with the XYZ*

deliverable and not telling us, causing at least a 20% increase in communication problems."

INFORMATION-GATHERING TECHNIQUES (page132): Many people ask me how risks are identified. That is the subject of a risk management class. You should know that there are many ways to identify risk and that risk identification can be an art form. Luckily, you need not be a risk management expert to pass the exam.

The list of ways to identify risk outlined in the *PMBOK® Guide* is an extremely narrow and general list. There are twenty more techniques for accomplishing this effort in risk management classes. The exam should be straightforward here and simply require you to know that you will be doing the following to identify risks:

- Brainstorming: Usually done in a meeting where one idea helps generate another
- Delphi technique: Described in the Scope chapter
- Interviewing: Also called expert interviewing on the exam and consists of the team or project manager interviewing an expert to identify risks on the project or a specific element of work
- Strengths, weaknesses, opportunities and threats analysis: An analysis that looks at the project to identify its strengths, etc., and thereby identify risks

TYPES OF RISK: Risks can be classified under two main types:

1. Business – Risk of a gain or loss
2. Pure (Insurable) Risk – Only a risk of loss (e.g., fire, theft, personal injury)

OUTPUTS FROM RISK IDENTIFICATION (page 133):
- Risks
- **RISK TRIGGERS** (Symptoms, page 133) – A project manager should determine what are the early warning signs (indirect manifestations of actual risk events) for each risk on a project so that they will understand when to take action.

STEP 3: **QUALITATIVE RISK ANALYSIS** (page 133): Is a *subjective* analysis of risks to:
- Determine which risk events warrant a response
- Determine the probability and impact of all risks identified in step 2, in a subjective manner
- Determine which risks to analyze more fully in risk quantification or to skip risk quantification in favor of going directly to risk response planning. (This decision depends on many factors, including the importance of the project and the potential affect of the project on the performing organization.)
- Document non-critical, or non-top risks
- Determine the overall risk ranking for the project

PROBABILITY AND IMPACT (see the picture on page 136): One of the ways to help rank risks is to analyze the probability of a risk occurring and the effect (or impact or consequences) of the risk on the project.

- Determine the probability of each risk occurring – usually in the form of taking an educated guess (e.g., Low, Medium, High or 1 to 10)
- Determine the consequences (amount at stake, or impact) of each risk occurring – also in the form of taking an educated guess (e.g., Low, Medium, High or 1 to 10)

ASSUMPTION TESTING (page 135): or "What assumptions have been made?" Before the project manager can use the risk information collected, assumptions made must be identified and tested. Too many unknown guesses make the data unreliable. The *PMBOK® Guide* suggests that testing include evaluating the stability of each assumption and consequences if each assumption is false.

DATA PRECISION RANKING (page 135): or "How well understood is the risk?" Before the project manager can use the risk information collected so far, they must also analyze the precision of the data – how good is the data? The *PMBOK® Guide* suggests that this include the following activities and that each risk be rated for its precision.

- Extent of the understanding of the risk
- Data available about the risk
- Quality of the data
- Reliability and integrity of the data

RISK RATING MATRIX (page 135): In order to sort or rate risks so a determination can be made as to which risks will move on through the risk process, a risk rating matrix (shown on *PMBOK® Guide* page 136) may be used. Such a matrix results in a consistent evaluation of low, medium or high (or some other scale) for the project and for all projects, an improvement in the quality of the data and the risk rating process being more repeatable between projects.

OUTPUTS FROM QUALITATIVE RISK ANALYSIS (page 136): The results of qualitative analysis of the risk of a project may include:

- Risk rating for the project
- List of prioritized risks
- List of risks created for additional analysis in risk quantification or risk response planning
- Non-critical or non-top risks documented for later revisit during risk monitoring and control

Risk qualification can also lead to:
- The project can be compared to the overall risks of other projects
- The project could be selected, continued or terminated
- Resources could be moved between projects
- A full benefit/cost analysis of the project may be able to be completed
- Trends in project risk identified if risk qualification is repeated

STEP 4: **QUANTITATIVE RISK ANALYSIS** (risk quantification, page 137): A *numerical* analysis of the probability and consequences (amount at stake or impacts) of the highest risks on the project to:

- Determine which risk events warrant a response
- Determine overall project risk (risk exposure)
- Determine the quantified probability of meeting project objectives – e.g., "We only have an 80% chance of completing the project within the six months required by the customer," or "We only have a 75% chance of completing the project within the $80,000 budget."
- Determine cost and schedule reserves
- Identify risks requiring the most attention
- Create realistic and achievable cost, schedule or scope targets

Risk quantification involves the following activities:

- Further investigation into the highest risks on the project
- Determination of the type of probability distribution that will be used – e.g., triangular, normal, beta, uniform or log normal distributions (See chart, page 140)
- Interviewing experts
- Sensitivity analysis – determining which risks have the most impact on the project
- Monte Carlo simulation (simulation) – described later
- Decision tree analysis – described later

PMI® suggests that the quantitative method (also referred to as quantification) is preferable to qualification because it is less subjective and is a better approximation of actual probabilities and consequences. NOTE: Steps 2 through 4 combined can be referred to as *risk assessment*.

EXPECTED MONETARY VALUE (OR **EXPECTED VALUE**): The product of two numbers, probability and consequences (impact or the amount at stake). Questions can ask, "What is the expected value of a task or of a series of tasks?" Expected value questions can also be asked in conjunction with decision trees noted in this chapter.

Exercise: Test yourself! Complete the following chart.

Task	Probability	Consequences	Expected Value
A	10%	US $20,000	
B	30%	US $45,000	
C	68%	US $18,000	

Answer:
I hope it makes you feel better that something on the exam is easy!

Task	Probability	Consequences	Expected Value
A	10%	US $20,000	US $2,000
B	30%	US $45,000	US $13,500
C	68%	US $18,000	US $12,240

DECISION TREE (page 139 and a picture on 141): There have traditionally been only one or two questions about decision trees on the exam. See the diagram on *PMBOK® Guide* page 141. You should understand the following:

- A decision tree takes into account future events in trying to make a decision today
- It calculates the expected value (probability times consequences) in more complex situations than the expected value previously presented
- It involves mutual exclusivity (previously explained in the Quality chapter)

You should be able to answer questions about decision trees and calculate a simple one like the one on page 141 of the *PMBOK® Guide*. Read the question carefully. It could ask you to calculate the expected value (or just "value") of a path or the value of your decision.

The following exercise shows a picture of a decision tree. The box represents a decision to be made and the circles represent what can happen as a result of the decision.

Exercise: A company is trying to determine if prototyping is worthwhile on the project. They have come up with the following consequences of whether the equipment works or fails when it is used. Based on the information provided below, what is the expected value of your decision?

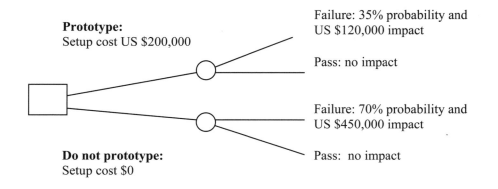

Prototype:
Setup cost US $200,000

Failure: 35% probability and US $120,000 impact

Pass: no impact

Do not prototype:
Setup cost $0

Failure: 70% probability and US $450,000 impact

Pass: no impact

Answer: If one just looks at the setup cost of prototyping it would seem like an unwise decision to spend money on prototyping. However, the analysis proves differently. Taking into account only one future event, the decision is that it would be cheaper to do the prototyping. The answer is US $242,000, or to prototype.

Prototype	35% x $120,000 = US $42,000 plus US $200,000 = US $242,000
Do not prototype	70% x $450,000 = US $315,000

MONTE CARLO SIMULATION (page 44, 75, 139, the chart on page 142, and referred to as "simulation" in the *PMBOK® Guide*): This simulation "performs" the project many times and uses the network diagram and estimates to simulate the cost or schedule results of the project. See also the discussion of this topic in the Time chapter. There have traditionally been only one or two questions about Monte Carlo analysis on the exam. This could change over time.

Monte Carlo Simulation:

- Evaluates the project, not the tasks
- Provides the probability of completing the project on any specific day, or for any specific amount of cost
- Provides the probability of any task actually being on the critical path
- Provides a percent probability that each task will be on the critical path
- Takes into account path convergence (places in the network diagram where many paths converge into one task)
- Translates uncertainties into impacts to the total project
- Can be used to assess cost and schedule impacts
- Is usually done with a computer-based Monte Carlo program because of the intricacies of the calculations
- Results in a probability distribution

OUTPUTS FROM QUANTITATIVE RISK ANALYSIS (page 139): When completed, quantitative risk analysis results in:

- Prioritized list of quantified risks
- Forecasts of potential project costs or schedule
- Listing of the possible project completion dates and costs with their confidence levels
- Probability of achieving the required project cost or schedule objectives
- Trends in risk as risk quantification is repeated throughout the project
- Documented list of non-critical, non-top risks

STEP 5: **RISK RESPONSE PLANNING** (page 140): This step involves figuring out "what are we going to do about it." It involves finding ways to make the negative risk smaller or eliminate it entirely, as well as finding ways to make positive risks more likely or greater in impact. All risk on a project cannot be eliminated. During this step:

- Strategies are agreed upon in advance by all parties
- Primary and backup strategies are selected
- Risks are assigned to individuals or groups to take responsibility
- Strategies are reviewed over the life of the project for appropriateness as more information about the project becomes known

RISK OWNER (page 141): Each risk must be assigned to someone who will help develop the risk response and who will be assigned to carry it out or "own" the risk. The risk owner is then free to take predetermined action when risks occur resulting in faster action and less cost, time and other impacts on the project.

> Think about how the application of risk management can change your real-world projects. Using risk owners means a substantial decrease in the need for meetings when a problem arises. If you use risk owners you have a prearranged and preapproved plan for action, and someone to carry it out, already in place. No meeting is needed.

RISK RESPONSE STRATEGIES (Sometimes called risk mitigation strategies, page 141): Developing options and determining actions to enhance opportunities and reduce threats. This may involve changing the planned approach to completing the project – e.g., changes to the WBS, quality plan, schedule and budget. These strategies cannot eliminate all risk. In each case, communication of risks and strategies is necessary as part of the strategy.

The choices include:
- **AVOIDANCE** – Eliminate the threat by eliminating the cause

- **MITIGATION** – Reduce the probability or the consequences of an adverse risk and increase the probability or consequences of an opportunity

- **ACCEPTANCE** – Do nothing and say, "If it happens, it happens." Active acceptance may involve the creation of contingency plans and passive acceptance may leave actions to be determined as needed. A decision to accept a risk must be communicated to stakeholders.

- **TRANSFERENCE (DEFLECTION, ALLOCATION)** – Make another party responsible for the risk through purchasing of insurance, performance bonds, warranties, guarantees or outsourcing the work. Here is where the strong connection between risk and procurement (or contracts) begins. One must complete risk assessment before a contract can be signed! Transference of risk is included in the terms and conditions of the contract.

When selecting risk strategies, it is important to remember:
- Strategies must be timely
- The effort selected must be appropriate to the severity of the risk – avoid spending more money preventing the risk than the impact of the risk would cost if it occurred
- One response can be used to address more than one risk
- Involve the team, stakeholders and experts in selecting a strategy

Exercise: For each strategy described, determine the name of its strategy. Remember to include mitigate probability and mitigate impact.

Description of strategy	Name of risk response strategy
Remove a task from the project	
Assign a team member to visit the seller's manufacturing facilities frequently to learn about problems with delivery as early as possible	
Notify management that there could be a major cost increase if a risk occurs because no action is being taken to prevent the risk	
Remove a troublesome resource from the project	
Provide a team member who is less experienced with additional training	
Train the team on conflict resolution strategies	
Outsource difficult work to a more experienced company	
Ask the client to handle some of the work	
Decide to prototype a risky piece of equipment	

Answer:

Description of strategy	Name of risk response strategy
Remove a task from the project	Avoidance
Assign a team member to visit the seller's manufacturing facilities frequently to learn about a problem with delivery as early as possible	Mitigation of the impact
Notify management that there could be a major cost increase if a risk occurs because no action is being taken to prevent the risk	Acceptance
Remove a troublesome resource from the project	Avoidance
Provide a team member who is less experienced with additional training	Mitigation of the probability
Train the team on conflict resolution strategies	Mitigation of the impact
Outsource difficult work to a more experienced company	Transference
Ask the client to handle some of the work	Transference
Decide to prototype a risky piece of equipment	Mitigation of the probability

OUTPUTS FROM RISK RESPONSE PLANNING (page 143):

INSURANCE: A response to certain risks such as fire, property or personal injury (e.g., pure risks) is to purchase insurance. Insurance exchanges an unknown risk for a known risk because the consequences of the risk are known.

CONTRACTING: Hiring someone outside your company to complete the work when it would decrease project risk. NOTE: You cannot remove all the risk from a project by contracting. For example, if there is a risk of damage in transport for a project component, hiring someone else to do the transportation will not make the move risk-free.

RESIDUAL RISKS (page 143): Some risks will remain after risk mitigation or risk response planning. Though these risks may have been accepted, they should be properly documented and revised throughout the project. What was thought of as an acceptable risk during planning may not have the same ranking during executing.

SECONDARY RISKS (page 143): Included in risk response planning should be an analysis of the new risks created by the risk response strategies selected. Frequently, what is done to mitigate one risk will cause other risks to occur. For example, a risk of fire can be allocated to an insurance company but also cause the risk of cash flow problems. Cash flow should then be analyzed and if appropriate, added to the risk management process.

CONTINGENCY PLANNING (planned responses, page 143): Planning the specific actions that will be taken if a risk event occurs, or *planned response*. These plans can be put in place later, if needed, without meetings or increased impact to the project caused by delayed action.

FALLBACK PLANNING (page 143): Specific actions that will be taken if the contingency plan is not effective.

RISK RESPONSE PLAN (risk register, page 143): A written document that captures the risks you identified and what you plan to do about them. The project manager should also record non-critical risks so that they can easily be revisited during the executing phase.

REVISED PROJECT PLAN (page 144): The efforts spent in risk management will result in changes to the project plan. Tasks could be added, removed or assigned to different resources. Thus, planning is an iterative process.

RESERVES (contingency, page 144): Formulating the amount of time or cost that needs to be added to the project to account for risk. These are sometimes called management reserves (to account for "unknown unknowns," items you did not or could not identify in risk management) and contingency reserves (to account for "known unknowns," items you did identify in risk management). Reserves should be managed and guarded throughout the project life cycle. PMI® recommends a reserve of at least 10% or better yet, it can be calculated based on the expected value of project risks. Let's try an example.

Exercise: You are planning the manufacture of an existing product's modifications. Your analysis has come up with the following. What is the cost reserve that you would use?

- 30% probability of a delay in the receipt of parts with a cost to the project of US $9,000
- 20% probability that the parts will be US $10,000 cheaper than expected
- 25% probability that two parts will not fit together when installed, costing an extra US $3,500
- 30% probability that the manufacture may be simpler than expected, saving US $2,500
- 5% probability of a design defect causing US $5,000 of rework

Answer: The answer is US $1,075.

30% x US $9,000	Add US $2,700
20% x US $10,000	Subtract US $2,000
25% x US $3,500	Add US $875
30% x US $2,500	Subtract US $750
5% x US $5,000	Add US $250
TOTAL	US $1,075

The exam often asks questions such as:

- *What do you do with non-critical risks? Answer: Document and revisit periodically.*

- *Would you select only one risk response strategy? Answer: No, you can choose a combination of choices.*

- *What risk management activities are done during the executing phase of the project? Answer: Watching out for non-critical risks that become more important.*

- *What is the most important item to address in project team meetings? Answer: Risk.*

- *How would risks be addressed in project meetings? By asking, "What is the status of risks? Any new risks? Any change to the order of importance?"*

STEP 6: **RISK MONITORING AND CONTROL** (pages 144 - 145): This step involves managing the project according to the risk response plan and may include the following activities:

- Keeping track of the identified risks
- Implementing risk responses
- Looking for the occurrence of risk triggers
- Monitoring residual risks
- Identifying new risks
- Ensuring the execution of risk plans
- Evaluating the effectiveness of risk plans
- Developing new risk responses
- Communicating risk status and collecting risk status
- Communicating with stakeholders about risks
- Determining if assumptions are still valid
- Revisiting low ranking or non-critical risks to see if risk responses need to be determined
- Taking corrective action to adjust to the severity of actual risk events
- Looking for any unexpected effects or consequences of risk events
- Reevaluating risk identification, qualification and quantification when the project deviates from the baseline
- Updating risk plans
- Making changes to the project plan when new risk responses are developed
- Creating a database of risk data that may be used throughout the organization on other projects

CONTINGENCY PLANS (page 143): *Planned responses* to risks, or putting in place the contingency plans set up during risk response planning.

RISK RESPONSE AUDITS (risk audit, page 145): Examining and documenting the effectiveness of the risk response and the person managing (owning) the risk. This is an important step in order to see if the plans put in place are effective and if changes are needed. An audit, like all audits mentioned in the *PMBOK® Guide*, allows lessons to be learned for the project and for other projects in the organization.

RISK REVIEWS (page 145): Questions that always seem to come up on the exam are those that require you to know that the team needs to periodically review risk plans and adjust as required. Therefore, risk should be a major topic at team meetings to keep focus on risks and to make sure plans remain appropriate. Remember that a result of such reviews may be additional risk analysis or qualification and quantification.

OUTPUTS FROM RISK MONITORING AND CONTROL (page 146):

- **WORKAROUNDS** (page 146) – *Unplanned responses* to risks, or dealing with risks that you could not or did not anticipate. Which do you think are more frequent, contingency plans or workarounds? Most project managers will say workarounds because that has been the project manager's experience. In fact, with proper risk management, workarounds become less frequent than contingency plans.

- Corrective action

- Changes to the project – it is important to realize that the risk management process will change the project plan during planning and during executing/controlling

- Updates to the risk response plan – it is wise to always re-evaluate whether the plans need any correcting or adjusting after each unidentified or identified risk occurs

- Other updates to risk database, checklists, etc.

EXTRAS: Since many people do not have training in risk management, or make common errors, risk questions on the exam require you to have some experience in performing risk management in the workplace. The following is a synopsis of my presentation, "Common Stumbling Blocks in Risk Management," designed to help you think about common risk management errors and thus help you prepare for the exam.

- Risk identification is completed without knowing enough about the project. (See Inputs to Risk Management).

- Project risk is evaluated using only a questionnaire, interview or Monte Carlo techniques and thus does not provide a detailed, per task analysis of risk.

- Risk identification ends too soon, resulting in a brief list (20 risks) rather than an extensive list (hundreds) of risks.

- Steps identification through quantification are blended, resulting in risks that are evaluated or judged as they come to light. This decreases the number of total risks identified and causes people to stop participating in risk identification.

- The risks identified are general rather than specific (e.g., "communications" rather than "poor communication of customers' needs regarding installation of system XXX causing two weeks of rework").

- Some things considered risks are not uncertain, but facts, and are therefore not risks.

- Whole categories of risks are missed such as technology, cultural or marketplace.

- Only one method is used to identify risks (eg., only using a checklist) rather than a combination of methods. A combination helps ensure that more risks are identified.

- The first risk response strategy identified is selected without looking at other options and finding the best option or combination of options.

- Risks are not given enough attention during the project executing phase.

- Project managers do not introduce risk management to their team during the planning phase.

- Contracts are usually signed long BEFORE risks to the project are discussed.

Chapter 10
Risk Management

Practice Exam for the CAPM® and PMP® Exams
Risk Management

1. All of the following are factors in the assessment of project risk EXCEPT?

    A. Risk event
    B. Risk probability
    C. Amount at stake
    D. Insurance premiums

2. If a project has a 60% chance of a US $100,000 profit and a 40% chance of a US $100,000 loss, the expected monetary value for the project is:

    A. $100,000 profit
    B. $60,000 loss
    C. $20,000 profit
    D. $40,000 loss

3. "An uncommon state of nature, characterized by the absence of any information related to a desired outcome," is a common definition for:

    A. An act of God
    B. An amount at stake
    C. Uncertainty
    D. Risk aversion

4. Assuming that the ends of a range of estimates are +/- 3 sigma from the mean, which of the following range estimates involves the LEAST risk?

    A. 30 days, plus or minus 5 days
    B. 22 - 30 days
    C. Optimistic = 26 days, most likely = 30 days, pessimistic = 33 days
    D. About 28 days

5. Which of the following risk events is MOST likely to interfere with attaining a project's schedule objective?

    A. Delays in obtaining required approvals
    B. Substantial increases in the cost of purchased materials
    C. Contract disputes that generate claims for increased payments
    D. Slippage of the planned post-implementation review meeting

6. If a risk has a 20% chance of happening in a given month, and the project is expected to last five months, what is the probability that this risk event will occur during the fourth month of the project?

    A. Less than 1 %
    B. 20%
    C. 60%
    D. 80%

7. **If a risk event has a 90% chance of occurring, and the consequences will be US $10,000, what does US $9,000 represent?**

   A. Risk value
   B. Present value
   C. Expected value
   D. Contingency budget

8. **Risks will be identified during which phase of the project management life cycle?**

   A. Initiating
   B. Planning
   C. Executing
   D. All phases

9. **What should be done with non-critical risks?**

   A. Document them for historical use on other projects
   B. Document them and revisit during project execution
   C. Document them and set them aside because they are already covered in your contingency plans
   D. Document them and give them to the customer

10. **All of the following are always inputs to the risk management process EXCEPT:**

    A. Historical information
    B. Lessons learned
    C. Work breakdown structure
    D. Project status reports

11. **Risk tolerances are determined in order to help:**

    A. The team rank the project risks
    B. The project manager estimate the project
    C. The team schedule the project
    D. Management know how other managers will act on the project

12. **All of the following are common results of risk management EXCEPT:**

    A. Contract terms and conditions are created
    B. The project plan is changed
    C. The communications plan is changed
    D. The project charter is changed

13. **Purchasing insurance is BEST considered an example of risk:**

    A. Mitigation
    B. Transference
    C. Acceptance
    D. Avoidance

14. **You are finding it difficult to evaluate the exact cost impact of risks. You should evaluate on a(n):**

    A. Quantitative basis
    B. Numerical basis
    C. Qualitative basis
    D. Econometric basis

15. **An output from risk response planning is:**

    A. Residual risks
    B. Risks identified
    C. Prioritized list of risks
    D. Impacts identified

16. **Workarounds are determined during which step of risk management?**

    A. Risk identification
    B. Risk quantification
    C. Risk response planning
    D. Risk monitoring and control

17. **During which step of risk management is a determination to transfer a risk made?**

    A. Risk identification
    B. Risk quantification
    C. Risk response control
    D. Risk response planning

Risk Questions Only For the PMP® Exam

18. **A project manager has just finished the risk response plan for a US $387,000 engineering project. Which of the following should he probably do NEXT?**

    A. Determine the overall risk rating of the project
    B. Begin to analyze the risks that show up in the project drawings
    C. Add tasks to the project work breakdown structure
    D. Hold a project risk review

19. **A project manager asked various stakeholders to determine the probability and impact of a number of risks. He then tested assumptions and evaluated the precision of the risk data. He is about to move to the next step of risk management. Based on this information, what has the project manager forgotten to do?**

    A. Evaluate trends in risk analysis
    B. Identify triggers
    C. Provide a standardized risk rating matrix
    D. Create a fallback plan

20. A project manager has assembled the project team, identified 56 risks on the project, determined what would trigger the risks, ranked them on a risk rating matrix, tested their assumptions and measured the precision of the data used. The team is continuing to move through the risk management process. What has the project manager forgotten to do?

    A. Simulation
    B. Risk mitigation
    C. Overall risk ranking for the project
    D. Involvement of other stakeholders

21. You are a project manager for a major new manufacturing plant that has never been done before. The project cost is estimated at US $30,000,000 and will make use of three sellers. Once begun, the project cannot be cancelled, as there will be a large expenditure on plant and equipment. As the project manager, it would be MOST important to carefully:

    A. Review all cost proposals from the sellers
    B. Examine the budget reserves
    C. Complete the project charter
    D. Perform an identification of risks

22. During risk planning, your team cannot come up with an effective way to mitigate or insure against a risk. It is not a task that could be outsourced, nor could it be deleted. What would be the BEST solution?

    A. Accept the risk
    B. Continue to investigate ways to mitigate the risk
    C. Look for ways to avoid the risk
    D. Look for ways to transfer the risk

23. A project manager is quantifying risk for her project. Several of her experts are offsite, but wish to be included in the risk assessment portion of the project. How can this be done?

    A. Use Monte Carlo simulation using the Internet as a tool
    B. Apply the critical path method
    C. Determine options for corrective action
    D. Apply the Delphi technique

24. An experienced project manager has just begun working for a large information technology integrator when the project manager wants to begin to identify all of the project risks. Which of the following would BEST help in this effort?

    A. An article from PM Network Magazine
    B. Her scope statement from the project planning phase
    C. Her resource plan from the project planning phase
    D. A conversation with a team member from a similar project that failed in the past

25. You have been appointed as the manager of a new, large and complex project. Because this project is business-critical and very visible, senior management has told you to analyze the project's risks and prepare mitigation strategies for them as soon as possible. The organization has risk management procedures that are seldom used or followed, and has had a history of handling risks badly. The project's first milestone is in two weeks. In preparing the plan to manage risks, input from which of the following is generally LEAST important?

    A. Project team members
    B. Project sponsor
    C. Individuals responsible for risk management policies and templates
    D. Key stakeholders

26. You were in the middle of deploying new technology to field offices across the country. A hurricane caused power outages just when the upgrade was near completion. When the power was restored all of the information was lost, with no way of retrieving it. What should have been done to prevent this?

    A. Purchase insurance
    B. Plan for a reserve fund
    C. Monitor the weather and have a contingency plan
    D. Schedule the installation outside of the hurricane season

27. A system development project is nearing closure when an unidentified risk is discovered. This could potentially affect the project's overall ability to deliver. What should be done NEXT?

    A. Alert the project sponsor of potential impacts to cost, scope or schedule
    B. Qualify the risk
    C. Mitigate this risk by developing a risk response plan
    D. Develop a workaround

28. The CPI of a project is 0.6 and the SPI is 0.71. The project has 625 tasks and is being completed over a four year period. The team members are very inexperienced and the project received little support for proper planning. Which of the following is the BEST thing to do?

    A. Update the risk identification and analysis
    B. Spend more time improving the cost estimates
    C. Remove as many tasks as possible
    D. Reorganize the responsibility matrix

29. While preparing your risk responses, you identify additional risks. What should you do?

    A. Add reserves to the project
    B. Document the unknown risk items and calculate the expected monetary value based on probability and impact that result from the occurrences
    C. Determine the unknown risk events and the associated cost, then add the cost to the project budget as a reserve
    D. Add a 10% contingency

30. You have just been assigned as the project manager for a new telecommunications project. There appear to be many risks on this project, but no one has evaluated them to assess the range of possible project outcomes. What needs to be done?

    A. Risk identification
    B. Risk quantification
    C. Risk response planning
    D. Risk monitoring and control

31. During project execution, a team member identifies a risk that is not in the risk response plan. What should you do?

    A. Analyze the risk
    B. Get further information on how the team member identified the risk, because you already performed a detailed analysis and did not identify this risk
    C. Disregard the risk, because risks were identified during planning
    D. Inform the customer about the risk

32. During project execution, a major problem occurred that was not included in the risk response plan. What should you do FIRST?

    A. Create a workaround
    B. Re-evaluate the risk identification process
    C. Look for any unexpected effects of the problem
    D. Tell management

33. The customer requests a change to the project that would increase the project risk. Which of the following should you do before all the others?

    A. Include the expected value of the risk in the new cost estimate
    B. Talk to the customer about the impact of the change
    C. Analyze the impacts of the change with the team
    D. Change the risk management plan

Risk Management Answers

1. **Answer:** D

    Explanation: Insurance premiums come into play when you determine which mitigation method you will use.

2. **Answer:** C

    Explanation: Expected monetary value is another name for expected value. It is computed by EV = Probability X Impact. We need to compute both positive and negative values and then sum them. 0.6 X $100,000 = $60,000. 0.4 X ($100,000) = ($40,000). Expected Monetary Value = $20,000 profit.

3. **Answer:** C

    Explanation: Understand this definition of uncertainty so you can answer questions concerning certainty.

4. **Answer:** C

    Explanation: This one drove you crazy didn't it? Reread the question! It means, "Which range has the least risk?" When you look at the ranges of each choice, you will see that A is ten days, B is eight days and C is seven days. Therefore, the answer is C. Practice reading questions that are wordy and have extraneous data.

5. **Answer:** A

    Explanation: Notice the words "post-implementation" in choice D. It will not definitely interfere with the project schedule. Contract disputes (choice C) or cost increases (choice B) will not necessarily interfere with schedule. The first choice is the only one that deals with a time delay.

6. **Answer:** B

    Explanation: Don't feel too silly. Many people miss this one. No calculation is needed. If there is a 20% chance in any one month the chance in the fourth month must also be 20%.

7. **Answer:** C

    Explanation: Expected value is computed by multiplying the probability times the impact. In this case EV = 0.9 X $10,000 = $9,000.

8. **Answer:** D

    Explanation: Though risks are primarily identified during planning, risks will come to light during all phases of the project. Therefore, choice D is the best answer.

9. **Answer:** B

Explanation: Risks change throughout the project. You need to review risks at intervals during the project to ensure that non-critical risks have not become critical.

10. **Answer:** D

Explanation: Project status reports can be an input to risk management, however, when completing risk management for the first time, you would not have project status reports. Therefore project status reports are not always an input to risk management.

11. **Answer:** A

Explanation: If you know the tolerances of the stakeholders, you can determine how they might react to different situations and risk events. You use this information to help assign levels of risk on each work package or activity.

12. **Answer:** D

Explanation: A change to the project charter (choice D) is not always necessary. In fact, a change to the charter is a fundamental change to the project and may require a huge adjustment in all aspects of the project plan. There are many reasons the other choices could happen as a result of risk. The communications plan (choice C) could change as a way to mitigate a risk. The project plan (choice B) could change to include a modified WBS and new tasks related to mitigating a risk. Since a contract can only be created after risks are known (a contract is a tool to mitigate risks) it is common sense that choice A cannot be the exception. Choice D is the best answer.

13. **Answer:** B

Explanation: To mitigate risk (choice A) we either reduce the probability of the event happening or reduce its impact. Acceptance of risk (choice C) does not involve insurance. Avoidance of risk (choice D) means that we change the way we will execute the project so the risk is no longer a factor. Transference is passing the risk off to another party.

14. **Answer:** C

Explanation: If you cannot determine an exact cost impact to the event, use qualitative estimates such as Low, Medium, High, etc.

15. **Answer:** A

Explanation: Impacts (choice D) are generally created during risk quantification. Prioritized risks (choice C) are created during qualification and quantification. Risks are identified (choice B) during risk identification. The best answer is A.

16. **Answer:** D

Explanation: A workaround refers to determining how to handle a risk that occurs but is not part of the risk response plan. The project must be in risk monitoring and control if risks have occurred.

17. **Answer:** D

   Explanation: Transference is a risk response planning strategy.

18. **Answer**: C

   Explanation: It is important to note that the risk management process will cause additional tasks to be added to the project. These tasks cost money and time, but may reduce the overall cost and time for the project. Project risk review (choice D) occurs during risk monitoring and control, choice A during qualification, and the analysis of risk (choice B) is generally done before risk planning and should have already been done.

19. **Answer:** C

   Explanation: The activities of qualitative risk analysis are probability and impact definition, assumption testing, data precision ranking and risk ranking matrix development.

20. **Answer:** D

   Explanation: The process they have used so far is fine, except the input of other stakeholders is needed in order to identify risks.

21. **Answer:** D

   Explanation: Though a charter and good cost proposals are important, a risk identification would be the most proactive response and would have the greatest positive impact on the project.

22. **Answer:** A

   Explanation: This question relates real-world situations to the risk types. Based on the question, you cannot delete the task to avoid it, nor can you insure or outsource to transfer the risk. The best answer would be to accept the risk.

23. **Answer:** D

   Explanation: The Delphi technique is most commonly used to obtain expert opinions on technical issues, the necessary scope of work or the risks.

24. **Answer:** D

   Explanation: The best source of knowledge would be reviewing impressions with a person on a similar project that failed. This interview would be part of the information gathering to identify risks and would help uncover risks the team may not be able to uncover on its own.

25. **Answer:** B

   Explanation: The project sponsor is only involved in providing funding. Compared to the other choices here, they would have the least input.

26. **Answer:** C

Explanation: Avoiding an uncontrollable risk factor by scheduling the installation at a different time could have a large impact on the project schedule. The best choice would be to have a backup.

27. **Answer:** B

Explanation: A workaround (choice D) is an unplanned response to risk that is occurring. You could not mitigate the risk (choice C) until you qualified the risk. You would need to analyze the problem before you would talk to the sponsor (choice A).

28. **Answer:** A

Explanation: The *PMBOK® Guide* says, "When the project deviates significantly from the baseline, updated risk identification and analysis should be performed."

29. **Answer**: A

Explanation: Notice that choice D could be done, but since it is better to calculate a reserve based on detailed risks, choice D is not the best answer. Choice C is not best as it only talks about costs, not schedule. Choice B does not go far enough. It involves calculating, but not using the results. Choice A is the best answer.

30. **Answer:** A

Explanation: This is new project and even though assessing the range of possible outcomes is done in a later step, risk identification should be done first.

31. **Answer:** A

Explanation: First you want to determine what the risk entails and the impact to the project, then determine what actions you will take in regard to the risk.

32. **Answer:** A

Explanation: Following the right process is part of professional responsibility. Because an unidentified problem or risk occurred, it is important to perform choices B and C. However, they are not your first choices. You might need to inform management (choice D), but this is reactive, not proactive, and not the first thing you should do.

33. **Answer:** C

Explanation: This is a recurring theme. First you should evaluate the impact of the change with the team. Next determine options. Then go to management and the customer.

Procurement Management
(*PMBOK® GUIDE* Chapter 12)

Procurement management is currently the third-hardest knowledge area on the exam (after Integration and Time).

Many questions relating to the procurement process are similar to those in risk management and the project life cycle. You must MEMORIZE the steps of procurement management and what happens during each step as outlined in the *PMBOK® Guide*.

Read procurement questions carefully. HINT: Unless specifically stated otherwise, the questions on procurement are from the buyer's perspective!

Keep in mind the following general rules, especially if you find a question where the answer is not immediately apparent:
- A contract is a formal agreement
- All requirements should be specifically stated in the contract
- All contract requirements must be met
- Changes must be in writing and formally controlled
- Most governments back all contracts by providing a court system for dispute resolution

NOTE TO STUDENTS OUTSIDE THE USA: The exam has very few references to international contracts, but you should be aware that government contracting specialists in the US wrote many of these questions. PMI®'s process for procurement management closely follows what is done in the US, but it is different than how procurement is handled in many other parts of the world. In many parts of the world, the contract is an informal document and the relationship between the parties is more important than the contract. If you are not from the US, a key trick is to take a more formal approach to the procurement process when answering questions. The contract is most important, it must be followed and everything provided in it must be done. Study this chapter carefully.

Chapter 11
Procurement Management

DEFINITION OF PROCUREMENT MANAGEMENT (page 147): "Includes the processes required to acquire goods and services from outside the performing organization."

PROCUREMENT MANAGEMENT PLAN (page 151): A formal or informal component of the project plan that describes how solicitation planning through contract closeout will be managed.

WHAT DO YOU NEED TO HAVE A CONTRACT? (What do you need to have a legal contract?):

1. An offer
2. Acceptance
3. Consideration – something of value, not necessarily money
4. Legal capacity – separate legal parties, competent parties
5. Legal purpose – you cannot have a contract for the sale of illegal goods

A contract, offer or acceptance may be spoken or written, though written is preferred.

WHAT IS A CONTRACT: When you think of the word contract, what comes to mind? If you are like many others, you will think of all the legal words such as indemnification, intellectual property and other legal small print. People often think of only the preprinted or standard contract - boilerplate contracts - supplied to them from the contracts or legal departments. They are only partially correct.

The word contract actually refers to the entire agreement between both parties. Therefore, it includes legal language, but it also includes business terms regarding payments, reporting requirements, marketing literature, the proposal and the scope of work - all the requirements of the project.

Many project managers and business professionals think that the only relevant part of a contract is the scope of work because they are naturally most familiar with that aspect of the contract. However, the scope of work does not include all the requirements. In fact, some of the legal language can be more relevant than the scope of work. For example, think of a project to develop new software. Who owns the resulting program? Who owns the resulting program if it contains modules or pieces of programs previously used and planned for future reuse? How do you protect your rights and ensure that all source code is delivered? The ownership clause in a contract for such services might be more relevant than the scope of work itself.

A contract is a legally binding document. Therefore, all terms and conditions in the contract must be met. One cannot choose to not conform or to not do something required in the contract. Any changes to the contract must be approved by both parties and a formal change to the contract issued in order to be effective!

PROJECT MANAGER'S ROLE IN PROCUREMENT: The project manager must be involved in the creation of contracts and fulfills the following key roles:

- Identify risks and incorporate mitigation and allocation of risks into the contract
- Help tailor the contract to the unique needs of the project
- Fit the schedule for completion of the procurement process into the schedule for the project
- Be involved during contract negotiation
- Protect the integrity of the project and the ability to get the work done
- Protect the relationship with the seller

The project manager must be assigned before a contract is signed! This allows the project manager to complete a risk analysis before a contract is signed. However, if yours is like many companies, this comes as something of a shock. In companies where projects are created through winning a contract from an outside client, sales and marketing will have handled the whole proposal process and signed a contract before the project manager is assigned. The project manager then is handed a project that is already in trouble because the contract, its terms and conditions, and even the scope of work are not appropriate.

CENTRALIZED/DECENTRALIZED CONTRACTING: In centralized contracting, a separate contracting office handles contracts for all projects. In decentralized contracting, a contract administrator (contracting officer) is assigned to each project.

Exercise: Complete the following.

Describe the advantages of Centralized Contracting

Describe the disadvantages of Centralized Contracting

Describe the advantages of Decentralized Contracting

Describe the disadvantages of Decentralized Contracting

Answer:

Advantages of Centralized Contracting
Increased expertise in contracting
Standardized company practices
A clearly defined career path for contracting staff

Disadvantages of Centralized Contracting
May be difficult to gain access to contracting expertise
One contracts person may work on many projects

Advantages of Decentralized Contracting
Easier access to contracting expertise
More loyalty to the project

Disadvantages of Decentralized Contracting
No home for the contracts person after the project is completed
Difficult to maintain a high level of contracting expertise in the company
Duplication of expertise and inefficient use of resources
Little standardization of contracting practices from one project to the next

THE PROCUREMENT MANAGEMENT PROCESS (page 147): Procurement management
is a step-by-step process. The exam may ask questions that require you to understand the steps and
what happens during each step. Here is a summary chart. Review it and try the next exercise.

Steps to Procurement Management

THE CONTRACTING PROCESS

| PROCUREMENT PLANNING | SOLICITATION PLANNING | SOLICITATION | SOURCE SELECTION | CONTRACT ADMINISTRATION | CONTRACT CLOSEOUT |

STEP	What happens during "BUZZWORDS"	What do you have when you are done?
1. Procurement planning	Make or buy	Make or buy, contract type selected, scope of work drafted
2. Solicitation planning	RFP created	RFP ready
3. Solicitation	Q & A	Proposal created
4. Source selection	Pick one	Contract signed
5. Contract administration	Admin	Substantially complete
6. Contract closeout	Finish	Done

STEP 1: **PROCUREMENT PLANNING** (pages 149 - 152): The buzzword for this step is
"MAKE OR BUY." It refers to "identifying which project needs can best be met by procuring
goods or services outside the project organization." Procurement planning should be accomplished
during the scope definition effort and includes the following activities:

MAKE OR BUY (page 150): The project can make all it needs, buy all it needs, or any
range of solutions in between. (As simple as this sounds, it has been a question on the
exam!) PMI® advocates that the actual out-of-pocket costs to purchase the product as
well as the indirect cost of managing the procurement be considered in any "make or
buy" decision. The cost savings to purchase may be outweighed by the cost of managing
the procurement.

One of the main reasons to buy is to decrease risk (cost, time, performance or
scope of work). It is better to "make" if:
- You have an idle plant or workforce
- You want to retain control
- The work involves proprietary information or procedures

Sometimes the make or buy analysis involves a buy or lease question such as:

*You are trying to decide whether to buy or lease an item for your project. The
daily lease cost is $120. To purchase the item the investment cost is $1000 and
the daily cost is $20. How long will it take for the lease cost to be the same as
the purchase cost?*

ANSWER: Let D equal the number of days when the purchase and lease costs are equal.

$120D = $1,000 + $20D

$120D -$20D = $1,000

$100D = $1,000

D= 10. The lease cost will be the same as the purchase cost after 10 days. If you think you will need the item for more than 10 days, you should consider purchasing it to reduce total costs.

CONTRACT TYPE SELECTION (page 150): This is an important topic! You must understand the following contract types and be able to tell the difference. You should also be able to answer situational questions describing what you would do differently depending on the contract type. There are also questions that require you to pick the most appropriate contract type based on a described situation. Think through this section carefully!

The objective of contract type selection is to have reasonable distribution of risk between the buyer and seller and the greatest incentive for the seller's efficient and economical performance.

There are generally four types of contracts:
- CR – Cost reimbursable
- T&M – Time and material
- FP – Fixed price
- Purchase order

The following factors may influence the type of contract selected:
- How well-defined the scope of work is or can be
- The amount or frequency of changes expected after project start
- The level of effort and expertise the buyer can devote to managing the seller
- Industry standards of the type of contract used

COST REIMBURSABLE (CR, page 151) – The seller's costs are reimbursed but the buyer has the most cost risk because the total costs are unknown. This form of contract is often used when the buyer can only describe what they need rather than what to do (e.g., when the complete scope of work or requirements are unknown, as in situations of buying expertise). The seller will therefore write the detailed scope of work.

Common forms of cost reimbursable contracts include:

CPFF – Cost Plus Fixed Fee: This is the most common form of cost reimbursable contract. In this form, the buyer pays all costs, but the fee (or profit) is fixed at a specific dollar amount. This helps to keep the seller's costs in line because a cost overrun will not generate any additional fee or profit. Fees only change with approved change orders.

> EXAMPLE: Contract = Cost plus a fee of $100,000.

CPPC – Cost Plus Percentage of Costs: This is an illegal form of contract for the US Government and is bad for buyers everywhere. Can you guess why?

This type of cost reimbursable contract requires the buyer to pay for all costs plus a percent of costs as a fee. Sellers are not motivated to control costs because the seller will get paid profit on every cost without limit.

> EXAMPLE: Contract = Cost plus 10% of costs as fee.

CPIF - Cost Plus Incentive Fee: This type of cost reimbursable contract pays all costs and an agreed upon fee, plus a bonus for beating the incentive. See more on incentive clauses at the end of this topic.

> EXAMPLE: Contract = Cost plus a fee of $100,000. For every month the project is completed sooner than agreed upon, seller receives an additional $10,000.

CPAF - Cost Plus Award Fee: This type of cost reimbursable contract pays all costs and an apportionment of a bonus based on performance. This contract is very similar to the CPIF contract.

TIME AND MATERIAL (T&M or Unit Price, page 151) – This type is usually used for small dollar amounts. This form of contract is priced on a per hour or per item basis and has elements of a fixed price contract (in the fixed price per hour) and a cost reimbursable contract (in the material costs and the fact that the total cost is unknown).

In this form, the buyer has a medium amount of cost risk compared to CR and FP because the contract is usually for small dollar amounts and for a shorter length of time.

> EXAMPLE: Contract = $100 per hour plus expenses or materials at cost or $5 per linear foot of wood.

This contract type is most appropriate when the buyer wants to be more in control, when the scope of work is not known or is incomplete, and for short-term services. It is also used in an emergency to begin work immediately when a scope of work has not yet been completed. It should not be used for long-term projects because the amount of profit grows over time and there is little incentive for the seller to complete the work.

FIXED PRICE (FP, Lump Sum, Firm Fixed Price, page 151) – This is the most common form of contract in the world. In this form of contract, one price is agreed upon for all the work. In this form, the buyer has the least cost risk because the risk of higher costs is borne by the seller. Therefore, it could be said that the seller is most concerned with the scope of work in this type of contract.

This form of contract is most appropriate when the buyer can completely describe the scope of work. (Do you see anything different from what you are doing in the real world? Maybe having the wrong contract type is the root cause of some of your problems!)

EXAMPLE: Contract = $1,100,000.

FPIF – There are also incentives for fixed price contracts. This is called **Fixed Price Incentive Fee**. The incentive is the same as CPIF above.

EXAMPLE: Contract = $1,100,000. For every month you finish the project early, you will receive an additional $10,000.

FPEPA – Fixed Price Economic Price Adjustment. Sometimes a fixed price contract allows for price increases if the contract is for multiple years.

EXAMPLE: Contract = $1,100,000 but a price increase will be allowed in year 2 based on the US Consumer Price Increase report for year 1. Or the contract price is $1,100,000 but a price increase will be allowed in year 2 to account for increases in specific material costs.

PURCHASE ORDER – A form of contract that is normally unilateral (signed by one party) instead of bilateral (signed by both parties). It is usually used for simple commodity procurements.

EXAMPLE: Contract to purchase 30 linear meters of wood at US $9 per meter.

ADVANTAGES AND DISADVANTAGES OF EACH CONTRACT FORM: This exercise helps test if you really understand the different forms of contracts.

Exercise 1: In the chart below, write the advantages and disadvantages of each form of contract for the BUYER. Since CPFF is the most common form of cost reimbursable contract, we will use it here.

What are the advantages of a CPFF contract?

What are the disadvantages of a CPFF contract?

What are the advantages of a T&M contract?

What are the disadvantages of a T&M contract?

What are the advantages of an FP contract?

What are the disadvantages of an FP contract?

Answer 1: There can be more answers than listed here. Did you identify and understand these?

CPFF/Advantages	T&M/Advantages	FP/Advantages
Simpler scope of work	Quick to create	Less work for buyer to manage
Usually requires less work to write the scope than fixed price	Contract duration is brief	Seller has a strong incentive to control costs
Generally lower cost than fixed price because the seller does not have to add as much for risk	Good choice when you are hiring "bodies" or people to augment your staff	Companies have experience with this form
		Buyer knows the total price at project start

CPFF/Disadvantages	T&M/Disadvantages	FP/Disadvantages
Requires auditing seller's invoices	Profit is in every hour billed	Seller may underprice the work and try to make up profits on change orders
It requires more work for the buyer to manage	Seller has no incentive to control costs	Seller may not complete some of the scope of work if they begin to lose money
Seller has only a moderate incentive to control costs	Appropriate only for small projects	More work for buyer to write the scope of work
The total price is unknown	Requires the most day-to-day oversight from the buyer	Can be more expensive than CR if the scope of work is incomplete. The seller will need to add to the price for their increased risk

Exercise 2: Write the most appropriate contract type to use in the situation described.

SITUATION	TYPE OF CONTRACT TO USE
You need work to begin right away	
You want to buy expertise in determining what needs to be done	
You know exactly what needs to be done	
You are buying the services of a programmer to augment your staff	
You need work done but you don't have time to audit invoices on this work	

Answer 2: Try to think of other situations that you would use each type of contract.

SITUATION	TYPE OF CONTRACT TO USE
You need work to begin right away	T&M
You want to buy expertise in determining what needs to be done	CPFF
You know exactly what needs to be done	FP
You are buying the services of a programmer to augment your staff	T&M
You need work done but you don't have time to audit invoices on this work	FP

RISK AND CONTRACT TYPE: The exam may ask questions that connect risk with the different forms of contracts. For example:

> *Who has the risk in a cost reimbursable contract, the buyer or seller?*
> *Answer: Buyer! If the costs increase, the buyer pays the added costs.*

> *Who has the cost risk in a fixed price contract, the buyer or seller?*
> *Answer: Seller! If costs increase, the seller pays the costs and makes less profit.*

INCENTIVES: Allows an incentive (or bonus) on top of the agreed upon price for beating cost, time, performance, scope of work or quality. *An incentive helps bring the seller's objectives in line with those of the buyer.* With an incentive, both buyer and seller work toward the same objective, for instance, completing the project on time.

You should have some experience calculating the revised fee and total costs associated with this type of contract (see the next exercise). Such questions occasionally appear on the exam.

Chapter 11
Procurement Management

Exercise: The cost is estimated at US $210,000 and the fee at US $25,000. If the seller beats that cost they will share the savings; 80% to the buyer and 20% to the seller. If the actual costs come in at US $200,000, what is the final fee and final price?

Answer:

Target cost	$ 210,000
Target fee	$ 25,000
Target price	$ 235,000
Sharing ratio	80/20
Actual cost	$ 200,000

Fee	• $210,000 − $200,000 = $10,000 x 20% = $2,000 • $25,000 target fee + $2,000 = $27,000 fee
Final price	$200,000 + $27,000 = $227,000

TYPES OF SCOPE OF WORK (page 151): A scope of work describes what work is to be completed under the contract. It must be as clear, complete and concise as possible and describe all the work and activities that the seller is required to complete. The scope of work may be revised during the procurement process, but should become finalized (excluding changes) by the time the contract is signed. There are many types of scope of work. The choice among them should depend on the nature of the work and the type of industry.

- Performance – Conveys what the final product should be able to accomplish rather than how it should be built or what its design characteristics should be.

- Functional or detailed – Conveys the end purpose or results rather than specific procedures, etc. It is to be used in the performance of the work and may also include a statement of the minimum essential characteristics of the product.

- Design – Conveys precisely what work is to be done.

Performance and functional are commonly used for information systems, information technology, hi-tech, research and development and projects that have never been done before. Design is most commonly used in construction, equipment purchasing and other types of projects.

Components of a scope of work can include drawings, specifications, technical and descriptive wording, etc. No matter what it contains, you should realize that the scope of work becomes part of the contract.

© 2002 - 1998 Rita Mulcahy, PMP
PHONE: (952) 846-4484 - EMAIL: info@rmcproject.com - WEB: www.rmcproject.com

Exercise: Complete the following to describe how detailed the scope of work must be for each type of contract.

For a CR contract?	
For a T&M contract?	
For a FP contract?	

Answer:

- For a CR contract – In this case, the scope of work describes only the performance or requirements because we are buying the expertise of "how to do the work." We may not be able to say exactly what to do or when.

- For a T&M contract – The scope of work can be any of the choices but it will be brief, describing limited functional, performance or design requirements.

- For a FP contract – The scope of work must be extraordinarily complete because we are buying "do it," not "how to do it." In order for the seller to fix the price they need to know, in advance, ALL the work they are required to do.

  Be careful, this is a general approach. There are many reasons to handle contracts differently. However, using an inappropriate contract form can result in increased risk, conflict and project failure.

STEP 2: **SOLICITATION PLANNING** (page 152 – 153): The buzzwords for this step are "RFP created," and it consists primarily of putting together the procurement documents.

> **PROCUREMENT DOCUMENTS** (bid documents): The documents put together by the buyer to tell the seller its needs. Procurement documents may take one of the following forms:
>
> - REQUEST FOR PROPOSAL (RFP, sometimes called Request for Tender) – Requests a price, but also a detailed proposal on how the work will be accomplished, who will do it, resumes, company experience, etc.
> - INVITATION FOR BID (IFB, or Request for Bid, RFB) – Requests one price to do all the work
> - REQUEST FOR QUOTATION (RFQ) – Requests a price quote per item, hour or foot

Procurement documents may consist of the following parts:
- Information for sellers
  - Background information
  - Procedures for replying
  - Guidelines for preparation of the proposal
  - Evaluation criteria (described later)
  - Pricing forms
- Scope of work
- Proposed terms and conditions of the contract

Note that the proposed contract is included in the procurement (bid) documents. Can you answer why? The terms and conditions of the contract are also work that needs to be done and have costs associated with them (for example, warranties, ownership). The seller must be aware of *all* the work that needs to be completed to adequately understand and price the project.

Well-designed procurement (bid) documents can have the following effects on the project:
- Easier comparison of sellers' responses
- More complete proposals
- More accurate pricing
- Decrease in the amount of changes to the project

You should understand that sellers could make suggestions for changes in the procurement documents, including the scope of work and the project plan.

The choice of which procurement document to use depends on the form of scope of work and contract type selected. See the next exercise.

Exercise: Test yourself! In the space provided below, write the contract type (FP, CR, T&M) that applies next to the procurement document, and the type of Scope of Work (Performance, Functional or Design) to be used.

Procurement Documents	Contract Type	Scope of Work
Request for Proposal (RFP)		
Invitation for Bid (IFB)		
Request for Quotation (RFQ)		

Answer: This is a general approach to promote understanding. In the world of contracts, an infinite variety of procurement documents and contract types exist. The exam keeps things simple.

Procurement Documents	Contract Type	Scope of Work
Request for Proposal (RFP)	CR	Performance or Functional
Invitation for Bid (IFB)	FP	Design
Request for Quotation (RFQ)	T&M	Any

STANDARD CONTRACT (or boilerplate page 156): Companies frequently have standard, preauthorized contracts for the purchase of goods or services. These types of standard contracts need no further legal review if used as they are. If signed as is, they are legally sufficient and will form a contract. The exam requires that you understand standard contracts but also realize your role in special provisions (described next).

SPECIAL PROVISIONS (Special conditions): The project manager must be able to read and understand standard terms and conditions and determine what needs to be added to, changed or removed from the standard provisions so that the resulting contract addresses the particular needs of the project. The project manager would meet with the contract administrator, lawyer or whomever is handling the contract to discuss the needs of the project and determine the final contract terms and conditions. These additions, changes or removals are sometimes called special provisions and are a result of:
- Risk analysis
- The requirements of the project
- The type of project
- Administrative, legal or business requirements

TERMS AND CONDITIONS: Following are some of the terms and conditions in many contracts that make up standard and special provisions. You should be generally familiar with what all of these mean. Don't get overwhelmed! You do not need to memorize these but just be familiar with the impact they have on you, the project manager. This is new to a lot of people.

- **Acceptance** – How will you specifically understand if the work is acceptable?
- **Agent** – Who is an authorized representative of each party?
- **Arbitration** – A method to resolve disputes that uses private third parties to render a decision on the dispute. Whereas government pays for the court system, arbitration is paid for by the parties and is used because it is faster and cheaper than the courts.
- **Assignment** – Describes the circumstances under which one party can assign its rights or obligations under the contract to another.
- **Authority** – Who has the power to do what?
- **Bonds** – What payment or performance bonds, if any, must be purchased?
- **Breach/Default** – When any obligation of the contract is not met. Watch out, one breach on the seller's part cannot be fixed by a breach on the buyer's part,

e.g., not completing an item in the scope of work (seller's breach) cannot be handled by the buyer stopping ALL payments (buyer's breach).

- **Changes** – How will changes be made, what forms used, timeframes for notice and turnaround?

- **Confidentiality** – What information must not be made known or given to third parties?

- **Force Majeure** – An act of God such as fire or freak electrical storm.

- **Incentives** – What benefits can the seller receive for aligning with the buyer's objectives of time, cost, quality, risk and performance?

- **Indemnification (liability)** – Who is liable for personal injury, damage, accidents?

- **Independent contractor** – States that the seller is not an employee of the buyer.

- **Inspection** – Does anyone have a right to inspect the work during execution of the project and under what circumstances?

- **Intellectual property** – Who owns the intellectual property (patents, trademarks, copyrights, processes, source code, books) used in connection with or developed as part of the contract? May include warranties of the right to use certain existing intellectual property in performance of the contract.

- **Invoicing** – When sent, what supporting documents are required and to whom are they sent?

- **Liquidated damages** – Estimated damages for specific defaults, described in advance.

- **Management requirements** – Attendance at meetings, approval of staff assigned to the project, etc.

- **Material breach** – A breach so large that it may not be possible to complete the work under the contract.

- **Notice** – To whom should certain correspondence be sent?

- **Ownership** – Who will own the tangible items (materials, buildings, equipment) used in connection with or developed as part of the contract?

- **Payments** – When will they be made, late payment fees, reasons for nonpayment? Watch out for payment management questions. For example, as a response to inaccurate invoices, the buyer cannot stop ALL payments; this would be a breach. They can, however, stop payments on disputed amounts.

- **Reporting** – What reports are required, at what frequency, from and to whom?

- **Retainage** – An amount of money, usually 5% or 10%, withheld from each payment. This money is paid when all the final work is completed and helps ensure completion.

- **Scope of work** – If not listed separately.

- **Site access** – Any requirements for access to the site where the work will be performed.

- **Termination** – Stopping the work before it is completed.

- **Time is of the essence** – Delivery is strictly binding. Seller is on notice that time is very important and that any delay is a material breach.

- **Waiver** – Statements saying that rights under the contract may not be waived or modified other than by express agreement of the parties. A project manager must realize that they can intentionally or unintentionally give up a right in the contract through conduct, inadvertent failure to enforce or lack of oversight. Therefore, a project manager must understand all aspects of the legal and other contract parts to enforce them, even if a contract administrator is available to administer the contract.

- **Warranties** – Promises of quality for the goods or services delivered under the contract, usually restricted to a certain time period.

- **Work for Hire** – The work provided under the contract will be owned by the buyer.

LETTER OF INTENT: You should understand that this is normally NOT a contract but simply a letter, without legal binding, that says the buyer intends to hire the seller.

PRIVITY: Means a contractual relationship. You should understand the following because it explains privity and shows you how questions on this topic are asked.

Company A hires company B to do some work for them. Company B subcontracts to company C. The project manager for A is at the job site and tells company C to stop work. Generally, does company C have to listen?

The answer is no. Companies C and A have no contractual relationship. A needs to talk to B who needs to talk to C.

NONCOMPETITIVE FORMS OF PROCUREMENT: Sometimes work is awarded to a company without competition. This may be done when:
- The project is under extreme schedule pressure
- A seller has unique qualifications
- There is only one seller
- A seller holds a patent for the item you need, or
- Other mechanisms exist to ensure that the seller's prices are reasonable

You should be familiar with the following forms:
- Single Source – Contract directly with your preferred seller without going through the procurement process. This might be a company that you have worked with before and, for various reasons, you do not want to look for another.
- Sole Source – There is only one seller. This might be a company that owns a patent.

Can you think of situational questions involving noncompetitive procurements? What if the sole source provider is late with delivery? Wouldn't your answer in a situational question be different if there wasn't another company to go to for the goods or service? Can you think of what you need to watch for in each noncompetitive type of procurement? Wouldn't you need to watch time, cost and other parts of the triple constraint more closely? What if the seller goes out of business? Does the seller have the expertise for the work?

Exercise: Test yourself! What are the unique management challenges for the buyer in managing sole source or single source contracts?

Answer: Seller could go out of business and seller has no incentive to:

- Charge the lowest price
- Complete the project on time
- Provide good quality

EVALUATION CRITERIA (page 153): Evaluation criteria are included in the procurement document to give the seller an understanding of the buyer's needs and help them decide if they should bid or make a proposal on the work. During source selection, evaluation criteria become the basis by which the bids or proposals are evaluated by the buyer. Price may not be the primary factor in selecting a seller! Such evaluation criteria may include:

- Understanding of need
- Overall or life cycle cost
- Technical ability
- Management approach
- Financial capacity
- Project management ability (I had to put this in! How many of you require your sellers or vendors to use the project management techniques you have learned? How about asking for a WBS and network diagram?)

Evaluation criteria are not commonly used in an invitation for bid situation because the lowest bidder or lowest responsible bidder is usually selected.

STEP 3: SOLICITATION (page 153 – 154): The buzzwords for this step are "QUESTIONS AND ANSWERS (Q&A.)" It consists of answering the sellers' questions and the sellers preparing the proposal.

BIDDERS' CONFERENCE (Proposers' Conference or Pre-Bid Conference, page 154): Used in conjunction with any type of procurement, the bidders' conference is a meeting with prospective sellers to make sure that they all have a clear and common understanding of the procurement. Sellers have a chance to ask questions.

A bidders' conference can be THE key to making sure the pricing in the seller's response matches the work that needs to be done and is therefore the lowest price. Bidders' conferences benefit both the buyer and seller. Many project managers do not attend these meetings or realize their importance. The exam often asks what things the project manager must watch out for in a bidders' conference:

- Collusion
- Sellers not asking their questions in front of their competition
- Making sure all questions and answers are put in writing and issued to all potential sellers by the buyer as an addendum to the procurement documents. This ensures that all sellers are responding to the same scope of work.

QUALIFIED SELLER LISTS (or prequalified seller lists, page 154): The sellers' qualifications have been checked in advance and the companies' names are put on an approved or prequalified list. The procurement documents would then be sent only to the prequalified sellers.

ADVERTISING (page 154): To attract additional sellers, an advertisement may be placed in newspapers, magazines and other places. NOTE: The US Government is required to advertise most of its procurements.

STEP 4: SOURCE SELECTION (page 155 - 156): The buzzwords for this step are "PICK ONE." It consists of receiving and reviewing the proposals and selecting a seller. The evaluation criteria are used to assess the potential sellers' ability and willingness to provide the requested products or services. Because they are measured, the criteria provide a basis for quantitatively evaluating proposals to minimize the influence of personal prejudices. In this step:

- A seller may simply be selected and asked to sign a standard contract
- A seller may be asked to make a presentation and then, if all goes well, go on to negotiations
- The list of sellers may be narrowed down ("short-listed") to a few
- The short-listed sellers may be asked to make presentations and the selected seller then asked to go on to negotiations
- Or some combination of presentations and negotiations

The choice of methods depends on the importance of the procurement, the number of interested sellers and the type of work to be performed.

The sellers' proposals may be reviewed, compared or selected by any one of the following:
- Weighting system – Weighting the sellers according to each of the evaluation criteria.
- Screening system – Eliminating sellers that do not meet minimum requirements of the evaluation criteria.
- Independent estimate – Comparing the cost to an estimate created in-house or with outside assistance. This allows the discovery of significant differences between what the buyer and seller intend in the scope of work. Therefore, the buyer must have his or her own estimates to check reasonableness. The buyer cannot rely on the seller's cost estimates.
- Past performance history – Looking at the seller's past history with the buyer.

PRESENTATIONS: In many cases, some of the sellers will be asked to make a presentation of their proposal to the buyer so that the buyer can pick the most appropriate seller. This is often a formal meeting of the buyer's and seller's teams and it provides the seller with an opportunity to present their proposal, team and approach to completing the work. Buyers get a chance to see the team they may hire and ask questions to assess competency, knowledge and ability. Presentations are used most often when a cost plus fixed fee contract is used, but they can be used in other situations (there is more to assess and how the seller is going to do the work is of prime importance).

NEGOTIATION (page 155): The exam usually has only one or two questions about negotiations. Procurement may or may not involve negotiations. The project manager must be involved during negotiation if for no other reason than to protect the relationship with the other side. Many projects go bad because of how negotiations were handled.

OBJECTIVES OF NEGOTIATION – The objectives of negotiation are to:
- Obtain a fair and reasonable price
- Develop a good relationship with the seller

The second item surprises most people. If you press too strongly during negotiations and the negotiations turn from a win-win (preferable) situation to a win-lose situation, the seller will be less concerned with completing the work than with recovering what they lost in negotiation. If negotiations are win-lose (in favor of the buyer), the buyer's project manager will have to spend time making sure that the seller does not add extra costs, propose unnecessary work or initiate other activities to "win" back what they lost during negotiation.

NEGOTIATION TACTICS – This is another topic that is included in the exam but not covered in the *PMBOK® Guide*. You should be familiar with the types of negotiation tactics. Here are the simple explanations for each tactic. Do not memorize them. Simply be able to pick the negotiation tactic that is being used in a situation.
- ATTACKS – "If you don't know the details of your own company, perhaps you should get out of the business!"

- PERSONAL INSULTS – "If you do not understand what you are doing, perhaps you should find another job!"
- GOOD GUY/BAD GUY – One person is helpful to the other side while another is difficult to deal with.
- DEADLINE – "We have a flight leaving at 5 PM today and must finish negotiations before that time."
- LYING – Not telling the truth. This may be obvious or hidden.
- LIMITED AUTHORITY – "I can't agree to shorten the schedule by six months. I only have been authorized to offer three months." Limited authority statements may or may not be true.
- MISSING MAN – "Only my boss can agree to that request, and he isn't here. Why don't we agree to only do ____? I can agree to that."
- FAIR AND REASONABLE – "Let's be fair and reasonable. Accept this offer as it stands."
- DELAY – "Let us revisit this issue the next time we get together." This may also take the form of never actually getting down to negotiating until the last day of a planned visit.
- EXTREME DEMANDS – "We planned on giving you the year 2000 compliant software in June 2000."
- WITHDRAWAL – This can either be an emotional withdrawal or a physical withdrawal and can show a lessening of interest.
- FAIT ACCOMPLI – A done deal. "These government terms and conditions must be in all our contracts."

MAIN ITEMS TO NEGOTIATE (page 155) – PMI® says that the main items to negotiate on a contract are:

- Responsibilities
- Authority
- Applicable law – Under whose law will the contract fall
- Technical and business management approaches
- Contract financing
- Price

Remember that price may not be the primary selection criteria or the primary negotiating item. Also note that this list may differ from the "real" world.

STEP 5: **CONTRACT ADMINISTRATION** (page 156 – 158): The buzzword for this step is "ADMIN." It consists of assuring that the seller's performance meets contractual requirements. Project managers have a tendency to ignore the terms and conditions of a contract and focus on what the project manager knows best; the scope of work. This is not acceptable project management. The project manager must read and understand the contract and manage, or help manage, its administration. The terms and conditions of a contract include work that needs to be done!

Chapter 11
Procurement Management

Take a moment and think of what work must be done during contract administration and try the next exercise.

Exercise 1: Describe what a project manager might be involved in during contract administration.

Answer 1: Activities during this step include:

- Reviewing cost submittals
- Implementing change control
- Documentation
- Making and handling changes
- Authorizing payments
- Meetings
- Monitoring performance against the contract including all its components (terms and conditions, scope of work, etc.)
- Understanding the legal implications of action taken
- Correspondence
- Record keeping
- Disseminating changes to the appropriate parties
- Performance reviews
- Scope verification
- Identifying risks

© 2002 - 1998 Rita Mulcahy, PMP
PHONE: (952) 846-4484 - EMAIL: info@rmcproject.com - WEB: www.rmcproject.com

Exercise 2: Let's take it a step further. Describe what specific things a project manager must watch out for during contract administration for each of the three main forms of contracts.

FIXED PRICE

T&M

CPFF

Answer 2: This is not a complete list! Think of what else they may be doing.

FP

Checking to make sure all the work in the scope of work is actually being done
Watching for overpriced change orders
Checking for scope misunderstandings

T&M

Providing day-to-day direction to the seller
Attempting to get concrete deliverables
Paying close attention to project schedule (You may think you always need this, but can you tell why it is more important with this type of contract?)
Making sure the project length is not extended
Watching for situations when switching to a different form of contract makes sense (You determine the scope of work under a T&M contract and then switch to a fixed price contract for completion of the project)

CPFF

Auditing the seller's costs
Making sure all costs are applicable and chargeable to your project
Making sure the seller's work is progressing efficiently
Watching for the seller adding resources to your project that do not add value or perform real work
Watching for resources being shifted from what was said in the original proposal (More experienced people proposed and less experienced used, but charged at the higher rate)
Watching for seller charges that were not part of the original plan
Re-budgeting the project

CONFLICT: In most projects where a contract is used, another person controls the contract. This person may be called the contracting officer or contract administrator and, in many cases IS THE ONLY ONE WITH AUTHORITY TO CHANGE THE CONTRACT. We have already said that the contract includes the scope of work. You can see the potential for conflict between the contracting officer and the project manager. This type of conflict is frequently a subject of exam questions.

CONTRACT CHANGE CONTROL SYSTEM (page 158): A process for modifying the contract that should be included in the contract. Sometimes exam questions ask how project control is different in a contracted environment. The answer may include:

- You need to deal with a different company's set of procedures
- It is not as easy to "see" problems
- Greater reliance on reports to determine if a problem exists
- Greater reliance on relationships between the buyer's and seller's project managers

CHANGES: All contracts, like all projects, have changes. The first step to handle changes that arise on the contracted project is to analyze the impacts to the project, just as it would be on a project without contracts or purchase orders. The change procedures in the contract must also be followed and all changes should be made formally as modifications to the contract.

A large number of changes on a project are a major problem because it is difficult, if not impossible, to continue work on a task if you are not certain the change will be approved. In cases with many changes, or even one major change, it might be best to terminate the contract and start fresh through renegotiating a new contract or finding a new seller.

Expect situations where your actions regarding changes are different depending on the type of contract used! Also expect situational questions to require that you know how to evaluate and formally make every change.

CONTRACT INTERPRETATION: In the real world, project managers are always faced with the need to interpret the contract to answer many questions including "What does the contract really say?" and "Who is responsible for what scope of work?"

Contract interpretation is never easy and frequently requires the assistance of a lawyer. However, the exam may describe a simple situation about a conflict over interpretation of a contract and ask you to interpret the correct answer. Contract interpretation is based on an analysis of the intent of the parties to the contract and a few guidelines. One such guideline is that the contract supercedes any memos, conversations or discussions that may have occurred prior to the contract signing. Therefore, if a requirement is not in the contract, even if it was agreed upon, it does not have to be met.

The following is an exercise on intent. The correct answers show more clearly the intent of the parties to the contract.

Exercise: In each row, circle the item on the left side or the right side that would "win" in a dispute over contract interpretation.

Contract language	OR	A memo drafted by one of the parties describing proposed changes after the contract is signed
Contract language	OR	A memo signed by both parties before the contract is signed that describes what was agreed to during negotiations
Contract terms and conditions	OR	Scope of work
Common definition	OR	The intended meaning (without supplying a definition)
Industry use of the term	OR	Common use of term
Special provisions	OR	General provisions
Typed-over wording on the contract	OR	A handwritten comment on the contract that is also initialed
Numbers	OR	Words
Detailed terms	OR	General terms

Answer:

CONTRACT LANGUAGE	OR	A memo drafted by one of the parties describing proposed changes after the contract is signed
CONTRACT LANGUAGE	OR	A memo signed by both parties before the contract is signed that describes what was agreed to during negotiations
Contract terms and conditions	OR	Scope of work
The answer depends on the Order of Precedence Clause in the contract that describes which terms and conditions will take precedence over the others in the event of a conflict between them.		
COMMON DEFINITION	OR	The intended meaning (without supplying a definition)
INDUSTRY USE	OR	Common use of term
SPECIAL PROVISIONS	OR	General provisions
Typed over wording on the contract	OR	**A HANDWRITTEN COMMENT ON THE CONTRACT THAT IS ALSO INITIALED**
Numbers	OR	**WORDS**
DETAILED TERMS	OR	General terms

STEP 6: **CONTRACT CLOSEOUT** (page 158 – 159): The buzzword for this step is "FINISH" and consists of finishing all the loose ends of the contract. Be prepared for up to six questions about this topic. Make sure you know the difference between contract closeout and administrative closure (in Communications).

Contract closeout is done:
- When a contract ends
- When a contract is terminated before the work is completed

Exercise 1: Describe what a project manager might be involved in during contract closeout.

Answer 1: Such closeout will include:
- Administrative closure activities such as:
    - **PRODUCT VERIFICATION** – Checking to see if all the work was completed correctly and satisfactorily. Was the product of the contract the same as what was requested? Did the product of the contract meet the needs of the customer?

    - **FINANCIAL CLOSURE** – Making final payments and completing cost records.

    - **UPDATE RECORDS** – Updating contract records.

    - **FINAL CONTRACT PERFORMANCE REPORTING** – Analyzing and documenting the success and effectiveness of the contract.

    - **CONTRACT FILE** – (project archives in administrative closure) At the end of each contract a concerted effort must be made to put all files, letters, addenda, change orders, correspondence and other records of the contract into an organized file. This file will be stored for use as historical records and help protect the project in case of arguments or legal action regarding what was done and not done on the contract.

- **PROCUREMENT AUDITS**: (similar to lessons learned in administrative closure) A structured review of the procurement process. Do not think of this as an audit of costs, rather think of it as a lessons learned of the procurement process that can help improve other procurements. The seller may be involved in procurement audits or lessons learned activities.

- Special activities required in the contract such as:
  - Arranging for storage of contract records and drawings

  - Creating and delivering legal documents such as release of lien documents and formal acceptance letters

  - Return of property used on the contract to its owner

The following are the results or outputs of contract closeout:

- **CONTRACT FILE**

- **PROCUREMENT AUDIT RESULTS**

- **FORMAL ACCEPTANCE AND CLOSURE**: Once closeout is completed and formal sign-off that the products of the contract are acceptable is received from the customers the contract is closed. Expect many questions on the exam that provide you with situations and require you to determine if the contract is closed.

All projects must be closed out no matter the circumstances under which they stop, are terminated or completed. Closeout provides value to the performing organization and the customer and should not be eliminated under any circumstances. You will see situational questions on the exam asking if the project is closed. The exam also asks for the difference between administrative closure and contract closeout. Depending on what choices the exam gives you, the answer could be:

1. Contract closeout occurs first. All contracts would be closed out before the project is closed out. Therefore, at the end of the contract, the project manager would perform a procurement audit for each contract, administratively close out the contract, and then administratively close out the project when the whole project is completed.

2. Administrative closure may be done at the end of each project phase and at the end of the project as a whole. Contract closeout is done only once, at the end of the contract.

3. Administrative closure uses the term "lessons learned" and contract closeout uses the term "procurement audit."

4. Contract closeout requires more documentation than administrative closure.

Practice Exam for the CAPM® and PMP® Exams
Procurement Management

1. **Once signed, a contract is legally binding unless:**

   A. One party is unable to perform
   B. One party is unable to finance its part of the work
   C. It is in violation of applicable law
   D. It is declared null and void by either party's legal counsel

2. **With a clear scope of work a seller completes work as specified, but the buyer is not pleased with the results. The contract is considered to be:**

   A. Null and void
   B. Incomplete
   C. Complete
   D. Waived

3. **All of the following statements concerning bid documentation are incorrect EXCEPT?**

   A. Bid documents that are well-designed can simplify comparison of responses
   B. Bid documentation must be rigorous with no flexibility to allow consideration of seller suggestions
   C. In general, bid documents should not include evaluation criteria
   D. Well-designed bid documents do not include a scope of work

4. **The primary objective of incentive clauses in a contract is to:**

   A. Reduce costs for the buyer
   B. Help the seller control costs
   C. Synchronize objectives
   D. Reduce risk for the seller by shifting risk to the buyer

5. **All the following statements about change control are incorrect EXCEPT?**

   A. A fixed price contract will minimize the need for change control
   B. Changes seldom provide real benefits to the project
   C. Contracts should include procedures to accommodate changes
   D. More detailed specifications eliminate the causes of changes

6. **A routine audit of a cost reimbursable contract determines that overcharges are being made to the contract. If the contract does not specify corrective action, the buyer should:**

   A. Continue to make project payments
   B. Halt payments until the problem is corrected
   C. Void the contract and start legal action to recover overpayments
   D. Change the contract to require more frequent audits

7. **The primary objective of contract negotiations is to:**

    A. Get the most from the other side
    B. Protect the relationship
    C. Get the highest monetary return
    D. Define objectives and stick to them

8. **A seller is working on a cost reimbursable contract when the buyer decides he would like to expand the scope of services and change to a fixed price contract. All of the following are the seller's options EXCEPT:**

    A. Completing the original work on a cost reimbursable basis and then negotiating a fixed price for the additional work
    B. Completing the original work and rejecting the additional work
    C. Negotiating a fixed price contract that includes all the work
    D. Start over with a new contract

9. **Bidders' conferences are part of:**

    A. Solicitation planning
    B. Contract administration
    C. Solicitation
    D. Procurement planning

10. **All of the following need NOT be present to have a contract EXCEPT?**

    A. Detailed scope of work
    B. Acceptance
    C. Address of the seller
    D. Buyers' signatures

11. **Which of the following BEST describes the project manager's role during the contracting process?**

    A. Project manager has only minor involvement
    B. Project manager should be the negotiator
    C. Project manager should supply an understanding of the risks of the project
    D. Project manager should tell the contract manager how the contracting process should be handled

12. **What is one of the KEY objectives during negotiations?**

    A. Obtain a fair and reasonable price
    B. Negotiate a price under the seller's estimate
    C. Ensure that all project risks are thoroughly delineated
    D. Ensure that an effective communication plan is established

13. **Which of the following activities occurs during procurement planning?**

    A. Make or buy decisions
    B. Answering sellers' questions about the bid documents
    C. Creating the contract terms and conditions
    D. Creating the request for proposal or bid documents

14. **Which of the following is the BEST thing for a project manager to do in the solicitation phase of procurement management?**

    A. Evaluating risks
    B. Confirming that submittals have been sent
    C. Confirming that changes to the contract are made
    D. Answering sellers' questions about bid documents

15. **In a cost plus fixed fee contract, how can the fee change?**

    A. It cannot change
    B. It can change if change orders are issued
    C. It can only be increased by 10% if there is an unexpected cost overrun
    D. It can be decreased under certain circumstances

16. **In a fixed price contract, the fee or profit is:**

    A. Unknown
    B. Part of the negotiation involved in paying every invoice
    C. Applied as a line item to every invoice
    D. Determined with the other party at the end of the project

17. **Your project, performed under a cost reimbursable contract, has finally entered closeout. What must the buyer remember to do?**

    A. Decrease the risk rating of the project
    B. Audit seller's cost submittals
    C. Evaluate the fee it is paying
    D. Make sure that the seller is not adding resources

18. **An advantage of a fixed price contract for the buyer is:**

    A. Cost risk is lower
    B. Cost risk is higher
    C. There is little risk
    D. Risk is shared by all parties

19. **All of the following are generally part of the contract documents EXCEPT?**

    A. Proposal
    B. Scope of work
    C. Terms and conditions
    D. Negotiation process

20. **You are in the middle of a complex negotiation when the other party says, "We need to finish in one hour because I have to catch my plane." They are using which of the following negotiation strategies?**

    A. Good guy, bad guy
    B. Delay
    C. Deadline
    D. Extreme demands

21.   Which of the following is an advantage of centralized contracting?
    A.   Gives easier access to contracting expertise
    B.   Increases company expertise in contracting
    C.   Gives more loyalty to the project
    D.   Allows a contracts person to work on a single project

22.   With which type of contract is the seller MOST concerned about project scope?

    A.   Fixed price
    B.   Cost plus fixed fee
    C.   Time and material
    D.   Purchase order

23.   Your company has an emergency and needs contracted work done as soon as possible. Under these circumstances, which of the following would be the MOST helpful to add to the contract?

    A.   A clear scope of work
    B.   Requirements as to which subcontractors can be used
    C.   Incentives
    D.   A force majeure clause

24.   During what step in the procurement process does contract negotiation occur?

    A.   Procurement planning
    B.   Solicitation planning
    C.   Solicitation
    D.   Source selection

25.   The project team is arguing about the prospective sellers who have submitted proposals. One team member is arguing in support of one seller while another team member wants the project awarded to a different seller. What step of the procurement process is the team in?

    A.   Procurement planning
    B.   Solicitation planning
    C.   Solicitation
    D.   Source selection

26.   For which of the following procurement processes is a make or buy analysis used?

    A.   Contract administration
    B.   Procurement planning
    C.   Solicitation
    D.   Source selection

27.   A project manager is in the middle of creating an RFP. What step of the procurement process is he in?

    A.   Procurement planning
    B.   Solicitation planning
    C.   Solicitation
    D.   Source selection

Procurement Questions Only For the PMP® Exam

28. **A seller has withdrawn from your project. A new seller has been selected and his/her labor forces are arriving at the job site tomorrow. What is the FIRST thing you should do?**

    A. Establish yourself as the authority in charge
    B. Bring your team in for introductions and establish a communications exchange
    C. Take the new team on a tour of the site and show them where they will be working
    D. Bring out the project plan

29. **Your program manager has come to you, the project manager, for help with a bid for her newest project. You want to protect your company from financial risk. You have limited scope definition. What is the BEST type of contract to choose?**

    A. Fixed price contract
    B. Cost plus percent of cost contract
    C. Time and materials contract
    D. Cost plus fixed fee contract

30. **Negotiations between two parties are becoming complex, so party A makes some notes that both parties sign. However, when the work is being done, party B claims that they are not required to provide an item they both agreed to during negotiations, because it was not included in the subsequent contract. In this case, party B is:**

    A. Incorrect because both parties must comply with what they agreed upon
    B. Correct because there was an offer
    C. Generally correct because both parties are only required to perform what is in the contract
    D. Generally incorrect because all agreements must be upheld

31. **Your project has just been fast tracked and you are looking at bringing in a subcontractor quickly. There is no time to issue an RFP, so you choose to use a company you have used many times before. A PRIMARY concern in this situation is:**

    A. Collusion between subcontractors
    B. The subcontractor's qualifications
    C. The subcontractor's evaluation criteria
    D. Holding a bidders' conference

32. **The project manager and project sponsor are discussing the project costs and whether it is better to have their own company do part of the project or hire another company to do the work. If they asked for your opinion, you might say it would be better to do the work yourself if:**

    A. There is a lot of proprietary data
    B. You have the expertise but you do not have the available manpower
    C. You do not need control over the work
    D. You know you have the resources to complete your part of the project

Chapter 11
Procurement Management

33. A project manager is attending his first bidders' conference and has asked you for advice on what to do during the session. Which of the following is the BEST advice you can give him?

    A. You do not need to attend this session, the contract manager will hold it
    B. Make sure you negotiate project scope
    C. Make sure you give all the sellers enough time to ask questions. They may not want to ask questions while their competitors are in the room
    D. Let the project sponsor handle the meeting so you can be the good guy in the negotiation session

34. A seller is awarded a contract to build a pipeline. The contract terms and conditions require that a work plan be issued for the buyer's approval prior to commencing work, but the seller fails to provide one. Which of the following is the BEST thing for the buyer's project manager to do?

    A. File a letter of intent
    B. Develop the work plan and issue it to the seller to move things along
    C. Issue a default letter
    D. Issue a stop work order to the seller until a work plan is prepared

35. Contract closeout is different than administrative closure in that contract closeout:

    A. Occurs before administrative closure
    B. Is the only one to involve the customer
    C. Includes the return of the property
    D. May be done more than once for each contract

36. You have just started administering a contract when management decides to terminate the contract. What should you do FIRST?

    A. Go back to solicitation
    B. Go back to solicitation planning
    C. Finish contract administration
    D. Go to contract closeout

37. The project team is arguing about the prospective sellers who have submitted proposals. One team member argues for a certain seller while another team member wants the project to be awarded to a different seller. The BEST thing the project manager should remind the team to focus on in order to make a selection is?

    A. Procurement documents
    B. Procurement audits
    C. Evaluation criteria
    D. Procurement management plan

38. The company is taking a vote to see if the contracts department should be split up and reassigned to projects or remain intact. A contract professional might not want this split to occur because they would lose _____ in a decentralized contracting environment.

    A. Standardized company project management practices
    B. Loyalty to the project
    C. A clearly defined career path
    D. Expertise

Procurement Management Answers

1. **Answer:** C

   Explanation: Once signed, a contract is binding. Generally the inability to perform, get financing or one party's belief that the contract is null and void does not change the fact that the contract is binding. If, however, both sides agree to terminate the contract, the contract can move into closure and it is considered completed.

2. **Answer:** C

   Explanation: If the seller completes the scope of work specified, the contract is considered complete. That does not mean the same thing as contract closed. Contract closure must still occur. However, in this situation, the contract work is completed. Tricky!

3. **Answer:** A

   Explanation: Bid documents must contain all the work that is to be done, including the scope of work (choice D) and terms and conditions and evaluation criteria (choice C). This is so that the seller can price the project and know what is most important to the buyer. Often the seller is required to inform the buyer of anything that is missing or unclear in the bid documents (choice B). It is in the buyer's best interest to discover missing items, since it will save the buyer money and trouble to correct the problem early. Choice A is an important point for the real world and is the best answer.

4. **Answer:** C

   Explanation: Incentives are meant to bring the objectives of the seller in line with those of the buyer. That way both are progressing toward the same goal.

5. **Answer:** C

   Explanation: In choice D, the word "eliminate" implies that changes will not occur. As that is not true, this cannot be the best answer. There are always good ideas (changes) that can add benefit to the project so choice B cannot be the best answer. Since there can be changes in any form of contract, choice A is also not the best answer.

6. **Answer:** A

   Explanation: Choice D does not solve the problem presented. Choice C is too severe and cannot be done unilaterally. Notice that choice B is really saying "halt ALL payments." Halting all payment would be a breach of contract on the buyer's part. A choice that said, "Halt payments on the disputed amount" would probably be the best answer, but it is not offered. The best answer is A.

7. **Answer:** B

   Explanation: As a project manager, you want to develop a relationship during negotiations that will last throughout the project.

8. **Answer:** D

Explanation: The seller does not have the choice to start over. The contract that exists is binding. Both parties could agree to start over, but this is a drastic step.

9. **Answer:** C

Explanation: Expect many questions on the exam that require you to know in what step of the procurement process activities are done.

10. **Answer:** B

Explanation: One set of signatures (choice D) is not enough; you must have sign-off (i.e., acceptance) from both parties. Though a scope of work is required, a detailed one (choice A) is not required in order to have a contract. The address of the seller (choice C) is also not required.

11. **Answer:** C

Explanation: As the project manager, you are the only one who knows what the project risks are. You need to make sure that provisions are included in the contract to address these risks.

12. **Answer:** A

Explanation: Choices C and D are good ideas, but not the key objective. Negotiations should be win/win, so choice B is not the best choice. A fair and equitable price (choice A) will create a good working atmosphere. Otherwise, you will pay later on change orders.

13. **Answer:** A

Explanation: Answering sellers' questions (choice B) occurs during solicitation, the contract and RFP (choices C and D) are created during solicitation planning.

14. **Answer:** D

Explanation: During solicitation you normally answer questions submitted by the sellers. Risk identification is done before the procurement process begins, as procurement is a risk mitigation tool. Contract changes may be made in source selection and contract administration. Submittals are sent during contract administration.

15. **Answer:** B

Explanation: The only way to change the fixed fee contract is to negotiate a change to the contract, normally in the form of a change order. A change order should include an additional fee if additional work is added to the contract.

16. **Answer:** A

Explanation: To the seller, it is known. But this question is from the buyer's perspective. You do not know what profit the seller included in the contract.

17. **Answer:** B

Explanation: Although choice D may be a concern during contract administration, it is not common during closeout. Choices A and C are definitely not correct. Choice B is part of the procurement audit and financial closure.

18. **Answer:** A

Explanation: If you had trouble with this one, you might remember that the questions are asked from the buyer's perspective unless otherwise noted. In this case the seller has the most cost risk, and the buyer's risk is lower.

19. **Answer: D**

Explanation: Because the negotiation process is not a document, this is the best answer. Remember that a contract is more than just the scope of work.

20. **Answer:** C

Explanation: Giving a time limit to the negotiation is an example of Deadline.

21. **Answer:** B

Explanation: Choices A, C and D are all advantages of decentralized contracting. By centralizing contracting, you increase the company's expertise in contracting, allowing individuals to learn from each other.

22. **Answer:** A

Explanation: In a fixed price contract, the seller has the cost risk and therefore wants to completely understand the scope of work before bidding.

23. **Answer:** C

Explanation: A clear scope of work (choice A) helps by eliminating some confusion, but the best answer is incentives. Incentives help to bring the seller's objectives in line with the buyer's.

24. **Answer:** D

Explanation: Negotiation occurs during the source selection step. You need to know the process and what happens in each step.

25. **Answer:** D

Explanation: The seller creates his proposal during solicitation, but it is not received and selected until source selection.

26. **Answer:** B

Explanation: A make or buy decision is needed before the rest of the procurement process can occur. It therefore must be one of the earlier steps of the procurement process.

27. **Answer:** B

Explanation: In solicitation planning we create the documents that will be sent out during solicitation. The request for proposal is one of those documents.

28. **Answer:** A

Explanation: The best answer here is to establish roles and responsibilities for the project. Those arriving at the job site do not know who is who - they were probably not part of any negotiations for the contract. Based on what is written in this question, the FIRST choice would be A, followed closely by B.

29. **Answer:** D

Explanation: Of the options given, the only contract that limits fees for large projects with limited scope definition is cost plus fixed fee.

30. **Answer:** C

Explanation: You are only required to deliver what is defined in the contract.

31. **Answer:** B

Explanation: Although you have used this contractor before, how can you be sure they are qualified to do the new work unless it is exactly like previous work? This is the risk you are taking.

32. **Answer:** A

Explanation: It is generally better to do the work yourself if using an outside company means you have to turn over proprietary data to the other company.

33. **Answer:** C

Explanation: The contracting officer usually holds the bidders' conference, so choice D is incorrect. However, the PM should attend, so choice A is incorrect. Negotiations (Choice B) occur after the seller is selected, not during the bidders' conference. Choice C describes one of the many challenges of a bidders' conference and is therefore the best answer.

34. **Answer:** C

Explanation: Any time that a seller does not perform according to the contract, the project manager must take action. The preferred choice might be to contact the seller and ask what is going on, but that choice is not available here. Therefore, the best choice is to let him know he is in default.

© 2002 - 1998 Rita Mulcahy, PMP
PHONE: (952) 846-4484 - EMAIL: info@rmcproject.com - WEB: www.rmcproject.com

35. **Answer:** A

   Explanation: Choice B cannot be correct since the customer may be involved in lessons learned and procurement audits and would certainly be involved in formal acceptance. Choice C cannot be correct since both are involved in the return of property. Contract closeout is done only once, at the end of the contract, so choice D could not be correct. Choice A is correct because contracts are closed out before the project is closed out with administrative closure.

36. **Answer:** D

   Explanation: If the contract is terminated, the project needs to enter closure. You need those results for historical purposes.

37. **Answer:** C

   Explanation: The evaluation criteria are the primary tools for evaluating potential sellers and should be used by the entire team in order to make a selection.

38. **Answer:** D

   Explanation: In a decentralized contracting situation there is less focus on maintaining the skill or expertise of the contracting department.

Professional Responsibility

(Not covered in the *PMBOK® GUIDE*)

Hot Topics

- Do the right thing
- Follow the right process
- Act ethically, fairly and professionally
- Watch for conflicts of interest or the appearance of conflicts of interest
- Report violations
- Increase knowledge and practices
- Deal with problems
- Ensure individual integrity
- Contribute to the project management knowledge base
- Enhance individual competence
- Balance stakeholders interests
- Interact with team and stakeholders in a professional and cooperative manner

Professional responsibility is not a new topic, but it has been reorganized into its own topic and reemphasized on the exam. Most people get less than 5 out of the 29 questions in this area wrong! Some of the topics within professional responsibility are generally easy. You should review and understand PMI®'s code of conduct which you will need to sign when you send in your application. Many professional responsibility questions relate to that code. Professional responsibility is often combined with cost, time and other topics.

As certified project managers (or soon to be) we have a responsibility to uphold and support the integrity and ethics of the profession. This involves ensuring that our actions are always in line with legal requirements and ethical standards. By doing so, we are upholding the needs of our stakeholders and the part of society impacted by our projects.

Still worried about this topic? Let me show you a major trick for getting professional responsibility questions correct on the exam.

Exercise: Describe what you think professional responsibility means by writing only a few phrases. Do not look at the answer until you have thought this through!

| |
| |
| |
| |
| |
| |
| |

Chapter 12
Professional Responsibility

Answer: (TRICK): The trick for all the professional responsibility questions is to MEMORIZE the following phrases. In a broad sense, professional responsibility means:

- Do the right thing
- Follow the right process
- Act ethically, fairly and professionally
- Watch for conflicts of interest or the appearance of conflicts of interest
- Report violations
- Increase knowledge and practices
- Deal with problems

The exam breaks professional responsibility down into the following categories. As you read them, see how easy most of them are to understand:

- Ensure individual integrity
- Contribute to the project management knowledge base
- Enhance individual competence
- Balance stakeholders interests
- Interact with team and stakeholders in a professional and cooperative manner

ENSURE INDIVIDUAL INTEGRITY: Or, ensure individual integrity and professionalism by adhering to legal requirements and ethical standards in order to protect the community and all stakeholders. This topic may require you to know that a project manager:

- Tells the truth in reports, conversations and other communications
- Follows copyright and other laws
- Does not divulge company data to unauthorized parties
- Values and protects intellectual property
- Does not put personal gain over the needs of the project
- Prevents conflicts of interest or the appearance of conflicts of interest and deals with them when they do occur
- Does not give or take bribes or inappropriate gifts
- Treats everyone with respect
- Follows PMI®'s Code of Professional Responsibility (described throughout this chapter)
- Does the right thing
- Follows the right process
- Reports violations of laws, business policies, ethics and other rules

Tell the truth in reports, conversations and other communications – You should realize what this means. PMI® wants you to report the real project status (e.g., that the project will be late) in project reports, conversations and meetings, even if you are asked not to.

Do the right thing – Many of these topics are interrelated. Do the right thing means being ethical, reporting violations, treating others with respect and following the right project management process. Notice this as you continue reading the rest of this chapter.

Follow the right process – This is one of the two hardest topics in professional responsibility! By including professional responsibility on the exam, PMI® is really saying, no more fooling around! It REQUIRES you to follow the project management process outlined in the rest of this book. It means that you MUST have a project charter, in fact it is unethical not to. It means that you MUST have a work breakdown structure, it is unethical not to. Why?

You should realize that not having a project charter hurts your project and at the least, causes increased costs and wasted time. Not having a WBS means that the project will have rework and that requirements will be undefined until later in the project. If you are serious about project management, professional responsibility is an exciting turn of events.

In previous sections of this book, I have strongly suggested that you understand and memorize the Life Cycle Game. Now you can see why. A project manager must understand the project management process in order to do the right thing!

Often the project manager is not given the authority required to get the project done. Imagine a situation where the project manager is given only the authority to write reports and transmit them to others. With no one directing the integration of the work, the project will probably be late and individuals working on the project will waste valuable time in rework. Professional responsibility REQUIRES the project manager to obtain the authority necessary to manage the project.

Project managers are often given unrealistic project completion deadlines or milestones. Many project managers just make the project happen as best as they can and wait to see what happens. Professional responsibility REQUIRES the project manager to handle the unrealistic schedule problem up front. This may mean saying, "Assign the project to someone else!" or "You have requested that the project be completed within six months. Our analysis makes us very certain that we can meet that due date only if we adjust the scope, cost or quality on this project. If we cannot make any changes, the project will be completed in eight months."

Professional responsibility in today's project management world also means saying, "I am sorry that you do not want to support my efforts in planning the project and want me to get started producing work right away. I can somewhat adjust, but as a certified PMP®, I am ethically bound to do project management correctly for the best interests of the project and the company. This means that I must have a project charter and at least a high-level work breakdown structure." The project manager is REQUIRED to do the right thing and stand up for the right process! When you pass the exam, start showing this book to your management. They can blame me instead of you when you want to do the right thing.

Chapter 12
Professional Responsibility

Exercise:

1. Your management has told you that you will receive part of the incentive fee from the customer if you can bring the project in early. Later, while finalizing a major deliverable, your team informs you that the deliverable meets the requirements in the contract but will not provide the functionality the customer needs. If the deliverable is late, you know that the project will not be completed early. What action should you take?

2. You are asked to make a copy of a magazine article and include it in new software you are writing. You see that the article has a copyright notice. What is the best thing to do?

3. Your company is in competition to win a major project for the government of country X. You are told that you must make a large payment to the foreign minister in order to be considered for the project. What is the best thing to do?

4. You provide a project cost estimate for the project to the project sponsor. He is unhappy with the estimate, because he thinks the price should be lower. He asks you to cut 15% off the project estimate. What should you do?

Answer: The answer depends on the exact wording of the choices, but generally:

1. Review the situation with the customer; review what is required in the contract
2. Ask the copyright owner for permission
3. Find out if there are any laws against such a payment
4. Look for alternatives by crashing, fast tracking, re-estimating or changing scope

Report violations – This is a hard topic for many people to deal with on the exam. Some of the questions describe situations that seem trivial (e.g., someone did not follow company policy). There may be other situations that are PMI®-isms. For example, depending on how they are written, many questions on the exam require the project manager to immediately report violations of policies, laws or ethics to a manager or supervisor instead of going to the person themselves. Questions on these topics should be reviewed carefully before answering.

© 2002 - 1998 Rita Mulcahy, PMP
PHONE: (952) 846-4484 - EMAIL: info@rmcproject.com - WEB: www.rmcproject.com

CONTRIBUTE TO THE PROJECT MANAGEMENT KNOWLEDGE BASE: Or, contribute to the project management knowledge base by sharing lessons learned, best practices, research, etc., within appropriate communities in order to improve the quality of project management services, build the capabilities of colleagues and advance the profession. This is a relatively easy topic to understand.

This topic may require you to know that a project manager:

- Shares lessons learned from the project with other project managers in the company
- Writes articles about project management
- Supports the education of other project managers and stakeholders about project management
- Coaches or mentors other project managers
- Performs research to discover best practices for the use of project management and shares the results with others
- Performs research on projects done within the company for the purpose of calculating performance metrics

ENHANCE INDIVIDUAL COMPETENCE: Or, enhance individual competence by increasing and applying professional knowledge to improve services. This is also a relatively easy topic to understand.

This topic may require you to know that a project manager:

- Works to understand their personal strengths and weaknesses
- Continues to learn
- Plans their own professional development
- Constantly looks for new information and practices that will help the company or its projects
- Continues to learn about the industry or industries where they work

BALANCE STAKEHOLDERS' INTERESTS: Or, balance stakeholders' interests by recommending approaches that strive for fair resolution in order to satisfy competing needs and objectives. This is one of the two toughest aspects of professional responsibility questions because it relates to real-world practices of project management. Many people do not understand these before they take the exam! The following should refresh your memory and help you understand this topic. It will also refer you to some of the discussions in previous sections of this book.

Exercise: What a project manager should know is outlined in this exercise. Spend some time THINKING about balancing stakeholder interests while getting ready for the exam. This exercise will help you determine if you really understand the process summarized here. Go through each topic and put a checkmark next to the ones you understand. Put an X next to the ones you are able to do in the real world. Further study all boxes without marks.

Chapter 12
Professional Responsibility

Topic	Understand √	Can Do X
Works to get as clear and complete requirements as possible before starting the project. (See the next section!)		
Knows team cannot resolve competing needs and objectives if they did not identify the stakeholders and determine their needs and requirements.		
Resolves conflicting needs and objectives based on how they affect the project. (See the next section!)		
Knows that if any needs conflict with that of the customer, the customer's needs should normally take precedence.		
Reviews or creates needs and objectives for each project phase at the beginning of that project phase.		
Uses quality management to ensure that the project will satisfy the needs for which it was undertaken.		
Understands all the stakeholders on the project and their objectives.		
Looks for competing needs and objectives during planning, and doesn't just wait for them to show up during project execution.		
Deals with problems and conflicts as soon as they arise. (See the next section!)		
Realizes that the project manager will have to say "no" (and have the authority to say "no") to some of the competing needs and objectives.		
Realizes that the project manager can call on management to help resolve competing needs and objectives that the project manager and the team cannot resolve on their own.		
Will change the project when the project starts to deviate from the requirements rather than change the requirements to meet the results of the project.		
Knows that the project manager and team will need to look for alternatives – including alternatives for resolving competing needs and objectives, alternative ways of doing the project tasks.		
Works toward fair resolution of disputes that consider all stakeholders' needs as well as the needs of the project.		
Uses the conflict resolution techniques explained in the Human Resource chapter.		

Topic	Understand √	Can Do X
Uses negotiation techniques to resolve disputes between stakeholders.		
Uses effective communication as explained in the Communications chapter.		
Gathers, assesses and integrates information into the project.		

Resolves conflicting needs and objectives based on the following order - Many project managers have no idea how to weight needs and objectives. This is critical on the project as well as on the exam. I have two tricks for you. Use the CD-ROM version of the *PMBOK® Guide* and search for the words "needs" and "competing." That will help you understand what the *PMBOK® Guide* is saying in these areas.

The project manager should facilitate the resolution of conflicting needs and objectives by accepting objectives or needs that comply with the following:

1. The reason the project was initiated (market demand, legal requirement, etc. page 53).
2. The project charter including the project's needs and objectives as stated in the charter (page 54) and the initial product description contained in the charter and later progressively elaborated (page 53).
3. The project triple constraint (page 29). If the most important item of the triple constraint is schedule, then any objectives that would delay the schedule would not likely be accepted. Those that enhance the schedule (without a huge impact on the other parts of the triple constraint) would be more likely to be accepted.

In order to deal with competing needs and objectives, the project manager would take the following actions:

- Determine and understand the needs and objectives of all stakeholders
- Actively look for competing or conflicting needs and objectives
- Get the team and other stakeholders involved as appropriate and get management involved when the team cannot resolve the competing objectives
- Determine options for fair resolution of conflict
- Use conflict resolution, communication, negotiation, information distribution, team building and problem solving skills (see those topics in this book)
- Review the competing needs and objectives against those listed above. (Those needs that are in line with the items in 1, 2, and 3 listed above may be accepted, those that are not are rejected and may be sent to company management for inclusion in a future project)
- Look for alternatives by crashing, fast tracking, re-estimating, brainstorming and other project management and management-related techniques
- Hold meetings, interviews and facilitate discussions to resolve competing objectives
- Make decisions and changes that do not impact 1, 2 and 3 above

- Bring suggested changes to the project charter to management's attention for approval

Works to get as clear and complete requirements as possible before starting the project - Pay careful attention to this. The project manager and team should be spending effort up front to have as many of the requirements determined in advance as is possible. Any requirements not determined in advance are risks to the successful completion of the project and are very costly to add or change later. On some projects, determining requirements means meeting with the customer to determine their requirements. On other projects, it entails reviewing the scope of work (scope statement or some other term) received from the customer and making sure that all the stakeholders' needs are included and that the requirements are clear.

Deals with problems and conflicts as they arise - Many peoples' style is to avoid conflict (what PMI® calls withdrawal) instead of solving the problem. We often seem to hope that the problem will just go away on its own. The PMI® approach is to face the issues and deal with them as soon as they arise, or even before they arise if you discover them first. For some people this could be a PMI®-ism. Be careful to keep a proactive attitude!

INTERACT WITH TEAM AND STAKEHOLDERS IN A PROFESSIONAL AND COOPERATIVE MANNER: Or, interact with team and stakeholders in a professional and cooperative manner by respecting personal, ethnic and cultural differences in order to ensure a collaborative project management environment.

- This topic may require you to know that a project manager:
  - Understands cultural differences
  - Uncovers communication preferences when identifying stakeholders
  - Uncovers and respects different work ethics and practices of the team members
  - Provides training
  - Follows the practices in other countries as long as they do not violate laws

Understands cultural differences – Cultural differences can mean differences in language, cultural values, nonverbal actions and cultural practices. Without planning and control, these can easily impede the project. Cultural differences do not only occur between people from different countries. They may also occur between people from the same country. In many countries there are cultural differences between those from the east and west of their country or from those from the north and south. Therefore a project manager will do all the following and more to diminish the negative impact and gain positive impact of cultural differences. The project manager:
  - Embraces diversity – cultural differences can make a project more fun
  - Prevents culture shock – the disorientation that occurs when you find yourself working with other cultures in a different environment. Training and advance research about the different cultures will help prevent culture shock
  - Expects cultural differences to surface on the project

- Uses clear communication to the right people and in the right form, as outlined in the Communications chapter, to prevent cultural differences from becoming a problem
- Uncovers cultural differences when identifying stakeholders
- Asks for clarification whenever a cultural difference arises
- Has the topic of cultural differences discussed at most team meetings

Exercise: Other people may tell you there are only five topics in professional responsibility. Those topics are not enough to answer all the professional responsibility questions on the exam. The following is a more extensive list. Make sure you get your mind around any differences between the responsibilities listed here and how you are able to manage your real-world projects! There is no need to spend hours reading about it or memorizing the following topics. The process of going through this exercise (in a study group if possible) will help you to prepare for the exam!

Test yourself! For each topic listed next, describe one or more situations that would require you to remember such responsibilities. For example, you could describe how to ensure individual integrity or what to do when a project team member asks you to lie about the status of the project. This is not an easy exercise and because of the wide variation of experience, there are no "answers."

Area of Professional Responsibility	Describe a real-world situation
Ensure individual integrity	
Adhere to legal requirements and ethical standards	
Protect stakeholders	
Share lessons learned and relevant information with others within and outside your company	

Area of Professional Responsibility	Describe a real-world situation
Build the capabilities of colleagues	
Advance the profession of project management	
Improve your competencies as a project manager	
Balance stakeholders' interests on the project	
Strive for fair resolutions	
Satisfy competing needs and objectives	
Interact with others in a professional manner	
Respect personal, ethnic and cultural differences	

Area of Professional Responsibility	Describe a real-world situation
Ensure a collaborative project management environment	
Comply with all organizational rules and policies	
Provide accurate and truthful representations in cost estimates	
Provide accurate and truthful representations in project reports	
Report violations of policies, procedures and codes of ethics	
Be responsible for satisfying the complete scope and objectives of customer requirements	
Maintain and respect confidential information	
Ensure that a conflict of interest does not compromise the customer's legitimate interests	

Area of Professional Responsibility	Describe a real-world situation
Ensure that a conflict of interest does not interfere with professional judgment	
Disclose conflicts of interest to the customer, management and others	
Disclose circumstances that could be construed as conflicts of interest	
Refrain from offering or accepting inappropriate payments, gifts or other forms of compensation	
Adhere to all applicable laws or customs of the country where services are being provided	
Respect intellectual property developed or owned by others	
Act in an accurate, truthful and competent manner	

Practice Exam For the CAPM ® and PMP® Exams
Professional Responsibility

1. Near the end of your last project, additional requirements were demanded by a group of stakeholders when they learned they would be affected by your project. This became a problem because you had not included the time or cost in the project plan to perform these requirements. What is the BEST thing you can do to prevent such a problem on future projects?

   A. Review the WBS dictionary more thoroughly, looking for incomplete descriptions
   B. Review the charter more thoroughly, examining the business case for "holes"
   C. Pay more attention to stakeholder management
   D. Do a more thorough job of solicitation planning

2. The software development project is not going well. There are over 30 stakeholders, and no one can agree on the project objectives. One stakeholder believes the project can achieve a 30% improvement while another believes a 50% improvement is possible. The project manager thinks a 10% improvement is more realistic. What is the BEST course of action?

   A. Move forward with the project and hope more information comes to light later to settle the issue
   B. Average the numbers and use that as a goal
   C. Perform a feasibility analysis
   D. Ask the sponsor to make the final decision

3. Your management has decided that all orders will be treated as "projects" and that project managers will be used to update orders daily, resolving issues and ensuring that the customer formally accepts the product within 30 days of completion. The revenue from the individual orders can vary from US $100 to US $150,000. The project manager will not be required to perform planning or provide documentation other than daily status. How would you define this situation?

   A. Because each individual order is a "temporary endeavor," each order is a project - this is truly project management
   B. This is program management since there are multiple projects involved
   C. This is a recurring process
   D. Orders incurring revenue over $100,000 would be considered projects and would involve project management

4. A project team has completed all the technical project deliverables, and the customer has accepted the deliverables. However, the lessons learned required by the project office have not been completed. What is the status of the project?

   A. The project is incomplete because the project needs to be replanned
   B. The project is incomplete until all deliverables are complete and accepted
   C. The project is complete because the customer has accepted the deliverables
   D. The project is complete because the project has reached the due date

5. You are in the middle of a new product development for your publicly traded company when you discover that the previous project manager made a US $3,000,000 payment that was not approved in accordance with your company policies. Luckily, the project CPI is 1.2. What should you do?

   A. Bury the cost in the largest cost center available
   B. Put the payment in an escrow account
   C. Contact your manager
   D. Ignore the payment

6. During a meeting with some of the project stakeholders, the project manager is asked to add work to the project scope of work. The project manager had access to correspondence about the project before the charter was signed and remembers that the project sponsor specifically denied funding for the scope of work mentioned by these stakeholders. The BEST thing for the project manager to do would be to:

   A. Let the sponsor know of the stakeholders' request
   B. Evaluate the impact of adding the scope of work
   C. Tell the stakeholders the scope cannot be added
   D. Add the work if there is time available in the project schedule

7. When checking a calendar of a team member to schedule a meeting, you see she has scheduled a meeting with a key stakeholder that you were not informed of. The BEST approach would be to:

   A. Avoid mentioning it to the team member but continue to watch her activities
   B. Notify your boss about the problem
   C. Address the concern with the team member
   D. Address the concern with the team member's boss

8. The project manager is having a very difficult time keeping a project schedule on track. The project is 13 months long and requires 220 people to complete. All of the project problems have been fixed to the project manager's satisfaction, the SPI is currently 0.67, the CPI is 1.26, there are 23 tasks on the critical path and the project PERT duration is 26. Under these circumstances, the monthly status report should say that the project:

   A. Has too many people assigned to it
   B. Is behind schedule
   C. Cost is behind budget
   D. Is too risky

9. Your employee is three days late with a report. Five minutes before the meeting where the topic of the report is to be discussed, she hands you the report. You notice some serious errors in it. What should you do?

   A. Cancel the meeting and reschedule when the report is fixed
   B. Go to the meeting and tell the other attendees there are errors in the report
   C. Force the employee to do the presentation and remain silent as the other attendees find the errors
   D. Cancel the meeting and rewrite the report yourself

10. **A manager has been given responsibility for a project that has the support of a senior manager. From the beginning, you have disagreed with the manager as to how the project should proceed and what the deliverables should be. You and she have disagreed over many issues in the past. Your department has been tasked with providing some key tasks for the project. What should you do?**

   A.   Provide the manager with what she needs
   B.   Inform your manager of your concerns to get their support
   C.   Sit down with the manager at the beginning of the project and attempt to describe why you object to the project and discover a way to solve the problem
   D.   Ask to be removed from the project

11. **A large, complex construction project in a foreign country requires coordination to move the required equipment through crowded city streets. To ensure the equipment is transported successfully, your contact in that country informs you that you will have to pay the local police a fee for coordinating traffic. What should you do?**

   A.   Do not pay the fee because it is a bribe
   B.   Eliminate the task
   C.   Pay the fee
   D.   Do not pay the fee if it is not part of the project estimate

12. **A major negotiation with a potential subcontractor is scheduled for tomorrow when you discover there is a good chance the project will be cancelled. What should you do?**

   A.   Do not spent too much time preparing for the negotiations
   B.   Cut the negotiations short
   C.   Only negotiate major items
   D.   Postpone the negotiations

13. **You've been assigned to take over managing a project that should be half-complete according to the schedule. After an extensive evaluation, you discover that the project is running far behind schedule, and that the project will probably take double the time originally estimated by the previous project manager. However, upper management has been told that the project is on schedule. What is the BEST course of action?**

   A.   Try to restructure the schedule to meet the project deadline
   B.   Report your assessment to upper management
   C.   Turn the project back to the previous project manager
   D.   Move forward with the schedule as planned by the previous project manager and report at the first missed milestone

14. You are halfway through a major network rollout. There are 300 locations in the US with another 20 in England. A software seller has just released a major software upgrade for some of the equipment being installed. The upgrade would provide the customer with functionality they requested that was not available at the time the project began. What is the BEST course of action under these circumstances?

    A. Continue as planned, your customer has not requested a change
    B. Inform the customer of the upgrade and the impacts to the project's timeline and functionality
    C. Implement the change and adjust the schedule as necessary because this supports the customer's original request
    D. Implement the change to the remaining sites and continue with the schedule

15. You are working on your research and development project when your customer asks you to include a particular component in the project. You know this represents new work, and you do not have excess funds available. What should you do?

    A. Delete another lower priority task to make more time and funds available
    B. Use funds from the management reserve to cover the cost
    C. Follow the contract change control process
    D. Ask for more funds from the project sponsor

16. You are a project manager for one of many projects in a large and important program. At a high-level status meeting, you note that another project manager has reported her project on schedule. Looking back on your project over the last few weeks, you remember many deliverables from the other project that arrived late. What should you do?

    A. Meet with the program manager
    B. Develop a risk control plan
    C. Discuss the issues with your boss
    D. Meet with the other project manager

17. You have always been asked by your management to cut your project estimate by 10% after you have given it to them. The scope of your new project is unclear and there are over 30 stakeholders. Management expects a 25% reduction in downtime as a result of the project. Which of the following is the BEST course of action in this situation?

    A. Replan to achieve a 35% improvement
    B. Reduce the estimates and note the changes in the risk response plan
    C. Provide an accurate estimate of the actual costs and be able to support it
    D. Meet with the team to identify where you can find 10% savings

18. Your employee is three days late with a report. She walks into a meeting where the report is to be discussed and hands you a copy five minutes before the topic is to be discussed. You notice some serious errors in the report. How could this have been prevented?

    A. Require periodic updates from the employee
    B. Coach and mentor the employee
    C. Make sure the employee was competent to do the work
    D. Cancel the meeting earlier because you have not had a chance to review the report

19. You are in the middle of a project when you discover that a software seller for your project is having major difficulty keeping employees due to a labor dispute. Many other projects in your company are using the company's services. What should you do?

    A. Attempt to keep the required people on your project
    B. Tell the other project managers in your company about the labor problem
    C. Contact the company and advise it that you will cancel its work on the project unless it settles its labor dispute
    D. Cease doing business with the company

20. All of the following are the responsibility of a project manager EXCEPT?

    A. Maintain the confidentiality of customer confidential information
    B. Determine the legality of company procedures
    C. Ensure that a legal conflict of interest does not compromise the legitimate interest of the customer
    D. Provide accurate and truthful representations in cost estimates

21. In order to complete work on your projects, you have been provided confidential information from all of your clients. A university contacts you to help it in its research. Such assistance would require you to provide the university with some of the client data from your files. What should you do?

    A. Release the information, but remove all references to the clients' names
    B. Provide high-level information only
    C. Contact your clients and seek permission to disclose the information
    D. Disclose the information

22. You just found out that a major subcontractor for your project consistently provides deliverables late. The subcontractor approaches you and asks you to continue accepting late deliverables in exchange for a decrease in project costs. This offer is an example of:

    A. Confrontation
    B. Compromise
    C. Smoothing
    D. Forcing

23. **Management has promised you part of the incentive fee from the customer if you complete the project early. Later, while finalizing a major deliverable, your team informs you that the deliverable meets the requirements in the contract but will not provide the functionality the customer needs. If the deliverable is late, the project will not be completed early. What action should you take?**

    A. Provide the deliverable as it is
    B. Inform the customer of the situation and work out a mutually agreeable solution
    C. Start to compile a list of delays caused by the buyer to prepare for negotiations
    D. Cut out other tasks in a way that will be unnoticed to provide more time to fix the deliverable

24. **You have just discovered an error in the implementation plan that will prevent you from meeting a milestone date. The BEST thing you can do is:**

    A. Develop alternative solutions to meet the milestone date
    B. Change the milestone date
    C. Remove any discussion about due dates in the project status report
    D. Educate the team about the need to meet milestone dates

25. **While testing the strength of concrete poured on your project, you discover that over 35% of the concrete does not meet your company's quality standards. You feel certain the concrete will function as it is, and you don't think the concrete needs to meet the quality level specified. What should you do?**

    A. Change the quality standards to meet the level achieved
    B. List in your reports that the concrete simply "meets our quality needs"
    C. Ensure the remaining concrete meets the standard
    D. Report the lesser quality level and try to find a solution

26. **You are the project manager for a new international project and your project team includes people from four countries. Most of the team members have not worked on similar projects before, but the project has strong support from senior management. What is the BEST thing to do to ensure that cultural differences do not interfere with the project?**

    A. Spend a little more time creating the work breakdown structure and making sure it is complete
    B. As the project manager, make sure you choose your words carefully whenever you communicate
    C. Ask one person at each team meeting to describe something unique about their culture
    D. Carefully encode all the project manager's communications

27. **A project has a tight budget when you begin negotiating with a seller for a piece of equipment. The seller has told you that the equipment price is fixed. Your manager has told you to negotiate the cost with the seller. What is your BEST course of action?**

    A. Make a good faith effort to find a way to decrease the cost
    B. Postpone negotiations until you can convince your manager to change their mind
    C. Hold the negotiations but only negotiate other aspects of the project
    D. Cancel the negotiations

28. You are working on a large construction project that is progressing within the baseline. Resource usage has remained steady, and your boss has just awarded you a prize for your performance. One of your team members returns from a meeting and tells you the customer said they are not happy with the project progress. What is the FIRST thing you should do?

    A. Tell your manager
    B. Complete a team building exercise and invite the customer's representatives
    C. Change the schedule baseline
    D. Meet with the customer to uncover details

29. A project manager discovers a defect in a deliverable that is due to the customer under contract today. The project manager knows the customer does not have the technical understanding to notice the defect. The deliverable technically meets the contract requirements, but it does not meet the project manager's fitness of use standard. What should the project manager do in this situation?

    A. Issue the deliverable and get formal acceptance from the customer
    B. Note the problem in the lessons learned so future projects do not encounter the same problem
    C. Discuss the issue with the customer
    D. Inform the customer that the deliverable will be late

30. Management tells a project manager to subcontract part of the project to a company that management has worked with many times. Under these circumstances, the project manager should be MOST concerned about:

    A. Making sure the company has the qualifications to complete the project
    B. Meeting management expectations of time
    C. The cost of the subcontracted work
    D. The contract terms and conditions

31. The customer on a project tells the project manager he has run out of money to pay for the project. What should the project manager do FIRST?

    A. Shift more of the work to later in the schedule to allow time for the customer to get the funds
    B. Reduce the scope of work and enter administrative closure
    C. Stop work
    D. Release part of the project team

32. You are the project manager for a large project under contract with the government. The contract for this two year, multi-million dollar project was signed six months ago. You were not involved in contract negotiations or setting up procedures for managing changes, but now you are swamped with changes from the customer and from people inside your organization. Who is normally responsible for formally reviewing major changes to the project/contract?

    A. The change control board
    B. The contracting/legal department
    C. The project manager
    D. Senior management

33. **During project execution, a major problem occurred that was not included in the risk response plan. What should you do FIRST?**

    A. Tell management
    B. Look for any unexpected effects of the problem
    C. Re-evaluate the risk identification process
    D. Create a workaround

34. **During planning, a project manager discovers that part of the scope of work is undefined. What should the project manager do?**

    A. Issue a change to the project when the scope is defined
    B. Remove the scope of work from the project and include it in the upgrade to the project
    C. Do what they can to get the scope of work defined before proceeding
    D. Continue to plan the project until the scope of work is defined

35. **The engineering department wants the project objective to be a 10% improvement in throughput. The information technology department wants no more than 5% of its resources to be used on the project. Management, who is also your boss, wants the project team to decrease tax liability. The BEST thing you can do is:**

    A. Put a plan together that meets all the objectives
    B. Have these people get together and agree on one objective
    C. Include the engineering and information technology objectives but hold further meetings regarding management's objectives
    D. Include only management's requirements

Professional Responsibility Answers

1. **Answer:** C

   Explanation: Choice D is a procurement function. Choices A and B are good ideas, but they do not solve the problem presented in the question. The charter and WBS do not identify stakeholders.

2. **Answer:** C

   Explanation: This type of issue must be settled early in the project because the content and extent of the entire project plan depends on the deliverables and objectives. The best way to resolve the issue is choice C, which is a problem solving method. The other choices are really smoothing or forcing.

3. **Answer:** C

   Explanation: Because orders are of short duration and numerous, this situation is a process, not a project.

4. **Answer:** B

   Explanation: There is no mention of a due date so choice D cannot be best. Replanning (choice A) is a drastic step, uncalled for by the situation described. A project is complete when all work, including all project management work, is completed. The lessons learned are project management deliverables so choice C cannot be correct.

5. **Answer:** C

   Explanation: Project managers must deal with potentially unethical situations like the situation described. Choice D ignores it and choices A and B hide it. Only choice C deals with it.

6. **Answer**: C

   Explanation: Based on the information presented, there is no reason to try to convince the sponsor to add the work (choices B and D). Though one could let the sponsor know (choice A) the best choice would be to say no. A better choice would be to find the root cause of the problem, but this is not a choice.

7. **Answer:** C

   Explanation: Always look for the choice that deals with and solves the problem. Choices B and D would not be appropriate until you learn the root cause of the problem. Choice A is withdrawal.

8. **Answer:** B

   Explanation: The only data that definitely tells something is the SPI. Less than one is bad, so the project is currently predicted to be behind schedule. This must be honestly reported.

9. **Answer:** A

   Explanation: Choice C is penalizing the employee and making them lose face. Choices B, C and D all involve decreasing the employee's morale. Therefore the best choice, and the one that does not waste everyone's time, is to cancel the meeting, get to the root cause of the problem and then fix it and reschedule the meeting (partially mentioned in choice A).

10. **Answer:** A

    Explanation: We assume that proper project management was followed and your opinion was considered during project initiating. Therefore, the best choice would be choice A. You need to provide the work as approved by management.

11. **Answer**: C

    Explanation: This is fee for service paid to a government official and is therefore not a bribe.

12. **Answer**: D

    Explanation: Choice D is more ethical and demonstrates good faith. Why spend time in negotiations?

13. **Answer**: B

    Explanation: Generally, moving ahead (choice D) withdraws from the problem. Choice C is not possible. The wording of this question says that an evaluation (a restructuring, choice A) has already been completed. Because the situation is so severe, the best choice would be to tell management.

14. **Answer**: B

    Explanation: Professional responsibility includes looking after the customer's best interests. Therefore, choice A cannot be best. In this case, the schedule and scope are already approved and all changes must go through the change control process. Therefore choices C and D cannot be best.

15. **Answer**: C

    Explanation: This is a common occurrence on many projects. When you take the exam, always assume that a change requires evaluation and formal change (choice C) unless it says otherwise. The request from the customer is a change and should be handled as a change. Choices A and D could be done, but only after evaluation and customer approval and as part of choice C. Choice B could be done, but only if the situation was identified as a risk and included in the reserve.

16. **Answer**: D

Explanation: Professional responsibility dictates that you should confront the situation first with the other project manager (choice D) to find out if the other project is really on schedule and therefore confirm or deny your information. Choices A or C would be the second step if choice D validates your concern. Choice B would be a more likely choice if it referred to an earlier step in risk. But choice D remains the best answer.

17. **Answer**: C

Explanation: This is a common problem on projects that many inexperienced project managers handle by doing choice B or D. If your estimates are accurate, you are ethically bound to stand by them (choice C). Management's only option to cut cost is to support the project manager's looking for alternatives related to the triple constraint. Choice A does not address the issue at hand, costs.

18. **Answer**: D

Explanation: Both A and D could have prevented the outcome, but D is the only one that would ensure you were not sitting in a meeting with a document that had not been reviewed.

19. **Answer**: B

Explanation: There is no indication that the labor dispute has caused any problems, so there is no need to cease doing business with the company (choice D) or to cancel its work (choice C). Choice A puts your interests over those of your company so it cannot be the best choice. The best choice would be to inform others in your company (choice B).

20. **Answer**: B

Explanation: The project manager is not empowered to determine the legality of company procedures.

21. **Answer**: C

Explanation: Confidential information should be respected (not disclosed to third parties) without the express approval of the client. If you chose choice A, remember that the clients own the confidential information. See, not all professional responsibility questions are tough!

22. **Answer**: B

Explanation: Both parties are giving up something. This is a compromise.

23. **Answer**: B

Explanation: Choices A and D ignore the customer's best interests. Any delays would have already been resolved with other change orders, so choice C is not appropriate. The ethical solution is to talk with the customer (choice B). You might still be able to win the incentive fee and find a mutually agreeable solution. Think of the good will that will come from telling the customer.

24. **Answer**: A

Explanation: Choices B, C and D do not solve the problem, while choice A does. Choice C violates the rule to report honestly and choice B is also unethical.

25. **Answer**: D

Explanation: Choice C simply withdraws from the problem and is therefore not the best solution. Can you explain why A and B are unethical? The only possible choice is D. That choice would involve quality and other experts to find a resolution.

26. **Answer**: C

Explanation: You should have noticed that only choices A and C involve more people than just the project manager. Since this is an issue involving everyone, everyone should be involved. Choice A may be a good idea in all cases, however, it does not specifically address cultural issues. Therefore, the answer must be C.

27. **Answer**: A

Explanation: There is always a way to decrease costs on the project. How about offering to feature the seller in your next television ad? Therefore, the best choice is A.

28. **Answer**: D

Explanation: You should look for a choice that solves the problem. Choice A is not assertive enough for a project manager. Choice B might be nice, but it does not address the customer's concerns with the project. Changing the baseline (choice C) is not ethical under these circumstances. You need more information before talking to your manager. Problem solving begins with defining the causes of the problem. Therefore, D is the only answer.

29. **Answer**: C

Explanation: Choice A does not follow the rule to protect the best interests of the customer. Choice B might be nice, but it does not solve the problem. Choice D will cause a default of contract. Although the deliverable meets the contractual requirements, it is best to bring the problem to the customer's attention (choice C) so an option that does no harm can be found.

30. **Answer**: A

Explanation: The first thing that should come to mind is if this is an ethical situation and if it violates any company rules or laws. If it does not violate any of these, it would be best to check qualifications (choice A). There is no justification to rate choices B, C or D higher than any other choice.

31. **Answer**: B

Explanation: Choice B really means, "Provide the customer with whatever value you can for the money already spent and stop work." This gives the customer some value for their expenditure. In addition, every project must be closed, as administrative closure provides benefit to the performing organization. This makes choice C not the best choice. Choices A and D do not solve the problem, but just postpone it.

32. **Answer**: A

Explanation: It is the role of the change control board to review and approve changes. That board may include people representative of all of the other choices.

33. **Answer**: D

Explanation: Because an unidentified problem or risk occurred, it is important to perform choices B and C. However, they are not your first choices. You might need to inform management (choice A), but this is reactive, not proactive, and not the first thing you should do.

34. **Answer**: C

Explanation: This question is similar to others in this book, but not exactly the same. You may also see this occur on your exam. Carefully read the questions! A project cannot be effectively planned with undefined scope of work (choice D). The best answer would be to try to solve the problem (choice C). If it could not be solved, then it should become part of the risk analysis to be done on the project.

35. **Answer**: C

Explanation: Did this one catch you? All deliverables must be quantifiable. Management's deliverable cannot be measured and therefore, needs more work. That means choice A is not correct. All parties rarely agree on all objectives (choice B). All the objectives should be met, but they must be quantifiable, so choice D is not correct. You need to have more discussions with management so you can make their objective quantifiable.

Bibliography

Most experienced and trained project managers who use these materials and the *PMBOK® Guide* to study do not need other materials to pass the exam. However, if you are not so experienced or you have not had project management training by a PMP®, and there are some topics you would like to learn more about, let me recommend the following additional reading.

Please see some of these at discount prices on our website www.rmcproject.com.

Hundreds of additional questions on PMP® exam simulation software, and review "flashcards"
- Mulcahy, Rita. *PM FASTrack®*, PMP® Exam Simulation Software. RMC Publications 2003. ISBN: 09711647-8-9
- Mulcahy, Rita. *Hot Topics – Flashcards to Pass the PMP® Exam.* RMC Publications, 2003. ISBN: 09711647-6-2

This book provides a real-world step-by-step approach to using risk management on projects. Full of tricks of the trade and common errors from two international studies conducted by the author, this book is a primary text for risk management courses and getting ready for the PMP® exam.
- Mulcahy, Rita. *Risk Management Tricks of the Trade® for Project Managers.* RMC Publications, Fall 2003. IBSN: 0-9711647-9-7

A book that covers a lot of the topics unknown to many who are taking the PMP® Exam.
- The Project Management Institute. *Principles of Project Management*, ISBN: 1-880410-30-3. This book includes chapters on:
  - Conflict management
  - Contracts
  - Negotiation
  - Forms of organization for project management
  - Roles and responsibilities
  - Team building

Easy to understand and the most real-world book on project management:
- Verzuh, Eric. *Fast Forward MBA in Project Management.* ISBN:0-471-32546-5

Basic project management textbook often used at universities:
- Meredith and Mantel. *Project Management: A Managerial Approach.* ISBN: 0-471-01626-8

This book has some great coverage of scheduling and PERT.
- Lewis, James. *Project Planning, Scheduling and Control.* ISBN: 1-55738-869-5

Index

D

data precision ranking, 236
deal with problems, 298, 304
decision tree, 238
definition of a risk, 229
definitive estimate, 144
deliverables, 84, 86
Delphi technique, 81
depreciation, 149
design of experiments, 171
determine quality standards, 24
direct cost, 148
discretionary dependency, 103
do the right thing, 298
duration compression, 113

E

EAC, 138, 139, 141, 142, 143, 144, 150
earned value, (see EV)
earned value management, 48
effective listening, 214
ensure compliance with plans, 24
ensure individual integrity, 298
estimate at completion, (see EAC)
estimate to complete, (see ETC)
estimating, 24, 103, 151
estimating methods, 103
ETC, 138, 139, 141, 142, 143, 144
EV, 138, 139, 141, 142, 143, 144, 150
evaluation criteria, 274
executing, 24
execution, 242, 243
expectancy theory, 202
expected monetary value, 237
expected value, 237
expert power, 198
external dependency, 103

F

fallback planning, 242
fast tracking, 115
feedback, 214
financial closure, 24, 218, 283
fishbone diagram, 171, 173
fixed cost, 148
fixed price, (see FP)
fixed price incentive fee, (see FPIF)
float (see slack)
flowchart, 99, 171
follow the right process, 298, 299
forcing, 201
formal acceptance, 218, 284
formal power, 198
formal verbal, 214
formal written, 214
FP, 264
FPEPA, 264
FPIF, 264
free slack, 107
fringe benefits, 202

functional, 35, 38, 39
functional manager, 193

G

Gantt chart, 3, 48, 49, 82, 98, 99, 121, 197
GERT, 102
gold plating, 19, 47, 52, 167, 168

H

halo effect, 198
hard logic, 103
Herzberg's theory, 203
heuristics, 118
historical information, 24, 47, 77
how are the questions written, 5
human resource responsibilities, 196

I

identify changes, 24
IFB, 269, 270, 271
impact, 237
impact of poor quality, 170
incentives, 267
increase knowledge and practices, 298
indirect cost, 148
influencing the organization, 24
informal verbal, 214
informal written, 214
information distribution, 212
information gathering techniques, 235
initiating, 24
initiation, 76, 80, 144
inputs and outputs, 10
inputs to estimating, 134
inputs to risk management, 230
insurance, 242
integrated change control, 24, 55
interact with others in a professional and cooperative
    manner, 304
internal rate of return, 146
interpreting the pmbok® guide, 13
invitation for bid, (see IFB)
ISO 9000, 168
iterations, 24

J

just in time, 168

K

kickoff meeting, 19, 51
knowledge base, 301

PHONE: (952) 846-4484 - EMAIL: info@rmcproject.com - WEB: www.rmcproject.com

L

lag, 106
law of diminishing returns, 148
leadership styles, 198, 199
leading, 24
lessons learned, 24, 48, 218, 230, 232, 284
letter of intent, 273
life cycle, 23
life cycle costing, 149
logic diagram, 101

M

make or buy, 261
manage by exception to the project plan, 24
management by objectives, 81, 89
management plans, 24, 49
managing changes, 59
mandatory dependency, 103
marginal analysis, 168
Maslow's hierarchy of needs, 203
matrix, 35, 37, 39
McGregor's theory of X and Y, 202
mean, 174
meetings, 216
milestone, 98, 120, 121, 163
milestone charts, 98
mitigation, 240
Monte Carlo simulation, 105, 239
motivation theory, 202
mutually exclusive, 168

N

negotiating, 24, 276
negotiation tactics, 276
net present value, 145
network diagram, 24, 49, 99, 101, 120
nonverbal communication, 214
noncompetitive forms of procurement, 273
normal distribution, 169

O

objectives, 24
objectives of negotiation, 276
opportunity cost, 147
order of magnitude estimate, 144
organizations, 35
out of control, 174

P

paralingual, 214
parametric estimating, 135
Pareto diagram, 172
payback period, 146
PDM, 101
penalty power, 198

performance measuring, 24, 58
performance reporting, 24, 217, 218, 283
perquisites, 202
PERT, 103, 104, 105, 120
planned value (see PV)
planning, 24, 119, 144
PMI®-isms, 18
powers of the project manager, 198
present value, 145
presentations, 276
prevention over inspection, 168
privity, 273
proactive, 19, 211, 229
probability, 169, 237, 238
problem solving, 200, 201
procurement audit, 19, 24, 284
procurement documents, 269, 270, 271
procurement management, 258
procurement management plan, 258
procurement planning, 261
product description, 77
product of the project, 77, 78
product verification, 24, 218, 220, 283
professional responsibility, 297
program, 21
progress reporting, 137
project, 21
project archives, 218, 283, 284
project charter, 49, 75, 78, 79, 120, 214, 215, 220, 230
project closure, 218, 284
project coordinator, 40
project expeditor, 40
project life cycle, 23, 84
project management information system, 48, 53
project management life cycle, 23
project management processes, 13
project manager as integrator, 47
project manager's role in procurement, 259
project office, 40
project plan, 24, 43, 47, 49, 54, 61, 62, 64, 121, 195, 212, 220, 242, 247, 270
project plan approval, 51
project plan development, 50
project plan execution, 52
project plan updates, 24, 61
project planning methodolody, 48
project selection methods, 75, 148
project slack, 106, 107
projectized, 36, 39
purchase order, 264
PV, 138, 139, 141, 142, 143, 144, 217

Q

qualified seller lists, 275
qualitative risk analysis, 235
quality, 167, 168, 170
quality assurance, 171
quality audit, 19, 171
quality control, 24, 58, 170, 172, 177
quality control tools, 172
quality management, 168
quality management plan, 24, 170
quality planning, 171
quality philosophy, 167

quantitative risk analysis, 237

R

re-estimating, 115
referent power, 198
release resources, 24, 218
report violations, 298, 300, 307
reporting, 98, 99, 121
request for proposal, (see RFP)
request for quotation, (see RFQ)
requirements, 2, 22, 24, 86, 98, 102, 133, 167, 168, 171, 174, 177, 178, 232, 257, 262, 269, 271, 272, 276, 277, 305, 307
reserves, 242
residual risks, 242
resource Gantt chart, 197
resource histogram, 197
resource leveling, 118
resource management planning, 134
responsibility for quality, 169
responsibility matrix, 196
reward power, 198
RFP, 261, 269, 270, 271
RFQ, 269, 270, 271
risk, 234
risk and contract type, 267
risk averse, 230
risk factors, 229
risk identification, 233
risk management, 62, 229, 230, 233
risk management plan, 24, 233
risk management planning, 233
risk management process, 233
risk monitoring and control, 244
risk owner, 240
risk rating matrix, 236
risk response audits, 244
risk response plan, 242
risk response planning, 239
risk response strategies, 240
risk reviews, 244
risk tolerances, 230
risk triggers, 235
roles and responsibilities, 187
rule of seven, 174

S

schedule, 24, 49
schedule control, 24, 58
schedule development, 99
schedule management plan, 118
schedule performance index, (see SPI)
schedule variance, (see sv)
scheduling tools, 97
scope change control, 24
scope decomposition, 86
scope definition, 86
scope management, 75
scope management plan, 80
scope of work, (see sow)
scope statement, 49, 80
scope verification, 24, 57

secondary risks, 242
senior management, 19, 21, 40, 47, 51, 78, 98, 144, 191, 194, 195
shortening the schedule, 113
single source, 273
slack (float), 106, 107
smoothing, 201
social-economic-environmental sustainability, 22
soft logic, 103
sole source, 273
solicitation, 275
solicitation planning, 269
source selection, 275
SOW, 268, 270, 271, 277
special provisions, 271
specification limits, 174
SPI, 64, 138, 139, 140, 141, 142, 143, 144, 150, 151, 156
sponsor, 191
stakeholder, 21, 22, 86, 192, 197, 198, 211, 217
stakeholder management, 21, 24
standard contract, 271
standard deviation, 169
statistical independence, 169
statistical sampling, 173
straight-line depreciation, 149
strong matrix, 35
sunk costs, 148
SV, 138, 141, 142, 143, 144

T

T&M, 263
team, 21, 192
team building, 25, 197, 198
team development, 24, 197, 198
terms and conditions, 271
threshold, 22, 191, 233
tight matrix, 35
time and material, (see T&M)
time scaled network diagram, 101
total quality management (TQM), 168
total slack, 107
transference, 240
tricks for taking the exam, 8
triple constraint, 22
types of cost, 148
types of risk, 235

U

uncertainty, 229
updating records, 24, 218, 283

V

VAC, 138, 141, 142, 143, 144
value analysis, 149
variable, 148, 172
variable cost, 148
variance analysis, 118
variance at completion, (see VAC)

W

waiver, 273
war room, 202
watch for conflicts of interest, 298
WBS, 19, 43, 47, 49, 52, 81, 85, 86, 88, 89, 101, 103, 120, 133, 134, 135, 137, 192, 193, 197, 198, 231, 232

WBS dictionary, 24, 87
weak matrix, 35
withdrawal, 201
work authorization system, 24, 47, 52
work breakdown structure, (see WBS)
workarounds, 244
working capital, 148